Received from
**World
Journalism
Institute**
www.worldji.com

City Notebook

The pumice dune at land's end point, where the borough of Queens touches the East River and Newtown Creek, screens everything from view except the upper half of the Empire State Building.

City Notebook

A Reporter's Portrait of a Vanishing New York

McCandlish Phillips

 Liveright • New York

Copyright © 1974 by Liveright Publishing
Copyright © 1962, 1963, 1964, 1965, 1966, 1970, 1971, 1972,
1973 by The New York Times Company. Reprinted by
permission.
"Otto" Copyright © 1974 by McCandlish Phillips
All rights reserved. No part of this book may be
reproduced in any form without permission in writing from
the publisher.

1.987654321
ISBN: 0-87140-566-0
Library of Congress Catalog Card Number: 72-97491

Designed by Madelaine Caldiero
Manufactured in the United States of America

The author gratefully acknowledges the permission of
The New York Times to adapt or reprint here certain
material by him that first appeared in its columns. Thanks
must go, too, to Laurie Nevin Friedman, Mary Yastishak,
Julie Yastishak, Esther DiQuattro, and Daniel Voll for
their assistance in manuscript preparation. It was a great
pleasure for the author to work with his editor, Ned
Arnold, a man of wit, erudition, ebullience, and reason.
Finally, though it is very much out of fashion, the author
gladly affirms his daily reliance on the God of the Scriptures
and on His Son, Jesus Christ.

Except for "Flashing Hands" (p. 189) by Pat Ikeda and the
Ringling Brothers and Barnum & Bailey Circus photograph
(p. 314), all of the illustrations are from *The New York Times*,
photographs by: Tyrone Dukes ("Empire State," frontis-
piece, p. ii); Lee Romero ("Victoria," p. 22); Barton
Silverman ("Deckhand," p. 138); Ernie Sisto ("Smokestack,"
p. 169); Neal Boenzi ("Man with Beast," p. 174, and "Georgia
Woman," p. 230); Don Hogan Charles ("James Van Der
Zee," p. 235); and Jack Manning ("Automat Singer," p. 298).

In memory of
MILTON BRACKER
and
ROBERT ALDEN

superb reporters, gifted writers, men who loved their craft so well that they spent everything for it. My dear friends.

Contents

Preface   xi

City Beat
Mama   3
The Waiting Room   5
Star   11
The Day the Wall Went Down   12
Reunion   14
Ward   16
A Knock on Many Doors   18
Times Square After Hours   21

City Scenes
Horticultural Homicide   31
The Great Bee Roundup   35
The Magistrate and the Parrot   36
Bricklayers: A Fraternity of Strangers   38
Uriburu and the Blob   40
The Truck That Came to Dinner   41
Blackout   45
Old Shoes   48
Chamber Music: The Tin Can Suite   50
High Bidder   52
Fall Guy   55
The Small World of Melvin Krulewitch   57

Book Row
Book Row   61

Four Originals
The Man from I.Q. H.Q.	87
Mr. Quickfingers	89
The Last of the Red Hot Principals	97
The Titan and the Tots	104

Port City
Pier 39	111
Storm Rescue at False Hook	118
Going Home	122
Portrait of a River	125
The Canal to Nowhere	137
The Seafarer	143

In Cold Blood
In Cold Blood	149

Under One Sky
Explaining the Weatherman	165
Rainbow Rain	168
Icthyological Armageddon	171
Silent Jungle	173
Call It What You Like, It's Still "Grant's Tomb"	176
The Secret Hodgepodge: One Mask, Many Faces	184
A Many-Fingered Voice	188
I Heard Them Singing	193
Letter to McNulty	196

The Sweet Sell
Coconut Keynote	205
Cheese	209
The Return of a Big Loser	214

Lox, Bagels, and Auld Lang Syne
    The Night They Clobbered Lindy's   223
    The Horn of Plenty Closes   226
    The Campaign for Jefferson Davis   229
    The World of James Van DerZee   234
    Wurlitzer Lives!   239

Jazz City
    His Father's Son   247
    Dixie-on-Hudson   250

Bright Lights
    Open Call   285
    Barbara Loden—Up from Daisy Mae   289
    The Monks and the Bells   296
    Songbird of the Automat   299
    Vaudeville Days   303

Clown
    Otto   313

Epilogue: Beyond City Limits
    A Winter Walk Along the Shore   325

About the Author   333

Preface

If 10,000 writers were asked to write books about New York City, the books they produced would tell a good deal less about the City than there is to know, so the first thing you should know about this book is that there is nothing comprehensive about it. The writer's attitude can perhaps best be summed up in these few words: I am not awed by the City—so much of it is like plain pieces of Buffalo or Pawtucket stretched out to excess—nor am I in dazzled love with it, but I hold it in a certain respect and affection, and I find it a fabulous subject.

If anyone were to ask me for my credentials as an illuminator of New York City, I would suggest that a biopsy of my lungs might establish my authority. I work in the City and I live in the City. The air of the City is the only air I have breathed, except in very brief side excursions, for more than two decades. My work as a City reporter has thrust me at every hour of the day and night into almost every imaginable circumstance and place.

I have rattled homeward over the BMT to Brooklyn, the beloved borough, for some of my years here, and for the rest of them I have walked briskly along Eighth Avenue and Broadway or have cruised the IRT to my Manhattan perch overlooking Broadway. Every time the local stops, the screech of metallic brakes comes up through the subway gratings and through my windows and into my ears.

In vacations over more than twenty years, I can recall having strayed out of the City twice. When people ask me, "Where did you go on your vacation?" I tell them I went where I would have wanted to go if I lived anywhere else in the world.

That is, I grant you, parochialism—but the catholicity that is contained within that parochialism is more than enough for me.

City Notebook is a casual portrait of life in New York City. I have been rummaging around the place for quite a long time, poking my nose into a lot of its peculiar corners, and this book catches the City in some of its moods and scenes. It is called *City Notebook* because almost everything in it is drawn from notes made in a reporter's notebook.

My design is not to falsify the City or glamorize it, but to show it as it is—in a few selected parts. The whole life and rhythm, the pulse and population of New York City is a living mosaic made up of millions of pieces, and the most anyone can know about them is fragmentary. Here are a few more pieces in that vast picture, including some you may not have seen before, and some you may not have known to exist.

McCandlish Phillips

City Beat

Mama

Just about everybody knew "Mama" at the crowded, clangorous East Bronx intersection where Simpson Street, East 165th Street, Westchester Avenue and Fox Street all run together.

In her high-laced boots, Mama looked like a period piece as she shuffled along from store to store in the busy marketplace—where the sidewalks swirl with pedestrians, trucks rumble over cobblestone streets and IRT trains shake on the old elevated structure that shadows the crossing.

Even at eighty-eight, Mama, frail and threadbare, went on earning a thin living by peddling handkerchiefs at a dime each out of her brown shopping bag. For blocks in every direction the rectitude of Mama had become a legend.

She was a merchant, not a beggar. No one ever gave Mama more than a dime for a white handkerchief and got away with it. Ten cents was her price, based on a sensible markup. If a buyer gave her a quarter and walked away, she would chase him and make sure he got three nickels change.

For quite a few years a lot of kindly men in the neighborhood were pretty badly oversupplied with handkerchiefs, because no one who gave her money ever got away without the matching number of handkerchiefs.

"I got three dozen myself I bought from her," Raoul Mercado, owner-chef of Las Villas Restaurant, said over juke-box rhythms as he piled Spanish food high on dinner plates. "She came in 2:00 P.M. mostly every day. Everybody love her."

Mama walked her circuit daily, slightly stooped as the weight of her wares pulled on her ninety-five pound form, with a kerchief over her gray hair and tied under her chin. She had a worn but not ragged winter coat with two big front pockets for change.

Sometimes she would just sit on a wooden box near Shapiro's Appetizing, the eggs and delicacies store, or at her favorite spot in front of Lederman's Pharmacy, or near Kresge's entrance. Mostly she went into the cafeterias, the bars and pool halls.

Mama would push through the double set of swinging doors into Simpson's Cafe, put her shopping bag down by the juke box, take a pile of handkerchiefs out, and walk down the long red bar with its widely spaced wooden stools. "You want a handkerchief? Ten cents. Ten cents," she would say.

"The men feel sorry for her. They want to give her fifteen cents. 'No charity,' she said," according to Arturo Jusino, the bartender.

"She was about four-feet-eleven-inches and a little bad on the hearing. She was almost half blind because she would hold a dollar bill up an inch from her eyes."

One day a man came in and threw a quarter into her bag, and Mama bent down and emptied out all her goods, fished up the coin and gave it back to him.

"When you saw her you had to say human beings are indestructible," said the clerk at Jorjan's Remnants store. "When you see an octogenarian out pushing handkerchiefs, you know they're indestructible." He remembered her pinched face and faded coat.

In Klinger's Cut-Rate Bakery, Robert Klinger said: "When I tried to give her a piece of cake for fifteen cents, she would stand there and bargain with me to take more money from her."

At holidays, Mama would give out gifts—handkerchiefs. Also for weddings.

"I know her since I'm a kid—thirty-five or forty years," said Joe Schneider in his narrow baked goods and sausage store. "There were no gratings on the windows—you could have slept in the street. Now the winos and junkies come in here three and four at a time. A woman says 'Hey, mister, look, he's taking a salami!' Should I stop him? Isn't it better to lose a salami than lose your life?"

At Jacobson's old-world style bakery, stacked high with cakes and cookies and rolls and pies, Mrs. Sarah Jacobson said, "She would come in to buy three-day-old cakes for a dime. The old people have a cake for breakfast with coffee, and a cake for supper with tea. Maybe a piece of boiled chicken for lunch."

Mama, a widow, was known to few by her name, Mrs. Elsie Litt. She had a tiny apartment on 167th Street. In the early evenings she left her door open a crack so neighbors could drop in.

On March 2, someone entered and ransacked her apartment and strangled her. "Every time you turn around here, somebody's killed," a policeman said bitterly.

The Waiting Room

Two kinds of people sit in the waiting room of the Port Authority bus terminal near Times Square. Some are waiting for buses. Others are waiting for death.

At times transients cannot get a seat because so many of "the regulars" are there: old people, from about sixty to ninety years old, who have made the waiting room a kind of club. Some come almost every day, to sit and wait, but not for buses.

Most sit alone, in silence. A few read. Some are convivial and gabby. "Once you start to talk to somebody, you have to talk to them every day," one of the quiet ones said, explaining his social reticence.

Max Cohen struts around the waiting room with four or five cigars in his shirt pocket and one stuck in the side of his mouth. He is a very small, wiry man with plenty of vinegar who wears his bristly white hair cut short. He worked for fifty years as a newspaper deliverer. He often comes to the terminal twice a day.

"Why don't you go home, Max?" he was asked.

"What, to lay down and look at four walls?" he shot back. He lives in a small, sparely furnished room that rents for seven dollars a week. "Later on, I'll go out and sit in the park, when it gets a little warmer," he said.

To old people whose dwellings are tiny or dreary or places of endless boredom, the waiting room is a kind of indoor park. It never rains in the Port Authority bus terminal. The gleam of the overhead bulbs is as steady as the sun in a cloudless sky.

From 200 to 250 old men and women are known to come to the terminal regularly. Many more come now and then. Occasionally the Port Authority police come in to clear the room, but it is a futile game, the rules of which are known to both sides.

Two policemen arrived at 1:20 P.M. the other day and stood in the center of the room. One of them spoke in a loud, brassy voice:

"Ladies and gentlemen. This here area is for people with tickets only. If you have a ticket, fine. If not, please get up and leave. Now show us your tickets."

There was a shuffling exodus as the ticketless drifted out to the concourse or into the public toilets. For several minutes the room was the preserve of the ticketed minority, but within six minutes things were back to normal.

At 2:04, the police came again and, immediately, three old people departed. There is a comfortable anonymity in the crowd on the concourse. There was no announcement this time; the blue shadow was enough.

Some old people come and go like characters in a drama, having fixed roles to play. Two are known as "the Lovers." They come in separately, meet, sit and hold hands a while, then leave.

Romeo is in his early seventies, a tall, spare man with bony shoulders that seem like pipes under his jacket. Juliet is in her late sixties, short, round-faced.

"You would think they were sixteen years old and just in love," a woman said. "She always wears a veil on her hair. He wears a little cap, a couple of sizes too small, and they sit and holds hands."

Some sitters look invincibly alone—severe, motionless—figures in stone.

It was 5:55 P.M. For 2½ hours now, a tall elderly woman with fluffy hair of the purest white has been sitting alone, in a pink jacket and blue miniskirt, gazing straight ahead. Thin lips, painted a bright orange-red, are shrill in a rougeless face powdered white.

The watchers are watched three days a week, from noon to 4:30 P.M., by the friendly eyes of Mrs. Stella G. Trebony and Mrs. Mary Butler. The Port Authority, which regards the visitors as a mild form of nuisance, like an excess of pigeons on a veranda, has sanctioned a long-term study of the phenomenon.

"Never marry an old bachelor. They never change their ways," a woman in a red hat was saying to a woman named Mary. "I married an old bachelor. Selfish! Leave all kinds of pots and pans! He was terrible. I had to get rid of him."

For more than an hour, red hat ran on and Mary was held to brief expressions of assent.

"Don't forget this town is made up of all the little towns in the country," a woman in sunglasses said. "It's just another little town, except it's bigger. Everybody came here from somewhere."

One of the regulars is a woman who carries two bottles of

wine in a shopping bag. She comes in and sips from them during the day and sometimes, when she is feeling loose, she stands up and sings "Moon River," a little off key.

Another steady sitter of a bouncy, outgoing sort, speaks five languages "and he comes in and says 'Good morning' in all five languages," an elderly woman said.

At 7:15 P.M., the woman with the white fluffy hair was still fast in her place. It had been almost four hours now.

A few of the sitters seem to have stepped out of a George Price cartoon. Their attempts at elegance are irreparably gauche. Several old sitters are alcoholics. Yet a surprising number, over half, dress and behave like solid members of the middle class, the upper middle class at that.

One man cuts the figure of a diplomat. He wears striped trousers, a dark blue coat with a vest and a black hat that stands out against a thick fringe of white hair. He looks as though he might have been at the Versailles Conference. He sits erect, like a man posing for an oil portrait. He does not talk to strangers.

Mrs. Trebony, who still has the soft accents of her early years in Savannah, Georgia, offers assistance to any who need it and will take it.

When any of the regulars are missing, she and Mrs. Butler write a note, or drop in to see them. Sometimes they are sick—sometimes they are dead. A few, at death, are found to have had plenty of money.

Mrs. Trebony nodded toward a male sitter. "He's here because he and his wife sat here," she said. "He goes around to all the places where they used to go, hoping she'll come to get him. He says, 'Why do you think she never comes?' He goes every Tuesday to the grave. People say he's crazy. Now, you know, I don't think he's crazy. Do you?"

A woman who is ninety and beyond the joys of living said, "I really just wish I would die, Stella. I wonder when my husband will come and get me?"

"You better be careful now," Mrs. Trebony said. "Which

one of them do you want to come and get you?" The nonagenarian has been married three times.

Mrs. Trebony told of an old woman who came at last to the point at which she knew she needed public assistance, a day she had hoped never to see. "She wasn't even getting enough to eat," Mrs. Trebony said. "She had spent her reserve."

The woman held out for a while more, but finally agreed to make out forms for help. "I hoped I wouldn't live this long," she said. The next morning she was dead.

Mrs. Trebony and Mrs. Butler supply half-fare subway cards to those who need them, as often as they need them. In this city, that is not necessarily a one-time favor. Old people are often mugged, and they lose their half-fare cards with their money.

A few months ago an eighty-six-year-old man named August went into a hospital for seven weeks. When he came out, he had lost his rented room. With residential hotels quoting fourteen dollars-a-day rates, or seventy dollars-a-week, there were terrors in it for him. He came to the two women for help.

Their presence goes back a little over a year to the point at which the perplexity of Port Authority officials led to a call for help to Travelers Aid, which led to a plea to the New York City Office for the Aging.

Mrs. Stella B. Allen of the West Side Office for the Aging met with Marvin Weiss, the terminal manager, and five others to talk about what could be done.

"They wanted to get them out, but without being too harsh," Mrs. Allen recalled. "We decided we were not going to throw them out. That we knocked off the agenda first."

One approach was to make "a sort of survey" to find out "who is there, and why." It was decided to put a table in the waiting room and to let it be tended by elderly women. They counted on "the empathy of the old for the old."

Project Find, a private agency, sent Mrs. Trebony and

Mrs. Butler. The city office agreed to supply their salaries. Find stands for "friendless, isolated, needy, disabled."

In the early course of the work, Elizabeth Stecher of Project Find met Mrs. Trebony's son, Louis, and became Mrs. Elizabeth Stecher Trebony.

"Two chief terrors haunt the minds of older people," Mrs. Allen said. One is placement in a home for the aged. The other is going on welfare.

"They feel that either just cancels them out as a person. They feel that this is the end of them. That's why they struggle so hard to stay independent, 'to be free,' as they put it.

"They can live in the crummiest little hole in a third-rate hotel, with pipes on the ceiling and holes in the floor, but they'll hold onto it," Mrs. Trebony said. "They only need a little bit of help to stay free—just a little bit of help."

The Port Authority co-exists with its aged visitors with a kind of grudging tolerance, mixed with perhaps a touch of involuntary affection.

A scale model of a vest-pocket park, with thumb-high trees and tiny plastic people, that sits in the office suite in the terminal is management's vision of one thing that might be done: the Port Authority would create a park near Times Square to lure the old folks out of the waiting room. The approach is one of attrition-through-compassion.

It would not be likely to work. One of the attractions of the waiting room is shelter from bad weather.

Project Find plans to open a coffee house for the elderly in the area. It has already raised $10,000 for this, and is seeking $20,000 more.

At 8:45 p.m. the other night, the woman with the white, fluffy hair wrapped her black coat around her and now she drowsed, her head slumping to her shoulder. A policeman walked behind her. Gently he touched her shoulder. "Mom," he said. "Mom, wake up." She brought her head up straight.

The illusion that one is waiting for a bus is made less tolerable by an attitude of slumber.

Star

Manuel Vasquez, a nineteen-year-old East Harlem youth, played the lead role in *Dope*. He died in Metropolitan Hospital last night in circumstances strangely like those in the play.

On the stage, Tony Vasquez, as he was known to friends, played a junkie who struggles against addiction and narrowly wins out. The junkie dies at the final curtain after a vindictive pusher stabs him.

The young actor, who apparently died of a narcotics overdose, had been engaged in a similar struggle off-stage for over a year. He had seemed to be winning it, but friends said he got "shot up" on Saturday and, with that, he lost it forever.

He had joined the Soul and Latin Theater a year ago for street performances that a critic said were "full of the rage and gaiety and despair of the ghetto." The theater, at 174 East 104th Street, produces "street plays" based on ghetto themes, using untrained slum teen-agers, blacks and Puerto Ricans, as actors. *Dope* has been playing about twice a week in the non-summer months. The next performance was to have been at Rutgers University in a week but it has been cancelled.

Young Tony was a dropout from Benjamin Franklin High School, but as he had emerged from addiction he had showed renewed interest in education, and just last week he took a seven-hour series of tests as a preliminary to entering a makeup program to qualify him for college.

"His life was as typical of an experience in ghetto living that you could find anywhere on God's earth," John Weckesser, the general manager of the Soul troupe said last night. "But this young guy was exceptionally talented, gifted—intellectually, artistically, emotionally. He's a statistic now, I guess, but he was no statistic in the minds of anyone he ever performed in front of, or with whom he in any way came in contact."

Tony won the lead role when he agreed to take no more narcotics and he went to Beth Israel Hospital for detoxification treatment. He had been out for almost a month and was getting help at Exodus House, 102nd Street near Second Avenue. He lived with his mother, Candida Soto, on East 102nd Street.

"All the junkies in the whole neighborhood were trying to get him to get back," said Maryat Lee, the author of *Dope*.

"They lurk around like vultures. The other junkies are jealous, very deep down, that somebody else is out, so they want to prove that he's not making it, so they won't have to make the effort themselves. Well they proved it."

The Day the Wall Went Down

A driverless automobile in which three children were playing lurched from its parking place in Brooklyn yesterday morning and struck a steel supporting column in a four-story brick tenement. The column buckled. The building's brick facade trembled for a moment and then slid to the street in a shower of bricks, leaving a line of living rooms exposed.

An eighty-one-year-old man was caught in the brickfall

and suffered a fractured rib. A five-year-old child who almost slipped off the edge of the third story was yanked to safety by the hair.

The automobile's owner, D. D. Howell, thirty-six, of Manhattan, had parked in front of 156 Grattan Street in the Williamsburg section of Brooklyn at 11:30 A.M. in order to change places in the driver's seat with a passenger, William Hinson.

Both men got out of the car, leaving its motor running. In the back seat were four-year-old Donald Howell and two children of Mrs. Lizzeta Jackson, Geraldine, nine, and Annette, ten.

Annette hopped from the back to the front seat and accidentally hit the gas pedal. The car lurched forward and crashed into an empty first-floor store. The round supporting column, eight inches in diameter and sixteen feet high, toppled.

What followed was almost surrealistic. The bricks appeared to "melt." Slowly at first, they churned, slid and finally spattered to the street, leaving the building-front naked.

A pedestrian, Joseph Riccardelli, eighty-one, of 152 Grattan Street, fell under the brick bombardment. He was taken to St. Catherine's Hospital with a fractured rib.

On the third floor, Mrs. Gladys Ellin's three children were sitting on the rug watching television when the front wall disappeared, taking shades, curtains, window frames and wallpaper in a tangle with it. The floor tilted. Gladys, seven, and Frank, four, scrambled to safety, but Madelaine, five, began to slide forward toward the lip of the floor. Her mother grabbed her by the hair and pulled her to safety.

The three children in the car were somehow spared serious injury. A fourth-floor tenant, Philip Metzger, sixty-four, who had been having a late breakfast with his wife, Henrietta, was treated for shock. All occupants were safely evacuated and the bare-faced house was closed for repairs.

Its eight families were all resettled with relatives or friends. The police issued a summons to the driver of the errant car.

Reunion

A long while ago, in an evil time when to be born Jewish was a crime, a mother in a Polish village placed her two baby daughters on neighbors' doorsteps and fled into the forest. How fully they were protected from the Nazis and how carefully they were educated and reared she did not know.

Last night, in an airport waiting room, the mother saw her two daughters together for the first time since that appalling day in 1942.

The story began in the village of Sokoloff, Poland, during the German occupation. A Jewish family—father, mother and two small daughters—had lived since the invasion in 1939 in fear of internment and death. The father first went into the forest to join a group of Partisans. His wife, Mrs. Sabena Futersak, followed him in 1942.

She left her two daughters—Sonia, then less than two years old, and Dina, seven weeks old—each at the door of a different family. As it turned out, a Sokoloff family took Sonia, and Catholic nuns received Dina.

When Dina was eight, a childless couple, Mr. and Mrs. Wladisalwy Benedyk, adopted her and gave her the name Maria.

Mr. Futersak died of wounds in 1945, just before the liberation, and Mrs. Futersak, expecting a third child, went to Austria, where a son, Samuel, was born in 1946.

She returned to Poland and found Sonia, but Dina could not be traced. Mrs. Futersak's mother and brothers had come to the United States. In 1949 she joined them here, bringing Sonia and Samuel. She continued her search by letters to Poland—without success.

In 1959 she turned to Children's Salvation Inc., a small voluntary Jewish agency that seeks, by skillful searching and diplomacy, to unite families divided in World War II. There are still remnants of Jewish community life in central and Eastern Europe, and these provide a fragile network by which to locate missing persons.

Menashe Stein, honorary chairman of the agency, and Rabbi Moses E. Leiter, its director, helped find Dina, or Maria. Soon the natural and foster mothers began corresponding in Polish. Mrs. Futersak sent gifts by mail. Maria, who was taking teacher's training, said she would not come to the United States until she had finished, and that she would not come without her foster mother.

Mrs. Benedyk, by now a widow with no other children, found it hard to acknowledge another's prior claim on Maria, but finally she wrote Mrs. Futersak these gracious words: "I've given her an education. I've cared for her. Someday I will present you with your little princess."

Last night, she did.

Mrs. Benedyk and Maria flew in from Eastern Europe on a Sabena Belgian World Airlines flight that arrived here at 6:15 P.M.—twenty-one years after Mrs. Futersak had left her daughter and fled.

There is a large meeting room in the International Arrivals building that looks out into the Customs section. It has a picture window with Venetian style blinds whose slats run vertically. The room was filled with Futersaks, relatives, friends and rabbis.

When Maria and her foster mother came to Customs, a dozen of them pulled the slats apart and pressed their faces to the window. For the rabbis and Mr. Stein, this was a sweet culmination. After years of work, a Jewish family sundered by the war was now to be restored.

Maria entered the room first, half on the run, a fresh-looking girl of twenty-one with bright pink cheeks, wind-blown auburn hair and a trim silhouette. She took her mother's left hand and kissed it. They embraced. Mrs. Benedyk, a small woman in a white silk babushka, came in. There was a flurry of excited Polish chatter.

Sonia, twenty-two, now a stenographer, met the sister whom she had "never really believed could be alive." Samuel, seventeen, a student at Manhattan's Yeshiva High School, beamed with delight.

Maria, who speaks no English, hopes to remain here. Mrs. Benedyk's future plans are uncertain. Interpreters said they did not know whether Maria would practice the faith of the Futersaks or the Benedyks, or whether she would use the name Dina again.

Mrs. Benedyk and Maria joined the family group in three sedans and drove to Manhattan, where both will stay with Mrs. Futersak, Sonia and Samuel in the family's $4\frac{1}{2}$-room apartment, at 10 Avenue D, on the Lower East Side.

Ward

Nearly 200 mentally retarded children are housed in wards at the old Gouverneur Hospital at 621 Water Street on the Lower East Side, and hope there is measured in terms of modest goals.

If a four-year-old child who has always been fed flat on his back takes food in a semi-sitting position, that is a triumph. The triumphs are few.

The children there are "non-verbal." They don't talk. They are "nonambulatory." They can't walk. Most are in what was once called "the imbecile and idiot range, but now we call them profoundly and severely retarded," a physician explained.

Gouverneur, a creaking municipal institution that goes back to 1892, was closed by the City as antiquated and inadequate back in 1961. The state rented it as an annex to the Willowbrook State School for the mentally retarded on Staten Island, which is overcrowded. Stung by public criticisms that such places are "a reproach to us all," the director invited the press to take an unlimited look at conditions in the five-story brick building near the East River waterfront.

A very pale boy of four with abnormally thin legs lay in a narrow bed in a second-floor ward. A physician was asked if such a child would have to spend his entire life in bed.

"The prospect is that this child will never walk," he said. "He has severe cerebral palsy and a scissors deformity of the legs. But perhaps someday he will be less spastic, more comfortable, easier to wash or dress."

One child in the ward was squeezing a noisemaking rubber duck—honk, honk, honk. Butterfly mobiles, fixed to the head bars of several beds, twisted slowly. Two white-clad women attendants were going from bed to bed trying to get each child to take a small plastic glass of apple juice. It was a task requiring great patience.

A physician said two things were necessary to work with such children: "Protective mentality, so you don't go home and weep as I did twenty-one years ago—and I was a doctor—and an empathy for the children. If you don't have them you can't remain in this work for long."

There are occasional rewards, he said. "You walk along and all of a sudden you see a child who has never shown any facial expression at all and you get a faint smile or a grin. He does not recognize you as you, but he does recognize a person showing some interest in him."

The objective, he said, is to "do whatever you can to make their lives as pleasant as possible."

Gouverneur was reopened for retarded children after the state spent about $100,000 for repairs. It must have more than one employee for every child it cares for. "This building, while it's old, is safe and clean and it's one of the few such institutions anywhere that is not overcrowded," the director said. "I would rather have these children here than shoved in on top of crowded pediatric wards at Willowbrook."

A Knock on Many Doors

It was a splendid apartment house once, with a place in the sun on Morningside Heights; then it was chopped down into rooms. Now 400 people dwell there, each with a sink, a gas burner and a table-top refrigerator. On the wall at the end of each hallway there is a coin telephone and the green paint around it is sketched with half-names and numbers: "Liz RI 9-9379." "Morrisey TR 5-0744."

In order to squeeze more dollars out of every foot of space, dozens of once fashionable buildings lining upper Broadway have been partitioned into cheerless stalls, and the stalls have been rented to people of no apparent consequence or interest.

But if a man could walk down the long, dim corridors of these buildings, and knock on many doors, he would discover decent human beings whose faces were masks waiting to be lifted, whose lives were stories waiting to be told.

Heavy glass doors with iron frames swing into the small, white-tiled lobby of the twelve-story building at Broadway and West 113th Street. The lobby is furnished with five chairs and three tables in a style that might best be called rummage-sale Victorian. The pieces, all heavy as cement, bristle with brooding figures and protuberances carved in dark wood. A grim-looking woman of late middle age, a lobby lounger, fixes everyone who enters with a haddock stare.

"Tony the Painter" is always about with his ladder and buckets, refreshing the house with paint. He barters his art for his room.

Every surface in the building that is susceptible to paint is painted in a single shade of green—a hesitant green, mixed with blue. Too green to be sky, too blue to be grass; call it bleen. Tony never dips a brush into anything else.

The bilious monotony of bleen has its cause in a prudent economizing that takes the cash and lets the decor go. The woman who owns the house knows a source of surplus paint, cheap by any reckoning, but with an extra saving on massive orders.

In this emerald palace about 125 elderly women live—widows, pensioners, spinsters and welfare cases playing out their years in lonely anonymity. There are more than one hundred foreign nationals, many of them Columbia University students from South America and Asia. The rest are single men and women with routine jobs, though a few are artists, musicians or would-be writers. There is also an evangelist, and a playwright with an eye patch.

On the tenth floor there is a tiny, impossibly thin woman, well past eighty, as brittle and dry as a stick, who will reel off for anyone the dreadful catalogue of her ills, including a series of fractures so long that it threatens to contort the listener's countenance with a burst of involuntary laughter.

On the fourth floor there is a young man who is exquisitely polite. He is avoided by most of the men, ignored by many of the women, but held in high favor by some of the women, who find him a "nice young man" of a fawning sort too rare in the world.

Possibly the most vibrant personality in the building is a seventy-eight-year-old man called "Brother Russell," a name he got in church. His typical greeting to a young man is to take a classic boxer's stance—feet set apart, chest barreled, elbows and fists cocked—and to inquire with a wicked grin whether he cares "to go a couple of rounds?"

Many of the older people in the building have a slightly haunted aspect. They move a bit furtively in the halls and quickly snap the locks on their doors when they enter their rooms. They seem to be avoiding unnamed dangers. But the door to Brother Russell's ninth-floor room is rarely locked, night or day, and most of the time it is a foot ajar, a standing invitation to enter. Borrowers say he has about the fastest wallet-draw on Morningside Heights.

There is a certain almost comic charm about Christopher, a lean, slack-postured, redhaired southerner who dropped out of Columbia College and took a job selling toys at Macy's in the Christmas rush.

"I was about the only one in the place who wasn't an actor out of work," he said. "My father thinks the world came to an end when I quit Columbia—but this is me. I have an idea that what a guy's actually doing is the important thing about the guy. I mean it's a real thing about the person, and not somebody else's thing about him."

In the east wing on the eighth floor there is a woman who often protests that she harbors no dislike for any race or creed, but who has never been known to get along with any Jew who moved into the wing.

She charged one older Jewish woman with playing the radio too loudly; she intimidated a very young one by rapping sharply on her door and publicly scolding her for not leaving the bath in fresh condition; and the excellent violin playing of a Juilliard School student named Isaac greatly annoyed her. The violinist stayed on, the older woman moved to another floor, and the girl moved out of the house the day after she had been reproached.

A very elderly woman who used to travel widely giving lectures holds onto the illusion of her self-sufficiency with pitiful courage. Two years ago she began leaning on a cane as she walked to the store to buy her small provisions. Now she is badly stooped and lame, but still she refuses help. Soon, inevitably, she will fall, and the illusion will be finally, irrevocably shattered.

A young woman who sometimes works in the slant-roofed office under the stairs in the lobby, taking in the rent, lost her husband by defection some months ago. She was left alone with a three-year-old daughter, and there is now an austere and shriveled severity about her. She walks erectly, eyes focused straight ahead, and her set features melt into a smile only at the surest touch of friendliness. A halting attempt to speak kindly brings a rather curt "Hello." Some will not try a second time.

Already she seems an appropriate figure among the thousands of homeless housed on upper Broadway.

Times Square After Hours

In the long, lonely hours of early morning, Times Square changes. It ceases for a while to play its practiced role as glamour girl of the Western world. Pre-dawn visitors see it in what amounts to its cold cream and curlers.

The Square loses its self-consciousness, takes off its garish, neon-painted face and goes through various ablutions. The pedestrian streams that flow for more than sixteen hours a day—from about 8:00 A.M. to past midnight—diminish to a trickle, then stop.

The beggar's tin cup does not rattle; the target guns go silent in the slot-machine parlors; loud speakers do not pour scratchy melodies into the ears of passersby; curbstone evangelists shout final affirmations above the chorus of their hecklers and go home.

There is a point past 3:00 when the loudest noise a stray visitor hears in the Square is the click-click of the inner workings of a traffic-signal, switching lights.

A thin old woman, stooped and clutching a double bucket filled with dirty water, comes out of a tropical drink stand and struggles to the curb to dump it, quietly cursing a passerby.

Harry Miller of Brooklyn tends the all-night newsstand at Broadway and Forty-third Street. "How long I been here?—ask me that. Since 1937. It's in my blood," he said, setting up and knocking down his own question. The newsie works from midnight to 9:00 A.M. "I get the midnight rush—people who want the races, the ballgames—and the morning rush. I was nineteen years old when I started. The trolleys were here then.

"The crowd is different now. Lindy's is closed, Toffenetti's is gone, Hector's, the Astor. The Capitol Theater's gone, the Roxy, the Paramount. They brought a nice crowd here. Now there's a lot of riff-raff mixed in."

This is the diary of a summer night in Times Square:

10:30 P.M. The crowds are thick on the sidewalks and street vendors work on nearly every block. The litter baskets—they look like volcanoes of trash that have just erupted—are overloaded from a Sunday's use. Debris is strewn over the pavement and in the gutters. A wind stirs up scraps and creates a funnel of newspaper that swirls up in a mad ballet.

Two men in work chinos are leaning on a lamppost at Broadway and Forty-fourth Street. One has a flashlight jammed in a rear pocket. They watch the passing show, a look of faintly contemptuous amusement on their faces.

A wiry man shaved bald comes by in a red, white and blue striped undershirt. Their eyes follow him. Two flamboyantly effeminate males in bright satins strut north. The men's smiles widen and they exchange a knowing glance. Two patrolmen stand against a clothing store window, watching. Their faces say nothing. They have seen it all too many times.

Most of the strollers are young, in the late teens to early thirties. Many are alone. Some couples walk hand in hand. Few have the scrubbed, alert tourist look, but most are plainly dressed in casual summer clothing and the scene is only intermittently Halloween in Hades.

11:05 P.M. A hairy chested young man in an unbuttoned shirt bumps a plywood case mounted on roller skate wheels up the curb at Forty-sixth Street. He unsnaps several latches and opens it, revealing rows and rows of costume jewelry.

"One dollar each—no tax," he says.

11:15 P.M. An attempt to preach near Broadway on Forty-fifth Street has degenerated into an abrasive quarrel.

"Fact Two!" blurts a man who a moment earlier offered to cite three facts to prove a point.

"I'm still waiting for Fact One!" his adversary shouts.

A block away another exhorter is crying out reproach. "I have only been out here for fifteen minutes and I have lived a lifetime already. I am old," a listener remarks, evidently a man given to pithy philosophical formulations.

The Automat in Times Square is a quieter forum. There are twelve people seated at seven tables, as seen through a slot between two window posters. Three are eating. The rest are reading or talking. One of the three eaters is nursing a pink lemonade.

There are four hawkers of long-stemmed flowers of plastic-crystal from Forty-fifth to Forty-seventh Streets on Broadway. A fifth bearer carries his assortment into the zone of this glut. He sets his down exactly beside a young woman's display. She smiles. They chat. Macy's tells Gimbels.

A horse-drawn open cab is heading south with three sharply dressed riders in it. The driver is an old man with a hearing aid and a high silk hat and he has an old brown and white plug horse. The rig stops at Forty-fifth Street. The light changes. The old man gives his horse the go signal. The horse does not move. He pulls on the reins sharply. The horse, who may be hard of hearing, moves.

It is near midnight and a tall, bearded man about thirty is weaving the melodic line for a winging trio in the high, sweet notes of a recorder. They stand against the iron grating drawn across the wide entrance to the Bond store at Forty-fifth Street. A sad-faced youth with sunken cheeks, dressed all in black, plays the guitar. A black man strums a one-string wash tub, made out of a tub, a pole and a string.

They do solo turns, producing a kind of strung-out cool jazz with a clean line. Now and then the wash tub man switches off to another instrument—a lard can turned upside down on a wooden crate. He slaps the top lightly with a couple of wire brushes. The three men look as though they had just met, but they work well together. A neon sign blinks on and off, almost keeping the beat, and every flash lays orange streaks on their faces. The bearded player has a severe case of rhythm. His left foot taps and his whole body, linked to it as to a pedal, jerks. A crowd of about fifty stands in a semi-circle. The music stops. There is no applause.

The tall one picks up a big tin can and moves through the crowd, a little diffidently, as an artist stooping to commerce. The people prove more eager to listen than to pay. In a few seconds most of them are gone.

A bronzed man nearby holds up two empty hands and shows both sides to onlookers in an impromptu magic show. Suddenly, he has a red ball the size of a bing cherry in his fingers. A second one pops into view. There is nothing up his sleeve. He has no sleeve. He is in an undershirt.

A block away a blind man shakes his cup and listens to the scuff of feet going by. In the midst of forty men gathered in a tight knot where the preacher had stood, someone asserts that the ancient Egyptian civilization was black. A portly, bald man called "Pop" says, "I am willing to concede that this is true, in part. But there were some people who were not conventionally known as blacks. . . ."

"Right!" a voice interrupts. "They were not conventionally known as blacks because the history was written by whites—that's why."

There is a cracking sound. Strong fumes come up. Someone has dropped a bottle of ammonia at the curb. In less than half a minute, only two of the forty men are left. The anthropological seminar will not reconvene again tonight.

12:40 A.M. Charles Wilson is at the top of a ladder on Forty-second Street, rapidly unhooking the big letters on the marquee of the Times Square Theater, one of eleven film houses on the block whose lights are all still blazing.

Swiftly he shrinks the words "VAMPIRE" and "HELLCAT" to "PIRE" and "CAT." The letters weigh about a pound each and he brings them down in a stack of about a dozen.

"Depends on how you feel," he says, "If you don't feel good, you bring ten down. If you feel good you bring fifteen. It varies." A trick of his trade is to leave the quotation marks and a few vowels hanging on the blank face and move them to fit the new titles.

In a few minutes the lights on the marquees start going off and by 2:00 A.M. the street is dark. The moving news sign on the tower a block away is out, and the big advertising signs in the Square are switched off, too.

1:45 A.M. Irving Rosenblatt plunges a mop head into a bucket of soapy water and sloshes it quickly over the window of a pancake restaurant. Six quick downward strokes with a squeegee and the pane is clean.

"It's a pain in the neck with restaurants," he says, "but it's easier at night. You have to do the insides, too, and the eaters don't want to be pushed around. At nighttime, it's mostly hang-arounds, so you can move them pretty easy.

Daytime, some woman comes along and says, 'Oh! There's a drop on my stocking. Buy me a new pair.' "

"You must be crazy, lady," is his blunt reply to that appeal.

He says he does twenty-two places in a night. He is a solid, sun-browned man with a white mustache, and he just happens to have a red album of his handball triumphs over there in the glove compartment of his car. He gets it out and leafs through it. "I won two national handball titles," he says. "I'm fifty-nine and I still run some of these kids into the ground. Look at this—1968 nationals. I treasure all this here stuff."

Ten pancakes sit on the flat griddle in the front window, making three stacks of three, leaving one oversized one. The griddle man dumps a load of bacon and eggs on top of it.

2:30 A.M. There are four long benches in Duffy Square, but all of the space is taken, half by sitters, half by sleepers stretched full-length. Flashy young women are standing on some of the corners on the east side of the square, seemingly with nothing to do. Two sailors approach two of them. They stroll north, talking. One of the women suddenly steps out and hails a cab. All four get in and go off.

Eight stools are occupied in a tiny eatery on Forty-third Street. "Give me a bagel with a shmear," a man says, and he gets it with cream cheese. "Make it quick, I only got a half hour," he says.

"I got all night," the counterman says.

3:10 A.M. You can walk a block in the Square now and not pass a soul. Private garbage removal trucks dominate the action, backing up to curbs to receive huge deposits of refuse in plastic bags or barrels. The last of the moviegoers are straggling out of the darkened houses on Forty-second Street. A homeless woman uses the Nathan's main door for shelter. "She's here every night. I let her sit on a stack of papers," Harry Miller says.

The Times Square Motor Hotel's large lobby is empty,

with most of the seat cushions set up against the backs to discourage walk-in lobby loungers.

3:33 A.M. Trucks delivering ice, bread, milk and pies arrive before dawn. Vacuuming, sweeping, polishing, swabbing floors with wet mops goes on behind many glass facades.

A United City Ice truck is parked outside a fruit drink stand and a big man, bare to the waist, hoists a large cake into a motorized shredding machine near the tailboard. The machine shudders and makes a loud sputtering noise and spits out two buckets of shaved ice to be carried into the stand.

5:23 A.M. The sky is gray-blue now. Empty buildings stand like cardboard cutouts against the slowly brightening day. Pigeons lining the long ledge above the Astor and Victoria theaters, under the block-long ad sign, are stirring from sleep. One flutters out and perches atop the T in the Victoria sign. Then there is another, and another, and all but the second I is occupied.

A sleeper on one of the benches stretches slowly. The day is at hand. Soon the Square will be crowded with all of its regular users—taxis and buses, and pigeons and people.

City Scenes

Horticultural Homicide

May, 1960—In Central Park last week, workmen tore down a fifty-year-old arbor, the decaying host to five wisteria vines. This, in the view of John C. Georgi, was horticultural homicide.

The arbor stood near the junction of West Drive and the Seventy-second Street automobile entrance to the park. Winds blew part of it down one night. The Parks Department dismantled the rest the following day.

When Mr. Georgi, a wallpaper muralist, came upon the spot, he had many of the sentiments expressed by George Pope Morris in the lines:

> *Woodman, spare that tree!*
> *Touch not a single bough!*
> *In youth it sheltered me.*
> *And I'll protect it now.*

The difference was that by the time Mr. Georgi arrived, the vines had been cut to stumps.

Nevertheless, in an arboreal fever, Mr. Georgi called the Parks Department to make sure that two other arbors flanking the automobile entrance would not be touched. And they will not, the department said.

"I've made a pilgrimage every year for fifteen years to see that arbor," he said. The pilgrimage was not long (four stops by IRT express from his home at 232 West Tenth Street) but it was sincere.

This year he found no arbor—just twenty postholes in an asphalt walkway. And hacked stumps.

The gracious shelter of the eighty-foot-long pine arbor was a dreadful loss, he said—"wanton" and "irreparable."

Mrs. Georgi, a painter, had been there a few days before and had reported the vines "dripping with buds and ready to blossom."

The Parks Department said the stumps would send out new shoots, and it promised to build a new arbor for them to twine round. Mr. Georgi said the vines would take years to replace themselves.

"I don't expect them to take a public referendum every time they want to trim a privet hedge," he said, "but they could at least have left the arbor up while the vines are blooming." The more he talked about it the angrier he became.

"I telephoned the Garden Clubs of America," he spluttered. "Miss Hill there—horrified to hear of it, said she would bring it up at the annual meeting next day. She suggested I call the Parks Department, Mr. Constable.

"I called. Mr. Constable was not available. Talked to a Mr. White—horrified to hear the old wisteria vines had been destroyed. Said he would check and call me back. He suggested that the old supports had fallen down, which is not true. I called back and got put on to a Mr. Jenkins, who seemed to be the director of park maintenance. Jenkins said he, too, was very upset to hear of the destruction.

"I asked to know, 'Why?' 'Who gave the order?' He didn't know but said he would call me back later and tell me who had actually done it. I said I wasn't interested in who held the saw but would like very much to see a head or two roll in the upper supervisory staff who were responsible for the outrage. He promised an investigation of the matter would be made.

"I called the Brooklyn Botanical Gardens, Mrs. Sutcliffe, who, on my estimated dimensions of the double trunk of the oldest vine—approximately twelve by fifteen or eighteen inches—at its base, thought it must have been at least fifty, possibly sixty years old.

"A thing of great beauty is gone. Did it need pruning?

Probably. Did the supports need re-inforcing or replacement? Most likely. Was it infected with some dread plant disease? Highly improbable. But for lack of direction, all is lost. We will not see its like again in our lifetime, not in Central Park."

In acidulous terms, Mr. Georgi proposed a "salute" to the Parks Department: "While you crowd our city pavements with concrete pork barrels topped with a few desiccated tulips and tired privet, while you extend your greetings to Tokyo with a tasteless version of a Japanese garden in the heart of the city—while these were being installed, your department was cutting down truly venerable wisteria vines in Central Park, a thing of beauty which your Japanese guests would have known how to enjoy."

Here, Mr. Georgi rose to poetic utterance: "It was covered with buds, tender pendants of green with promise of a glorious cascade of pale mauve and purple blossoms. It would have been in full bloom about now.

"If it was rickety, as they say, they could have propped it up. If they didn't have the money, they could have sent out the clarion call for contributions. Anything, but not murder! It's absolute, sheer horticultural murder."

July, 1969—There are some who grieve well and some who grieve long, and there are some who grieve well *and* long, and John C. Georgi belongs in the latter category. He went to Central Park yesterday to place a wreath and conduct a memorial tribute at the site of a lovely old wisteria arbor that Parks Department workmen had hacked down nearly a decade ago.

He went, as he put it, to "the very spot where the fifty-year-old vines were slaughtered." The Parks Department had not, as it had promised at that time, put up a new arbor nor were any traces to be found of the old wisteria stumps.

Since nothing else was handy, Mr. Georgi had his memorial wreath set at the base of a lamppost, which happened to be three feet from a portable privy that had been installed for the use of workmen on another project.

Three long, purple ribbons streamed from a bow at the top of the wreath and silver letters spelled out the phrases: "IN LOVING MEMORY OF/THE WISTERIA VINES/MURDERED MAY 1960."

In his memorial tribute, Mr. Georgi said, "The wisteria vines and supporting arbor on this site were wantonly destroyed in May, 1960, by order of the Parks Department, for lack of funds to make repairs, or just plain lack of vision."

He told sadly of "a small section, a perfect little gem of landscaping," and recalled that, "This small arbor, seventy or eighty feet in length, with benches, was covered by six or eight gnarled and lusty wisteria vines, and in full bloom was a sight to see. It was a pleasant spot to rest a moment, a proper and welcome stop after crossing the bridle path by the ornamental bridge designed by Olmsted and Vaux. There was always the possibility of a run-away horse and rider to add to the day's excitement.

"It was the early 1900s when the vines were started. My last sight of it was in early spring, 1959. My wife and I, year after year, kept a check on its possible full flowering, weather being what it is here, and made a point of going for the occasion."

Thunder rumbled ominously overhead and a violent rain storm descended but Mr. Georgi held his ground. He recalled how he and his wife would "sit for a few hours" in the shade of the old arbor "and wonder at the beauty of it and enjoy the early afternoon."

"*That* spring day, a Sunday, happened to be 'I Am An American Day' with ceremonies at the Band Shell. As I watched them come up the walk, singly and in groups from the Seventy-second Street entrance, these new Americans, they passed beneath the arbor on the walkway. They would often pause, noticing the pungent, spicy scent of the abundant, pendant purple blooms.

"Sometimes you would see a smile, or at least a nod of the head in approval, as if to say, 'It can't be all bad if they can keep and protect all this beauty. Maybe I have done the right thing to come to this great City.'

"Of course, they couldn't know that next year this living, flowering archway would be demolished."

It was 2:30 and a second downpour came and Mr. Georgi was forced to retreat along the footpath, across the Drive and up through the remaining fragment of what had once been a long and lovely walkway-arbor, a stretch of sweet shade in a city whose citizens need all the blooming shelter they can get.

The Great Bee Roundup

The City's emergency forces massed yesterday on a hollow tree in the Inwood section of Manhattan to consider what might be done about a swarm of bees that had lodged in a topmost branch at the rear of 65 Hillside Avenue.

The bees had rashly sent emissaries into some of the apartments to make friendly overtures, but residents, mistaking their gesture for armed aggression, called the police.

The police came. They gazed up at the swarm eighty feet above the ground in the hilly, rocky wooded area behind the building. None of the techniques of law enforcement seemed applicable, so the police decided that bees in trees, like stranded cats, were the Fire Department's business.

Ladder Fourteen responded swiftly but could not maneuver

into the wooded section. The firemen did not have a portable ladder that would reach the treetop. If they had, they wouldn't have known what to do when they got up there, so they called the Parks Department.

The Parks Department said, sensibly, that it didn't have any tree pruners on duty. But even if a tree pruner had been available to cut the swarm's branch off, a beekeeper with a receptacle called a "bee retriever" would have had to be present. Otherwise, the bees, brought crashing to the ground, would create what the Fire Department described as a "condition."

By this time the very residents who had called the police were out, pleading with the City's finest and bravest not to do anything that would overexcite the bees. By 7:00 P.M. all forces had withdrawn and the bees were still up there, snickering.

The Magistrate and the Parrot

The Case of the Garrulous Parrot was resolved yesterday in East New York Magistrate's Court.

Mrs. Cecelia Amato, a day worker, had charged that the forty-year-old bird had repeatedly addressed her in "vile and indecent language" as she walked to a subway station in the mornings. But yesterday she withdrew her complaint of disorderly conduct against Sam Maiorana, who pledged to keep his parrot in a private place, out of earshot.

Pete's morning perch had been the back of a chair in front of 1257 Myrtle Avenue in Brooklyn's Bushwick section, where his master lives behind a vacant store. It was from this vantage that Mrs. Amato said the bird had repeatedly anathematized her in the rich argot of the waterfront.

In previous court appearances Mrs. Amato had given a kind of anagrammatic series of clues to the words she was sure she had heard. She gave the first letter of each word and told the number of letters that would complete it—leaving the rest to the knowing conjecture of the court.

On each of these occasions, Mr. Maiorana had also appeared, carrying his parrot on a stick. The bird was attired in a vivid mélange of jungle colors—pale green, a bit of orange on the wings, a splotch of bright yellow on the crown, a smidgin of blue on the beak.

Those who had hoped the bird would shatter the decorum of the court with one loud word of obscene rebuke to the whole judicial process were disappointed. Hour after hour, Pete sat silent—a figure of august propriety.

Yesterday, for the first time, Mr. Maiorana came without his parrot.

"Why isn't the parrot here today?" demanded Magistrate John F. Furey.

"I figured she got no case," Mr. Maiorana said, pointing at Mrs. Amato.

"Your honor, ask him if he's got one or two parrots," Mrs. Amato suggested.

"How many parrots have you got?" the judge asked.

Mr. Maiorana said he had one "boy parrot," to which Mrs. Amato replied: "Well, when he's out on the street he's talking, but when he's in court, he's quiet." Mr. Maiorana rejected the implication that he had brought a stooge parrot into court.

He then attempted to pass a piece of paper to the bench. "What's that, a character attestation for the parrot?" the judge asked, spurning it.

"If you've got anything else that talks, keep it away from this woman," Magistrate Furey directed after Mrs. Amato had withdrawn her complaint. Mr. Maiorana said afterward that he had an inarticulate male boxer, Baby, and Tommy, a silent solemn cat.

A bird expert, who asked to remain anonymous during a telephone interview, said that though the mechanism by which parrots mimic human sounds is not fully understood, parrots are known to have a highly developed "intelligence."

"Nothing verging on rational deduction, of course, but they have a pretty good memory," he said.

Bricklayers: A Fraternity of Strangers

An officer of Local 34 of the Bricklayers, Masons and Plasterers International Union yesterday denied that the bricklaying business is a family affair.

"That's a fallacy," declared Vincent Dee in the course of a bricklaying contest on the site of Cooper Union's new engineering building at Astor Place.

A few minutes later Mr. Dee was congratulating the winner, eighteen-year-old Kevin McCann, for having scored 273 out of a possible 300 points. Kevin's father, John, a bricklayer, stood nearby, beaming.

His grandfather would have been proud, too, for he had been a bricklayer before them. The McCanns live in Jackson Heights, Queens. Kevin also has a bricklaying uncle.

This did not seem to be the way to knock a fallacy into a cocked hat, but Hugh Murphy of the United States Department of Labor strongly supported Mr. Dee.

"Any boy who has a sincere desire to take up the trade is welcome to walk into the union's office and apply," he said. His background qualified him as an expert.

"My grandfather was a bricklayer, my father was a bricklayer, I was a bricklayer and my son is an apprentice bricklayer," Mr. Murphy added.

By placing first among fifteen apprentice bricklayers, young McCann earned the right to represent Local 34 at the state bricklaying finals at Syracuse in April. He also won one hundred dollars.

"I didn't think I did too good," Kevin said modestly, after a gilt cardboard crown had been placed on his head.

To an observer short on family background, who needed a few basic clues on the art of laying bricks, the contest was a series of minuscule revelations.

The fifteen competitors built structures that looked something like the tops of chimneys. The structures were called brick piers. A pier is anything that is an isolated piece of masonry, apart from a continuous wall.

There were six different plumbings in the five-course structures. A plumbing is a test applied to a corner to be sure that it is perfectly perpendicular. A course is a layer of bricks.

Red jumbo facebrick was used. It had a wirecut surface. Facebrick is normally laid where bricks will show and is fancier than hidden brickwork. A wirecut surface is not actually cut with wires, but it looks as though it had been, and it provides a certain esthetic effect.

The apprentices laid stretchers, not headers. Stretchers are bricks laid lengthwise, with one side showing. Headers are bricks that show one end.

The judges gave points for each of six technical categories and for a column headed "miscellaneous."

"That's in case a kid got sassy or decided to give one of the judges some lip," a judge explained.

Did anyone lose points for disrespect?

"Got no lip at all," he said.

Uriburu and the Blob

A bright green spot moved swiftly down the East River late yesterday afternoon. It was of mysterious origin to river viewers who did not know that it was a work of art.

The spot—a light, minty green—covered an area much larger than a tennis court. Borne along by ebb-tide currents, it slid under the Queensboro Bridge, swirled past the United Nations and Bellevue Hospital on its course to Wall Street and the harbor.

The work of art was unsigned, of course, but it was the latest creation of Uriburu, a thirty-year-old Argentine artist, who had made a similar green splash in the canals of Venice a few months ago. Uriburu is one of the new breed of environmental artists who take nature for their canvas and seize cities for background.

Uriburu thinks big. He will go to Paris to dye a patch of the Seine on June 15 and then on July 15, he will repeat the process in the Riachuelo River in his home city of Buenos Aires.

"So I do a very big triangle," he explained earnestly. The triangle, which spans the Atlantic in his conception, will have three corners, the green spots in the East River, the Seine, the Riachuelo.

It was 4:03 P.M. when the S. T. Boss, a green and red tug, pulled in near East 61st Street. Uriburu and two friends loaded ten large black cans onto the hired craft. Each can contained about twenty-five pounds of fluorescent sodium, a rust-colored powder, which the three men dumped into the water, chucking the empty cans overboard, too.

The rusty powder foamed white, then turned green. Streaks of green quickly twisted into serpentine lines, then spread out into a system of three large blobs. The blobs coalesced into a roundish shape, the ultimate work, roughly 175 feet by 50 feet.

A motorized craft moved downriver pushing two immense garbage scows heaped high with refuse. The blunt-nosed scows, river brutes of no poetic sensitivity, bashed the work. Uriburu took no offense.

"I like only transitory things," the artist said. "It is more interesting to do something that moves, that is not static. An artist has to be a free man. I do not want to work in an enclosed space. Out of doors!

"All the modern art is disappearing from the galleries and is coming out where it can be seen by all the people in a very big space.

"Venice is an eternal city, and they say no one can change it, but you can change Venice in a day, without damage, of course, by art in plastic forms. I used 30 kilos (about 66 pounds) of dye in Venice. It's expensive. Very expensive."

"I think it's beautiful," a bystander said. " To spend so much money for a moment."

"Excuse me, I have to wash my hands," Uriburu said, bending down to a rain puddle and rinsing his rust-colored palms. The puddle turned green. It was a small work.

The Truck That Came to Dinner

"VRRRRROOM!" said Mrs. Charles Gaines as she sat in her handsomely appointed, spacious apartment on West Fifteenth Street. "VRROOM, VROOM, VROOM, VROOM."

She was imitating the sound a huge tractor-trailer makes when it tries to start up a ramp over a dip in the street just outside her living room window. Mrs. Gaines is an expert. Her front windows look out on forty-two truck berths at a block-long loading platform for one of the largest express depots in the world—the Manhattan Assorting Terminal.

West Fifteenth Street has a split personality. The south side of the street is zoned R-8 (residential). The north side is zoned M1-5 (industrial). The invisible dividing line runs down the middle of the street. On the south side there are twenty-two apartment buildings, three to six stories high with front stoops and iron railings. The truck platform is on the north side. The Port Authority rented it out late in 1965 for the terminal's twenty-four-hours-a-day, seven-days-a-week loading and unloading operation.

Tenants in all the apartments facing it are living in acute distress. They have the mercantile equivalent of all-news radio—"all noise, all the time," the difference being that there's no knob to shut it off with. At almost any hour of the day or night there are seven to ten trucks in the street, scrambling to get into one of the berths.

The "CHIFF-CHIFF" of hydraulic brakes (like steam escaping from a narrow fissure), the scrunch of clashing gears, the thump of wooden boxes being unloaded, the blaring of a loudspeaker system, the growl of trucks being jockeyed in and out of position, the slamming shut of metal doors hardly ever stop.

"This was a window," Gerhardt Liebmann, an architect and artist, said in a front bedroom of his seven-room apartment. Now, instead of a window he can see out of, he almost has one he can't hear through.

Over the glass, in his effort to erect a sound barrier, Mr. Liebmann installed two thicknesses of composition board, a wooden shutter and burlap curtains: "and it still doesn't keep all the noise out." He does not want to brick it up.

Mrs. Mattie Dechner has three rooms with five windows, all facing the street. She has a tape recording she made one day, which she calls, "A Quiet Sunday Afternoon."

There has been a freight platform across the street since 1932, but it was only used from 8:00 A.M. to 6:00 P.M. on weekdays and residents had learned to live with it. Many of them were away at work from a little after 8:00 to a little before 6:00 anyway. On weekends the other side of the street was as silent and lifeless as a pyramid, and not having any neighbors over there had certain advantages in quietness, too.

"You try and park a freight train—that's what these are, they come right off the tracks—in such a narrow street," a resident said, referring to the piggyback trailers that are always being jackknifed into place at berths running from Eighth to Ninth Avenues.

The street is thirty-six feet wide. The big trailers are forty-two feet long, detached from their nine-foot-long driver cabs.

"The docking space recommended for trucks that long is fifty-seven feet," Mr. Liebmann said. "If they had the docking space they needed, that would put them sixteen feet into our bedrooms and right into our beds."

Drivers sometimes have to bump up over the curb onto the sidewalk to maneuver into position on the crowded street. They dent fences, crack stoops and make pedestrians shrink into doorways. Several weeks ago a distraught, rather elderly woman came out of the front door of her basement apartment and chased a driver down the block waving a hatchet, while people cheered from their windows. He got away.

Children can't play on the sidewalk, houses shudder, windows rattle, plaster cracks.

"There are two reverse gears, I've discovered," Mrs. Gaines said with crisp authority. "The second one is the noisy one, but it's faster. They don't sneak out of here at night. VRRRRROOM! they gun the motors to get out, then CHUME! into gear, CHUME! into the next gear, then they slam on the brakes at the corner."

Mrs. Gaines, the wife of an actor, also complained about "swearing, shouting and yelling" outside her windows. Bursts of outrage seem to be as indispensable to the wheels of commerce as grease is to a crankcase. She said she was building up "a monstrous anger" that she did not think was good for her.

"You come home. You've worked all day, you're tired," Mr. Liebmann said. "Now's the time to sit in a chair, relax and have a beer. But the hell of it is, when you're through they're just beginning, and you know they're going to go all night."

Whatever spirit of good will once had flourished on the block toward express trucking has been turned into a militant and almost warlike hatred, as residents chafe and "CHIFF," fume and "CHUME!" in their affliction. Mrs. Dechner, an activist, has been organizing tenant opposition and the terminal has had to pay some heed, if only to the point of arguing its own necessity.

"The terminal is a vital link in the service to the residents and the economy of New York City," a spokesman said. "Like the airlines, we're trying to do everything possible to ameliorate the noise, but we have to operate as we are operating to sort and dispatch inbound and outbound shipments to fifty states. This is part of the fabric of the absolutely necessary round-the-clock activity that supports the economic life of cities."

Hugh Graef, director of operations, addressed a letter to "All Drivers" last month that was handed to them with their pay, asking that "each of you consider at all times the welfare of these residents."

"I can best sum it up," he wrote, "that we should treat these residents as we would want any of our relatives treated who might be faced with the requirement of living near a truck terminal."

In reposing confidence in the capacity of truck drivers for empathy, residents believe Mr. Graef has hit upon a just about totally feckless noise-abatement scheme.

(The rights of a few hundred tenants being a poor match for rights-of-way affecting a million express parcels, the terminal stuck it out for five years until February, 1970, outlasting most of the tenants with front apartments on the block. Mr. Liebmann, who had once felt like a king in his seven-room, floor-through apartment, took it for two years before moving to SoHo. When the former occupants quit, some of the fine old apartments were remodeled into mice warrens and let out at three times the rent. The people who moved in were not fully aware of their jeopardy. The truck depot was silent—only because, the Port Authority said, there was "no tenant for it.")

Blackout

Midtown Manhattan was divided for a while last night—half-blaze, half-black—as the island's vital center became an odd patchwork of darkness and light.

The contrasts were everywhere and sometimes they seemed inexplicable: at points there was light east but none west, or light north but none south, or light low but none high.

Either you had it or you didn't, and there was a world of difference to be traversed from one curbstone to the next. Like the moon, Broadway had a light side and a dark side for a while. A man moving down the main stem from upper Manhattan had a margin of light to his right but he glanced eastward into thick blackness, like the blackness of a rain forest on a moonless night. Whiplash winds and driving rain with hail made it a rather eerie scene. Pedestrians huddled under movie marquees for semi-shelter, dashing out in clusters for the few taxis that came along.

The march of lighted street lamps on Forty-second Street from the Hudson River ended abruptly on the west side of

Fifth Avenue and there were no more lighted posts along the street to the East River. The Chrysler Building, all dark, was a silent silhouette stabbing the cloud cover and its top was snuffed from sight by rolling mists.

At Turtle Bay, the United Nations glass secretariat was a slab of ghostly gray, except for a spine of yellow emergency lights running up the middle.

The zone of light and the zone of darkness fell in eccentric patterns over the broad waist of mid-Manhattan. In spots, where the blackness was almost palpable, a man felt he could reach out and scoop in handfuls of it. The north face of the City at the end of Central Park was alight. Nearer Times Square, a hotel's swinging door swung into darkness.

A moving sign wrote in the night. The silhouette of a basketball player went right on dribbling across the animated electric board on Seventh Avenue at Forty-sixth Street. Hurrying pedestrians below stamped boot prints on the hail-speckled pavement.

The Great White Way suffered a kind of electrical schizophrenia. On the east side of Times Square, film shadows failed in the Criterion Theater. Hundreds of patrons sat in darkness for half an hour before leaving and getting their money back. The Victoria Theater's patrons on the west side of Broadway did not know that anything unusual had happened. A film called *Brewster McCloud* continued to unreel there.

The blackout left the wax museum on the west side alight, but it hit marquee and screen at Loew's State I and II, stopping *Love Story*—no spooning.

The spiral of light on the "Pure Wool" sign in Times Square cast its glow throughout the emergency, but opposite it the swirl of neon smoke curling from the yards-long Kent cigarette blacked out—no smoking.

Power is distributed to the city on a checkerboard grid, and many people and places found that they were sitting on the black squares. At first, dwellers in apartments untouched by the failure gazed out at buildings a few yards away where the only light was the occasional gleam of a match or cigarette lighter. The contrasts softened later. Instead of chunks of brightness and blackness in the moonless night, there were towers of light next to others emitting only the warm, dim glow of candlelight.

The temperature-weather beacon atop the Mutual of New York Tower functioned during the power-out but it seemed to be subject to mild electrical fits. At 9:50 P.M. it flashed the right time, but it gave the temperature as 3:30 (instead of 30 degrees).

Above Fiftieth Street, places that didn't need any were prodigal with light. A deserted Daitch-Shopwell supermarket was day-bright with fluorescent candles. In a store nearby, sunlamps kept bagels hot. The first word continued to chase the last word around the electric sign that spins along the brim of the hatbox entrance to the Paramount Theater at Columbus Circle.

An M104 bus moving along East Forty-second Street, headlights slicing the darkness, seemed a fitting symbol of the crisis. The fluorescent tubes in its front half were on but others were out and the rear of the bus was shadowed. Rain fell in twisting sheets in the light-cones of auto headlamps.

A curious and especially inconvenient combination of dark and light affected the Commodore Hotel. The closed and empty shops along its street level were ablaze, but the hotel's face was otherwise entirely dark, from lobby to roof. Guests were stranded high in their hotel rooms. Some could look down and see cops with flashlights directing traffic, their rapid motions creating quick-fading coils of light.

Tad's on Forty-second Street was all dark inside, but steaks were kept sizzling over the charcoal pit. Plumes of fire sent big orange streaks flashing across the frosted window, making the place look from the outside as if it were being gutted by fire.

The facade of Grand Central Terminal was lighted,

including the red and blue face of its clock, but across the street a Horn and Hardart Automat, with an "Open All Night" sign in its window, closed during the blackout.

People kept trying to enter. Raymond Murray, the security guard, got tired of shouting through the glass door and he lettered "NO COMING IN" in the steamy mist that had formed on the plate glass.

"They can't read that," objected Woody Piquette, a customer. "You have to do it backwards." Mr. Piquette then slowly lettered "DO NOT ENTER" backwards on the glass.

A group of nine patrons, mostly elderly, huddled like refugees at a table near the door. They listened to bulletins on a fist-size radio that Patricia Burnett had brought with her. "I wasn't going to take it, but then I did, and it comes in handy," she said.

Across the way, in the terminal, blackness prevailed for a time in the passages. As some newsmen groped to interview bemused passengers, the lights for television cameras pierced the dark interior. To cover a blackout for television, you've got to have plenty of light.

Old Shoes

A long time ago—on March 1, 1916—an itinerant shoe salesman billed a Cornell University student $9.50 for a pair of shoes. A few days ago, a check in that amount was received here, in full if long-deferred payment.

Yesterday the salesman, Ben Lowe, now seventy years old, talked by phone to his former customer, Howard Baylis Carpenter, sixty-five. Mr. Lowe thanked Mr. Carpenter for the check and told him, "Your credit is always good."

If the two should do business on the same principle again,

however, Mr. Carpenter would write the check when he was 109 and Mr. Lowe would receive it at 114.

Back at the time of World War I, Mr. Lowe went from campus to campus with a trunkful of shoes. "In those days, the boys dressed up," he recalled. "They didn't wear dungarees and sweaters."

Mr. Lowe's method was to set up shop in fraternity houses in the late afternoon and early evening, after which he joined the students in their recreation.

At Cornell, with just the right mixture of naïveté and sophistication, he sat in the "jigger shop" eating ice cream and smoking cigars. At Princeton, he quaffed ale and sang at the old Princeton Inn. At Williams, he shot pool.

Mr. Lowe figured that any boy enrolled at Cornell was a little bit of fiscal all right. Credit was freely extended. "All I did was take the father's name and home address and that was it," he said. "There weren't too many poor boys working their way through Andover Academy."

Up near the frozen waters of Lake Cayuga, over which he skated mornings, Mr. Lowe entered the Seal and Serpent Fraternity. He sold a boy a pair of shoes—tan scotch grain numbers with straps across the vamp.

That was January 3, 1916. The boy didn't have the cash. Mr. Lowe said, "Take the shoes," he would bill him later, which he did.

Unexpectedly, the boy, a senior, got a job offer in Cuba. He left school to take it. Later he served in the Navy. Mr. Lowe rose to executive vice president of the Whitehouse & Hardy shoe store. Mr. Carpenter became an engineer with the Esso Standard Oil Company. Years passed. The bill was forgotten.

Last fall, Mr. Carpenter retired. Two weeks later he suffered a stroke. During his recuperation at his home at 6 Tudor Court in Elizabeth, New Jersey, he found time to go over some mementos of his youth, which he found stored in a cardboard file book.

Among the items he found were four unpaid bills, all for

amounts under ten dollars. Two were from doctors. One was from Mr. Lowe. And one from A. Starr Vest, a clothing salesman of Chicago.

Mr. Carpenter, a member of the Plymouth Brethren and a believer in the Bible, realized that for a long time he had been considerably wide of the Biblical injunction to "Owe no man anything . . . ." (found in Romans 13:8). Mr. Carpenter sat down and wrote checks.

"If I wasn't a born-again Christian," he said, "I might have torn them up as old and dead. But the Lord has been good to me." The check to Chicago came back stamped, "Unknown."

Chamber Music: The Tin Can Suite

Chamber music was played yesterday in the middle of two blocked-off play streets in Harlem.

Michael Bartos, the conductor of the New Chamber Orchestra, is not the kind of man to wait temperamentally for a perfect silence to descend upon his audience. Instead, he is the kind who lifts his voice above the din and hollers, "Okay!—Bach!"

Concert lovers who suffer acute violations of sensibility when people clear their throats would possibly have writhed in anguish if they had heard what the game of tin shoes does to Haydn's Symphony No. 45 in F-Sharp Minor. Mr. Bartos is a young welfare worker. He organized the twenty-three-piece volunteer chamber orchestra last year and the average age of its players is twenty-three years.

Tin shoes is played by any number of children about eight years old. A boy begins by smashing in the middle of a soft drink can with a baseball bat. Then he wedges a sneaker into the depression and goes clanking down the street. It is very bad for Bach.

"What do you play—all slow songs?" a girl in pigtails with a chocolate-covered sherbet stick asked, as the orchestra tuned up on 130th Street near Madison Avenue. The rackety rumble of a New Haven train poured over the scene from the elevated structure on Park Avenue. The block was a splendid chaos of 250 screeching children until a priest came out of All Saints Church rectory, put his two little fingers between his teeth and let out a piercing whistle. "You want to hear a violin?" he asked. Some did.

Mrs. Sharon Daniel Diaz, a young mother who had left her three-year-old daughter with a sitter to come out and play her fiddle, said of Mr. Bartos, "He doesn't do this for a living, but he's really desperately dedicated to doing creative and unusual things with music." Nothing short of desperate dedication would have carried him through the afternoon. The players sat on folding chairs in the middle of the street and children weaved in and out among the music stands. Gusty winds kept twisting the portable aluminum stands, to which sheets of music were secured with pink and yellow plastic clothespins.

A nun in white and black sat in a steel chair next to a fire hydrant. Mothers, with children in their laps and arms, perched between the iron railings of twelve-step stoops outside four-story brick and brownstone tenements. A boy with a piece of silver towel rack sawed it across his shoulder in imitation of the violins. He lowered his head to the side and looked dreamily enraptured by his soundless music.

As Mr. Bartos conducted, he saw a strange montage: faces peering from behind window flower pots, boys playing poker on the curbstone, a man in a floppy old hat sitting on top of a rubbish tin, flying basketballs and a girl with a green balloon in her teeth. A tenor dog with operatic aspirations yelped off-key.

When the first concert was over at 4:30 P.M., the

players—fifteen men and eight women—picked up their chairs and instrument cases and walked two blocks west to 129th Street near Lenox Avenue, trailed by youngsters on skateboards, roller skates and bicycles, and dogs on leashes. Sally Warsaw, six, came over to nineteen-year-old Lillian Coster, who was sitting on a milk box, and took a toot on her bassoon. Two children stood perilously close to the far thrusts of Dr. Edward Tolstoi's fiddle bow. Dr. Tolstoi, a professor emeritus of medicine at the Cornell Medical College and a practicing internist, is the oldest member of the amateur but quite professional-sounding orchestra.

Children sat cross-legged on the street and adults stood ringed around the orchestra. A stout mother came over and sharply reproved her son for conduct unsuited to a concert, but that didn't stop the bub-bub-bub sound of inflated rubber balls bouncing on the pavements.

When it was over, Dr. Tolstoi, a freckled man with a fringe of red hair under a baldish dome, packed his fiddle into his case. "That's it," he said. "Now I've got to get right back to the hospital and see some sick people." The orchestra dispersed and the block was left to its own incessant obbligato.

High Bidder

When the auction began under the crystal chandeliers in the cream and gold hotel ballroom, sixty-three men were scattered through four sections of seats. Seven were puffing cigars and many looked like prosperous real estate operators.

"Big money boys," one of the auctioneer's aides said, pointing to the left, to a section dotted with shiny bald heads.

But way down in front, a bit to the right of the raised

lectern, an auto mechanic wearing a blue windbreaker jacket sat next to his wife and their five-year-old daughter, Angela. She wore a bright yellow sweater with a pink comb in her hair.

The Robert Joneses of 320 New York Avenue in the Crown Heights section of Brooklyn were the only family in the grand ballroom of the Hotel Roosevelt, Madison Avenue at Forty-fifth Street.

They sat silent as bids of $8,600 and $15,700 brought down parcels in a public auction of city-owned surplus real estate conducted by the Department of Real Estate.

Seated a few rows away, officers for the Carrano Construction Company of Brooklyn were waiting to make a winning bid of a quarter of a million dollars for an industrial lot on Newtown Creek at Vandam Street in Brooklyn.

When lot No. 53 came up—an irregularly shaped interior plot off 117 Underhill Avenue in Brooklyn, with a three-story frame dwelling on it—Mr. Jones sat up straight and made an opening bid at the stated minimum price—$600.

The bidding had been rather desultory through the morning. More than half the lots put up failed to draw an opening bid, but now suddenly four persons were making bids.

"$900," Mr. Jones signalled to auctioneer Stanley Siebert. But a bid of $950 came, then $1,150.

"$1,200," Mr. Jones said. Still the bids came—$1,300—$1,550—$1,750—$1,800—$2,400, on up to $2,800.

Mr. Jones waited while the auctioneer began to close the sale and then he called, $2,900." There was a bid from the back of the room, $3,000.

Mrs. Jones nudged her husband's elbow and Mr. Jones swallowed and made one more bid, $3,100.

There was silence. "First call." "Second call." "Third call," Mr. Siebert warned. Then—"Sold."

The mechanic and his wife, Gwendolyn, a cashier at the Brooklyn Jewish Hospital, and Angela, were the owners of a home, with what Mrs. Jones called "a pretty pink front," two blocks from the Grand Army Plaza and three blocks from the Brooklyn Museum in one of the best sections of the borough.

"I figured I'd bid up to $1,000—" Mr. Jones said.

"He's no gambler," his wife broke in.

"But she kept nudging me and I was surprised I bid so high," Mr. Jones said. "We'll have to draw the money out of our Christmas Club."

He said another man at work had told him about the City's occasional public auctions a week ago. He had not been inside the frame house yet. "We are going to see how it looks inside, what shape it's in, and see if we want to live there," he said.

The auction went on. No one wanted former Public School 83 on Vernon Boulevard in Long Island City, Queens, a four-story stone-and-brick building offered at a $92,000 minimum. Forty-six parcels were sold, out of 128 offered, for a total of $614,575.

When parcels are passed over, they are marked down. Lot No. 70, a vacant plot on Park Place near Hopkinson Avenue in Brooklyn, twenty feet wide by seventy-one feet deep, was put up for the eighth time—this time at a $100 minimum—but there were no bidders on the piece, which has an assessed value of $1,500.

Kenneth Diamondstone, a twenty-six-year-old counsellor to narcotics addicts at the Beth Israel Hospital, was glad to get "a beautiful brownstone" at 175 Bergen Street in Brooklyn for $15,700, but no one walked out of that ballroom looking more pleased than the Joneses.

Fall Guy

The man's feet suddenly shoot up in the air, flailing; his head sweeps down in a blur, and he is dumped onto his shoulder blades by the woman who once promised to love, honor and obey him.

A wife who throws her husband forcefully to the ground ten or twenty times a day, in front of thirty or forty other women, would seem to be trifling with her vows.

But when Ruth Horan sends her husband Nick sprawling to show other women how to protect themselves from strangers, her act is pro-social, benign and wifely.

Mr. and Mrs. Horan's newest series of "Judo Classes for New York Lasses" began this week in the gymnasium of the Central Branch of the Young Women's Christian Association, Lexington Avenue at Fifty-third Street. Participants range from teen-agers to motherly women in their forties and grandmotherly women in their fifties. One supple sixty-five-year-old woman has enrolled.

A group of more than thirty bare-footed brunettes, blondes, redheads and gray heads, some of them giggling, gathered the other night on a great white mat to be taught how to fend off uninvited advances. Miss Gene Gays, director of health education at the branch, said that, although judo could be fun, the classes were organized "for self-protection," not recreation.

The hour-long evening classes, with separate times for students at various stages of advancement, run for nine weeks. Beginners take no falls and are never thrown. The cost is two dollars a lesson and there is no extra charge for throwing Mr. Horan around.

His role in the classes is that of "the fall guy, or victim." He estimates that he takes "a couple of hundred falls a night." He stalks the advanced students with a rubber knife or a garroting belt to try their skills.

A surprising lot can be accomplished in judo with very little effort. Age, strength and weight are not important factors because an opponent's own weight or strength is used against him, and the force that he applies is turned quickly to his own disadvantage.

"It's all leverage," Mr. Horan explained, seizing a visitor's hand. "With just my two fingers set like this, I could break your wrist."

"I'll take it on faith," the visitor said. He jerked his hand out of the wrist-breaking zone, but Mr. Horan explained that there are many ways in judo to upset or disarm an opponent while damaging nothing but his dignity.

"A woman of 120 pounds can take a man of 200 pounds and flip him just like that," he said, snapping his fingers. "The bigger they are the faster they go over. We timed it, and it takes one-fifth of a second to have them on their backs." The course is especially popular with nurses and others who work shifts that oblige them to walk lonely streets at night.

"I'm just back from my judo class," one nurse told a man who was bothering her and he melted into the shadows.

Martha Altman, an eighteen-year-old City College student majoring in psychology, told why she had enrolled: "I live in the West Bronx and I go to school odd hours, and I didn't like the feeling when I was walking through the neighborhood at night that anything could happen to me. Now if anyone came at me with a knife, I'd break his arm— I wouldn't kill him."

The Small World of Melvin Krulewitch

Melvin L. Krulewitch, Republican candidate for Borough President of Manhattan, yesterday demonstrated a formidable capacity for establishing rapport with the voters. In a two-hour walking tour of the Lower East Side, the candidate found something in common with an astonishing variety of persons, including a few who expressed outright hostility.

Mr. Krulewitch started from in front of 205 East Houston Street at noon. He pointed out that he was no stranger to the neighborhood, having been born a few blocks south at 234 East Broadway. The tour began in a drizzle and ended in driving rain.

In the crowded bazaars of Orchard Street, Mr. Krulewitch drew on his Yiddish.

"Sholem aleichem," he said, entering the first of a dozen bargain dry goods stores. "Vee hut ihr gefastet?" In English it meant: "Peace brother. How have you fasted?"

It was the right note. Solemn faces, absorbed in study of the merchandise, brightened. After further brief amenities, Mr. Krulewitch handed his cards around, shook hands, asked to be remembered at the polls and left.

At one stop, a young man wore a left-out-of-it-all look.

"Que tal?" Mr. Krulewitch said, turning to him. "Usted vive en Manhattan?"

"Si," the man said, looking pleased. The candidate grabbed his hand and poured forth a stream of Spanish, the burden of which was "votar por Krulewitch."

Coming upon a man with a French accent, he lapsed into French. "Comment vont les affaires?" he said. "Vous demeurez en Manhattan?"

"Oui," the man said. Mr. Krulewitch asked him to vote row A all the way.

At another stop, a man said that he was Polish.

"Polish?" Mr. Krulewitch exclaimed in a voice full of the joy of discovery. "Krulewitch means 'king's son' in Polish!"

In a delicatessen, the candidate ran into a party that spoke no tongue but English. For a moment, it looked as though Mr. Krulewitch might not be able to establish the bonds of fellowship. Then he noticed a Friends Seminary emblem stitched on a boy's blazer. Mr. Krulewitch happens to have a son, Peter, seventeen, who goes to Friends Seminary.

To a man who accused the Republicans of being unfriendly to organized labor, Mr. Krulewitch took pains to show the tiny union label stamped on his campaign literature.

The last stop of the day was a bar and grill on Suffolk Street.

A short, heavy-set man who said he was a truck driver and proud of it challenged him to prove his friendliness by buying everyone a beer. That done, the man was still unconvinced. He took a belligerent stance—feet spread, hands on hips, jaw extended—about a foot from the candidate.

"I was in the Marines eight years and four days. How about you, buddy?" he demanded.

Here, Mr. Krulewitch merely drew from his wallet papers identifying him as Major General Melvin Krulewitch, United States Marine Corps Reserve, twice-wounded veteran of World War I, World War II and Korea.

The short man snapped quickly to attention and apologized. "I'm sorry, sir," he said.

It was an eventful day in the small world of Melvin Krulewitch.

Book Row

Book Row

New York City is full of mercantile enclaves. The financial district near the Battery at the tip of Manhattan and the garment center a little south of Times Square are known to nearly everyone. Among the many others, some are quite obscure. Between 121 and 200 Varick Street, for instance, there is a tiny loose-leaf-binders district. Wholesale florists are tightly ranked along West Twenty-eighth Street at numbers 41, 43, 44, 45, 46, 47, 48, 49, 53, 54, 57, 58 and again at twenty locations from numbers 100, 102, 104, 104A, on up to 132. There are also a few florists around the corner on Sixth Avenue (or, in its fancier designation, The Avenue of the Americas). It is a good place for a rose fever victim to stay away from.

In late September, 1969, I spent mellow days in the teeming stalls in book row south of Union Square, absorbed in the endless stacks, which I cruised in a reverie that spanned the ages and the continents. I spent hours in conversation with the men and women who own the shops and found them a rather special breed of characters, almost monkishly devoted to books. Most had decided early, as one of them put it, that nothing in life could be better than simply "to be among books." It is not a universal appreciation, as I discovered when one of the proprietors fixed his straightest gaze upon me and said, through a narrow aperture of teeth, "Listen, I *hate* books." Love had led to vocation, vocation to surfeit, and surfeit to hatred. The melancholy cycle had left him trapped in his declining years under an avalanche of books, lost beyond recall in a polyglut of prose.

Yet most of the owners showed a fondness for their trade

that ran deep. All had a knowledge of books from the buying and selling angle—a dealer usually knows the value of a book to a nickel at a glance—but many showed a knowledge of literature, of authors and subjects of scholarly breadth. Several were busy not only in book selling but also, in back rooms, in publishing—and publishing of an exceptionally high order.

"I am amazed how many New Yorkers do not even know there is a second-hand book center."

That astonishment was expressed through a sigh by Mrs. Ruth W. Carp, a widow I met in the Green Shop on Fourth Avenue during one of those pleasant September afternoons. The oversight, she said, was not only that of a large part of the general populace, but also that of the City government, which had neglected to act to save the special character of the enclave. She was carrying on her late husband's business and I encountered her in the first of two extended visits to the center, the first in 1969, the second in 1973.

By any reckoning, book row is a cultural resource of major scope. What Lincoln Center is to music, what the Broadway-Times Square sector is to theater, the book center is to rare, used and antiquarian books.

It is a haunt, a hunting ground. Its narrow aisles let out on amazing vistas and lead to the farthest horizons that man has searched or that human imagination has conjured.

The stores are profusely stocked and together they make up an enormous hoard of ideas and knowledge, with few amenities. Many are shabby, drab, cluttered. The late Meyer Berger affectionately called them "littered Dickensian dust bins."

Browsing is entirely free. Salesmen almost never accost. It can be carried out with unhurried carefulness, hour after hour, in store after store. The row will yield its treasures for very little money. Worlds can be bought there for a few spare coins. There are hundreds of thousands of volumes stacked on its tables and shelves or heaped on its bare wooden floors, all instantly available to browsers at prices ranging upward—and downward—from a quarter.

In less than a lunch hour's time a searcher can turn up the works of Rudyard Kipling for forty-eight cents, in a single volume of 1,004 pages; or a set of Anatole France for a song; a thick volume on "Diseases of the Heart" by Friedberg for just under a dollar; or he can reconnoitre the "Sywannee River: Strange Green Land" with Matschat for two dollars, or roll "Along the Great Rivers" with Gordon Cooper for three dollars.

If you would like to go "Head Hunting in the Solomon Islands" with Caroline Mytinger, you can get a good bit of it in by standing in the aisle and leafing through the pages. The full trip will cost you $2.50. Or you can go along while "A Southerner Discovers New England" with Jonathan Daniels for $1.50, a more placid journey at an appropriately reduced rate. When a browser selects more than one book he can often haggle off a quarter or fifty cents at the checkout point, if he cares to make the little effort it requires. Nearly twenty years ago, when I was new to the City and had to skim through a time of fiscal scarcity, when every dime counted, I went into a store on the row and found three books I very much wanted. Two were marked $1.50 and the other ninety-five cents. By holding out a little, I got them all for $2.50, even though the seller at first refused. I cannot easily tell you how rich I felt going home with those three books, each a prize clearly beyond my means.

It is entirely possible for a young person with an appetite for words and but little cash to go through the shops today and, by careful selection, acquire the foundation of a decent personal library for fifteen or twenty dollars. For that money, he will have no trouble in coming out with twenty or twenty-five books, each in good condition and each suited to his own taste from a vast selection.

If he restricts himself to books in the lowest price range or waits for the special sales, he could stagger homeward under a burden of fifty books. Second-hand is not necessarily second-rate. Librarians from England and all over the United States come to the row. Some of them browse and pick for two or three days, and leave orders running from about $300 up to $6,000 to be shipped to them.

An idea of the variety available is gleaned by noting the section signs in one store, which offer works in Economics, Philosophy, Psychology, Social Science, Music, Poetry, Religion, Drama, History, Journalism, Fiction, Aviation, Chemistry, Architecture, Electronics, Physics, Metals, Engineering, Art, Plastics, Dictionaries, Cookbooks, Travel and Labor—each populated with books stacked from floor to ceiling, eighteen shelves high.

"A delightful oasis in the desert of life," Arthur Fowler called the stores along book row. "No institution makes a richer contribution to the convenience, culture and limited means of booklovers than the second-hand book shops" clustered there just below Fourteenth Street on Broadway and Fourth Avenue, he said.

Scholars, writers, professors, students, celebrities, librarians, literary adventurers and what one dealer called "fiction addicts" scour the shelves for matter. Over the years, the White House has sent presidential orders to the row.

A big red sign at Broadway and Twelfth Street identifies the Strand Book Store, the biggest and busiest of the lot, a father and son business that has nearly tripled its space, going from about 10,000 to 30,000 square feet in five years.

If the Strand is the Macy's of book row, Schulte's around the block at 82 Fourth Avenue was its Gimbels. Surveying its barn-like main floor, its basement and three-sided balcony, an awestruck customer called Schulte's "a great amphitheater" in which there seemed to sit "arranged all the books that were ever penned."

When I visited it, every stair step and nearly every floor board in the place creaked with nearly every footfall, but there were 140,000 books on its shelves, and, if a person could not find what he wanted, there were these lines to reassure him: "The Mounties always get their crook/ And Schulte's always get their book," in proud, if flawed, poesy.

If there wasn't enough on the main floor, it was upstairs to Asia, Africa and Religion, two land masses leading on to infinity—up there amid pipes and low-hanging bare light bulbs, which customers turned on and off as they moved from section to section. Tables were heaped with books in stacks running thirty high and, if you saw a title that looked tempting near the base of a stack, it was quite a trick to slip it out without spilling a tower of books.

The whole atmosphere of Schulte's was about as warm, and about as cracked and withering, as old leather book bindings. When it was closed and its huge stock sold off, it looked for a while as though no booklover would ever again make its old boards groan. The store had been there since 1917, but now it stood empty and lifeless and dark. Then, suddenly, a younger dealer moved in, half motivated by ambition and half by a yearning to see a great tradition carried on—not merely restored but revived to something like the pace of its best years. He put 35,000 books on display, held 15,000 more in reserve, and talked hopefully, if a little doubtfully, of keeping the old barn in the book business for years to come—if the rent is not raised too fast. With some paint and refixturing and perhaps a new front, the place could be made over into a linoleum sales showroom and let for easily twice the rent. Just a glance away, on the other side of the street, the winey aura of a book stall has given way to the bright interior glaze of the Plastic Center of New York ("All forms of plastic cut to size") and, in that, surviving book dealers think they see the neon writing on the wall.

Biblo & Tannen at 63 Fourth Avenue has the stamped metal ceilings and splintered floors that make most of the book shops seem antiquated, but it is headquarters for a highly respected publishing and reprinting business that has won the praise of "The Classical Journal" and other periodicals of scholarly stamp. Jack Biblo and Jack Tannen preside, with a lively and sometimes intellectually argumentative air, over their own gray brick building which, with its sober, rather narrow front and three neat rows of three upper windows, looks as if it had been brought over from London, circa 1885. It is five stories chock full of books, including basement.

The two men also run Canaveral Press, which reprints popular titles, and, as an affair of the heart, they issue the Biblo & Tannen series of "distinguished reprints for librarian and scholar." The firm takes landmark books that are out of print or scarcely available and reissues them under its own imprint at prices generally lower than new novels or nonfiction.

Customers who hand two singles and some change to the natty Mr. Tannen, standing at the counter near the door, and watch him wrap the three books they have chosen hardly suspect him of being involved in so exalted a labor. He is one-half of the reason for the present availability of such works as Arland Ussher's *Journey Through Dread,* a study of Kierkegaard, Heidegger and Sartre; John Devitt Stringfellow Pendlebury's *The Archeology of Crete;* and E. A. Wallis Budge's *The Mummy,* an exhaustive examination of Egyptian hieroglyphics, among dozens of other titles.

Both Jacks are lean, energetic, fast-talking; both wear mustaches and horn-rimmed glasses; in summer both wear short-sleeved dress shirts with ties and sharply pressed trousers, looking rather like a couple of nimble hoofers from an old-time vaudeville act. Both are not quite a decade younger than the century.

When they are together the two men talk in an interlinear way, which makes them essentially co-authors of their discussion, and it is more than a little hard to know which of them has said what afterward. Sometimes one would start a thought and the other would finish it, or modify it, or elaborate, or contradict.

"This is becoming a lost art," one of them said. "No kids today are interested in going into the book selling field. When our generation dies off, they'll be very, very few second-hand book stores."

"We came from a slum neighborhood—East New York in Brooklyn," Mr. Biblo said. "In those days, a penny was a lot, but a bunch of us were terribly interested in books and the rental of a Tarzan book in a store on Pitkin Avenue was ten cents for three days.

"Five of us kids each chipped in two cents, and all five of us read that whole book in three days. We didn't need a quick-reading course."

"To work for one dollar a day in a bookstore—just to be in a bookstore—that was nirvana," Mr. Biblo said. "Kids today won't start for ninety dollars a week. It's nothing today for a boy ten years old to come in and pull out a ten dollar bill. It's quite a different world."

"We started the business in 1928," Mr. Tannen said. "We slept in the back room and we worked eighteen hours a day and we each took a dollar-a-day out for the first three years."

"We didn't have hours. As long as a customer was in the place, we stayed open," Mr. Biblo said.

"If a customer came in and spent one dollar—big sale—we'd go out and have coffee and," Mr. Tannen said, implying Danish.

Biblo & Tannen is a little less hungry now, a little more formal; the shop is kept open from 10:00 A.M. to 5:30 P.M. six days a week. It has something over 40,000 books on open shelves, out of a total stock of about 100,000. "We own this building—that's the reason we can stay in business," Mr. Biblo said. "The chances are we could not have survived otherwise; the rents would be prohibitive."

The partners say they spent $46,000 to reprint the six thick volumes of the 1898 J. G. Frazer translation of *Pausanias Description of Greece,* whose introduction begins: "It may be reckoned a peculiar piece of good fortune that among the wreckage of classic literature the *Description of Greece* by Pausanias should have come to us entire." It notes also that "Without him, the ruins of Greece would be for the most part a labyrinth without a clue, a riddle without an answer: His book furnishes the clue to the labyrinth . . . "

By printing 1,000 sets—each with 189 illustrations sprinkled among its 3,129 pages—Biblo & Tannen hoped to do the same favor for libraries, making the odyssey of that intelligent and observant traveler available for $87.50, with no royalties to the author, who has been dead for about 1,800 years. The sets sold slowly, steadily. By 1974, more than 600 had been sent out.

Switching to his Canaveral Press identity, Mr. Tannen said, "We're the ones who started the Edgar Rice Burroughs renaissance back in 1963 by reprinting a couple of dozen of his public domain books in hard cover (*At the Earth's Core, Lost on Venus, Tanar of Pellucidar,* etc.).

"It caught on. Movies, television, paperbacks—all made money out of it. In soft cover, 80 million copies were sold. Everybody got rich out of it but us. We feel like the small prospector who discovered a uranium mine, and then the big boys come along and take it over."

Biblo & Tannen's "Colossal Book Sale" was in progress. Every book—excluding fiction—on the shelves was selling for seventy-five cents for two weeks (including many marked $2.50 and higher) and, for ten days after that, every book would sell for fifty cents.

"We work like dogs," Mr. Tannen said. "We could earn more money in almost any other business in America, but we didn't go into this to make money, we went into it as a labor of love."

"Of 1,000 books we buy today, one per cent are good,"

his partner said. "Ninety-nine per cent are junk. This is what we live for, to get that one book out of 1,000 that is needed by somebody for the perpetuation of knowledge.

"People come in here all the time with family heirloom books from the last century—gross volumes, overillustrated junk. The age of a book has nothing to do with its value, except if it is published before 1510—then it means something. It's rarity, not age, that counts."

"You know, you have a dream about finding a rare book," Mr. Tannen said. "You go out to visit a library for sale, you never know what you're going to find. Just the feel of a book like this gives me a shiver." He ran his fingers lightly over the top of a fantastic book, "Biblia Sacra Polyglotta," dated London 1657, by the printer Thomas Roycroft. It had long columns of Samaritan, Greek, Chaldean, Syriac, Arabic, Ethiopian, Persian and Latin running side by side, and it was in its original leather cover.

"We got it from the library of a good scholar. He was living with about six cats," Mr. Tannen said. "It's worth around $35,000. We have an offer of $22,000."

"It's funny," he said, "but a book got me into the book business: Christopher Morley's *Haunted Bookshop* did it."

Did he have any regrets? "You know," he said reflectively, "I'm still thrilled with it. I would by all means do it again. You don't retire. You die in this business."

Another dealer thought longevity was one advantage of the trade. "Lots of old booksellers live to a ripe old age," he said. "My theory is that through the years they absorb so much dust that their lungs are calcified and *nothing* can hurt them."

The speaker was Louis Schucman, who was standing in his long, narrow world of books a couple of doors away. There were ladders here and there leading to the upper shelves and piles of books had accumulated on the floor, in sections where they would eventually be alphabetized into place.

"I don't hurry," the bookman said. "The customers go for the stacks on the floor." The book business changes as "the tides of ideas ebb and flow," he said, and changes in taste change the speed at which books move on certain shelves. Marxism and Thomism had both fallen way off, but books on art and movies were up in sales.

Mr. Schucman's fingers plucked *Logical Positivism* by A. J. Ayer from a shelf. "Ten years ago, we'd have sold this right away," he said. "Logical positivism was a strong stream in philosophy and Ayer was a major figure in it. Today, what with this and that, the logical positivists are less sure of their position. We'll sell it, but maybe not for months.

"Twenty-five years ago, the real sellers were books on Marxism. Not now. The structure of radicalism has changed. Ten or fifteen years ago, Thomism was a great seller. Today, with all the changes in the church, there's very little call for it.

"College kids used to come in and ask for books on literary criticism. Now they ask for books on movies and directors."

A young man stepped in the store and asked if Mr. Schucman had a certain book. "No," the bookseller replied instantly. How did he know what might or might not be among the roughly 50,000 books in stock?

"If I didn't know, I would be out of business," he said. "I can tell you ninety-five per cent of what we have in stock—some can do better—but I can always tell you one hundred per cent of what we haven't got.

"This is really one of the last strongholds of pure capitalism in that market demand is everything," Mr. Schucman said.

A customer came to the small counter. "Two dollars?—I thought it was twenty cents," he objected when the owner told him the price.

"You go to a movie, it costs you $2.50 or $3.50—a family

of four is $10," Mr. Schucman told him. "Maybe you'll do that ten or twenty times a year. What have you got left?—memories. Think of the books you can buy for ten dollars and keep."

The customer was unconvinced by this line of reasoning and did not take the book.

The average customer spends "fifteen to twenty minutes browsing" before deciding whether or not to buy, the owner said. Others are more careful. "Some people will spend hours and hours going through hundreds and hundreds of prints and will end up buying three prints for ten cents each," he said.

Customers who haggle over prices apparently go on the "theory that each morning an angel comes down and leaves me a basket of books at no charge," Mr. Schucman said.

"People come in and they want a set of encyclopedias for their children. The set is worth $275, but they think they can get it for $20 here; when they find it's closer to $150, they're surprised."

For that eventuality, Mr. Schucman has a couple of little speeches, the first a reasoned pitch about amortizing the cost, the second a rather bald attempt at inducing parental shame.

"Think of it this way," he tells them, "You'll pay the $150 now, but you're amortizing the cost of the set over the years a child will use it."

If they don't go for that, he asks more bluntly—"Isn't your child worth $10 a year?"

"You know something?" Mr. Schucman said. "To some, they're not."

The owner mimeographs his own catalogue in a little space next to the water cooler by his desk, stacked so high with books that if a customer doesn't stand just so he can't look past them to the man seated there. He has to line up with the see-through slot the owner has left.

A thin, olive-skinned young man with a string of beads around his neck wheeled in a shopping cart with about fifteen books in it that had hardly been used. "Do you buy books?" he asked.

"Yeah," Mr. Schucman said laconically, giving them half a look. "What do you want for all this?"

"Twenty-five dollars," he said.

It was no sale, and it took less than a minute. The young man went out.

"Dessicated classics," Mr. Schucman said. "Nobody reads them." Some books, especially fancy sets or mass-printed, special-offer volumes may look good but they are a drug on the market.

"Always look at the bottom, not at the top—that's how you can tell a nice new book," Mr. Schucman said, puffing dust from the top of a book. The little, black, wheeled wagons out front, with neat-painted yellow lettering, offered books at "twenty-five cents. Five for one dollar."

Income varies widely in the trade. "On a per-hour basis my income would be much less than a person who works for the City," Mr. Schucman said after nearly thirty years on book row.

"You can go to dental school and come out and earn one hundred dollars a day as a dental assistant," Mr. Tannen said, warning that no one should attempt to get into the business if he had illusions. "It's a rough business, but if you love books and don't mind starving, go right into it."

The owner of a moderately busy and obviously well-managed store said that he had got his business to the point at which he can take home $400 a week the year round, but at year's end there are no profits left in the till. The owner of a far less successful shop said, "I don't think anyone goes into this because you're out for money. You get a job, you can *make* five dollars an hour."

"In England, you know, booksellers are knighted," still

another dealer said. "In America, booksellers are third rate citizens."

To earn a decent living, dealers work long hours, nearly always in six-day weeks, and they must spend some evenings and Sundays making rounds and inspecting private libraries put up for sale. They must maintain inventories vastly larger than their sales turnover because, in their business, it takes barrels of stock to produce a teacup of profits. Handling and processing so many books is a physically exhausting job, usually done on a hopelessly backlogged schedule. The necessary glut leads to high shelves reached only by ladders, to piles on the floors, and just behind the scenes in most shops, unsorted mountains of books, or cartons heaped to the ceiling.

Mr. Schucman called overstocking "one of the curses of the book trade."

"It's a disease with most booksellers to buy, buy, buy," Fred Bass said in the Strand. "We're worse than our best customers. You get your capital all tied up in books. My instinct tells me, get everything. So you get piles on the floors. I just can't get them up on the shelves. The customers seem to go for the books piled on the floor. Once I got all the piles off the floors and onto the shelves and, you know what?—business stopped."

There was a certain logic in the geographical situation of the used book center in its earlier years, but time has effaced that logic and the center has remained fixed by a combination of tradition and inertia. The second-hand book stores grew up around the publishing houses that once flourished near Fourteenth Street. "Most of the publishers grew affluent and moved uptown, and the bookstores stayed," Mr. Bass said. A few publishers are left scattered in the area, including Fairchild Publications which puts out the spicy little journal called *Womens Wear Daily,* a skillfully compounded blend of trade news and gossip, further enlivened by a dash of political coverage along with reviews and editorial judgments that manage somehow to be saucy, imperious and authoritative all at once.

On my first long visit I found the widow Carp in her blue smock jacket in the Green Book Shop, a typically shaped stall almost sixty feet deep and about eighteen feet wide. She talked of her delight in helping young people who come in "when they're just discovering books and they are so eager and enthusiastic."

There is an advantage not only to customers, but also to sellers, in having the stores grouped so closely. "We take in each other's washing," Mrs. Carp explained. "If I am short a couple of books for a mail order, I go through the street with a list in my hand and get what I need, and usually there's a twenty per cent discount we give to each other."

Grace Church, the famous old Episcopal house of worship on Broadway at Tenth Street, owns the eight-story loft building whose gymnasium-sized first floor is now the home of the Abbey Book Shop. It moved in from a far smaller site when Schulte's shut up shop forever, ending what had been a glorious history on Fourth Avenue.

The older store had known its best days in the 1920s and the 30s and, though it had retained all of its size and selection and much of its charm, business had diminished while the rent went up. That seemed to be the end until George Foss of the Abbey, established in 1965, waxed bold enough to pack up a relatively small collection and move in, hoping not merely to survive but eventually to bring the place back to its prosperity and bustle.

Mr. Foss keeps the Abbey open from 11 A.M. to "8:00 or 9:00 or 10:00 P.M., as long as I'm here it's open" six days a week. "One night I pulled up at 1:30 A.M. and the policeman outside said, 'Isn't this an unusual hour?' and I said, 'Yes, but it's a very unusual business I'm in.'

"A kid today won't work for less than three dollars an

hour, so I have to work alone here. Come over here and let me show you something," Mr. Foss said, leading to the side shelves. He pointed through a space in a shelf and there, under a wooden stairway in the dim light, was an old time-clock with twenty-five side slots for time cards.

"This store used to have twenty-four people working in it," Mr. Foss said. "I wouldn't sell that clock for anything. $500."

"No, it's an antique," his visitor agreed.

"It isn't that," Mr. Foss said. "I like it."

Schulte's became the Abbey in July, 1971. "They weren't even able to meet the $700 rent anymore," Mr. Foss said. "With no salaries to pay, I've been able to meet it so far, but if they don't give me a deal I can afford, I'll hold the biggest sale you've ever seen and clear out."

The store is seventy feet deep and over thirty feet wide. It has a three-sided haymow balcony that Mr. Foss has cut off to the public. Barrels of books are hidden behind the last public shelves. The owner is a big, amiable slave to books in early middle age. He has a large face in the Nordic or Viking mold with blond hair and blue eyes and a build that would do credit to a wrestler.

Mr. Foss was pawing through twenty or thirty cartons of books near the front of the store. "I get a big kick out of going through these boxes seeing what I'll find," he said. "Nothing rare, you know, but there's a fascination in it." He held out an open book whose flyleaf was ink-marked "9/23/22 from the collection of Mrs. Frederick L. Shepherd."

"I went to a warehouse and bought this all for $200," Mr. Foss said. "I had to pack them into cartons, truck them over here, unload them, and now I'm starting to process them. If you like books, it's a pleasure. There's something about books . . . it's something, I don't know, I guess you just have to like them," he said, spraying shrapnel over his verbal target while not quite hitting the bullseye.

"I got into this just by chance," he went on. "I was just walking along the other side of the street one day, minding my own business—I was in Civil Service then—and a fellow asked me to help him with a load of books he'd just got from a large estate. He had the store over there." The man had a heart attack while the books were being sorted, and Mr. Foss found himself in deeper than he had expected. Later, he bought the shop.

A booklover can, if he chooses, spend all day and part of the night in the Abbey. When the store is closed, Mr. Foss places a cane laterally across the window in the front door, with a closed sign hanging on it. Glancing in through that window, a visitor remembered Schulte's with its incredible array of second-hand books. Franklin P. Adams sang of the store years ago in "The Conning Tower" column and the Reverend Fred V. Christ, a Pennsylvania minister, had called it "an infinite Elysian field of mental pasture" in which he often fondly grazed.

In August, 1959, the Post Office had dutifully delivered a letter from San Bernardino, California, addressed only to "The Largest Bookstore in the World, New York City, New York" in childish scrawl. The last owner, David J. Butler, kept that among the store's treasured papers in his old cage office at the rear.

"I came here in 1929 in the shipping rooms, under old Mr. Schulte," Mr. Butler said the last time I saw him. Theodore E. Schulte, who died in 1950 at eighty-three, was the dean of antiquarian booksellers and his store had been doing business at 82 Fourth Avenue since 1917. Schulte's had its origin in the old American Baptist Publications Society, for which Mr. Schulte had once worked. The store became a notable repository for second-hand theological books, Bibles, church and Sunday School materials, as well as general stock. Boys filled with a new-born love of literature would come in, jingling their change, to exercise great care in picking out a new adventure for twenty cents or a quarter. In its brightest days, the store had many branches, especially at resorts, one of them in a large frame house at Lake Placid. A photograph showed a stand out front dominated by Billy Sunday hymn books.

With 50,000 books in the store and with by no means all of them on open display, Mr. Foss is running a shadow of Schulte's, yet he hopes later to have the substance and the glory of it, too. The present collection is not a notable one. He has a reserve collection of 28,000 books in Elizabeth, New Jersey, and, if the rent on Fourth Avenue does not run out of reach, he expects to close the other place and cart those books over to enrich the Abbey's stock.

"I just use them for filler," Mr. Foss said of the long rows of Reader's Digest condensed books lining the upper shelves at the rear of the store, out of reach. "There are certain books that are re-saleable and certain books that are not re-saleable. You develop an idea after a while, you get burnt so many times," he said.

"I bought 700 cartons of old books seven months ago," he remarked, but they are all in the basement waiting to be opened if he gets a favorable lease. The Abbey is like a big rummage sale of old books during the weeks-long sales Mr. Foss likes to put on. In his dollar sales, close to 25,000 books are available at that price.

"I had a best seller in here a few months ago, fifteen of them, and I didn't know it was on the list, and I was selling them for one dollar," he said. As he talked, a man with a beautiful collie strolled the aisles, pausing occasionally to pick up a book and inspect it.

"It'll be pot luck if you find it," Mr. Foss assured a customer who asked him for a certain title. A novelist, R. Leslie Gourse, came in looking for copies of her 1962 book, *With Gall and Honey*. She did not find it.

"Sometimes I'm groggy," Mr. Foss said. "But I've been able to make a living, pay my taxes. I've been able to pay the rent since I moved here, and I'm always on time. A store that rented for $300 fifteen years ago now goes for around $1,500. That's why you see all these antique stores in the area now.

"See this bowl?" he said, picking up a large, decorative fruit bowl from a shelf near the cash register. "I bought it because I like it. An antique store will get an old bowl in, and the owner will look it over and he'll say, 'This is from the eighteenth century,' and he'll sell it for $700. If you can make three of those sales a month, you're okay. That's why they're renting these places to antique stores. They're forgetting one thing; a used bookstore can withstand a depression and survive, but an antique store can't. If people only have ten cents, they'll still buy a book."

"There's room in this business for everybody," said Fred Bass at the giant Strand, the most aggressive seller on the row. "Another store could open across the street and my business would increase. People like to browse from shop to shop."

"We would welcome an increase of twenty stores," another dealer said.

In 1969 there were twenty-one stores in five blocks in a rather quaint sector south of Union Square, running from Ninth to Fourteenth Streets. In 1947 there had been thirty stores. There is fear among dealers that the book center may become just a footnote in the City's history.

Mrs. Carp said that rising rents had driven dealers out of the row and into lofts, where they handle mail order sales only. "It's deadly to be stashed away in some loft when you're used to the open door," she said.

"Look, frankly, in two years when my lease is up, the landlord is going to ask for more rent, like double, and I won't be able to stay here," Mr. Schucman said in his stuffed, medium-sized shop. "In order to exist at all, you have to have a large space in a fairly busy area at a rather low rent, and that is no longer available." As it turned out, Mr. Schucman was right. His shop is no longer there.

Mrs. Carp said that when she and her husband saw the trend, they got together with the other owners and petitioned the City to relocate the whole group in one area "and they wanted to move us into the concourse in a subway station," she said.

She spoke hopefully of holding an outdoor book sale in the spring or fall "a little bit like the thing they have in Paris all the time. Or maybe we'd have pushcarts loaded with books. It might become a semi-annual event—'Come to the Fourth Avenue outdoor book sale,' " she said.

A stroll along those same blocks in 1974 yields a count of nine surviving book stores—a loss of exactly a dozen stores in a little over four years.

Sometimes when he looked at the then 128-year-old brick building in which his store, the Vanity Fair, had space, Herbert Oxer, the owner, wondered how much longer it would be left standing. (The building was torn down and the tract is now a parking lot). He sold books, prints, circus posters, theater broadsides, and old American pictorial weeklies—*Harper's Weekly, Leslie's, Gleason's* and others.

He had a November 1871 copy of *Harper's Bazaar* in the window, a little scarred because of a literary cat who "likes to paw through old periodicals," as Mr. Oxer said.

"I don't see the sense in calling this Fourth Avenue," Mr. Oxer griped that day. "Whoever heard of Fourth Avenue?" It is just a short stretch linking the Bowery to Park Avenue South. "They should call it Book Row," he suggested. "It would identify the area much better, and you could write to me at 108 Book Row, New York, New York, 10003." He thought that might help save the used book center.

Diagonally across from the Abbey, where a nondescript book den had been situated, there is now a sterile, efficient insurance office. Yet thanks chiefly to the bulging Strand, the total number of books available has risen even as stores have closed. On one check, there were 555,000 books in three neighboring stores—350,000 in one, 140,000 in the next,

65,000 in the third. The Strand had about 500,000 books in 1970. That number rose to one million in the next two years, the figure used in the store's advertisements and on the sides of its shopping bags, but Mr. Bass thinks he has a million and a half. "I haven't had the time to count them lately," he remarked.

"Most of my libraries are bought at night," he said, guessing that he looks at thirty to forty collections in a week. He prefers to see a library of 1,000 books or more, but worth also depends on what is in it, and he goes out to see anywhere from 100 up to 25,000 books. People frequently walk in the door, unannounced, to say they have a load of books parked at the curb outside.

"The only way to do it is to look at each book," Mr. Bass said. He pointed to eighty cartons he had just purchased holding close to 3,000 books. "Took ninety minutes," he said. His method is to go from book to book, carrying a little scratch pad in his palm and marking down estimated values, not for every volume but for each section of about fifteen books.

"Rare books are rare," he said. "You don't really find them in garbage heaps. But we find many, many scarce items selling for $100 to $150 or more."

The Strand has a roster of "thirty-eight employees, plus me and my dad," according to Mr. Bass. The business was started in 1930 by Benjamin Bass, who opened a store at 95 Fourth Avenue. He moved to the present Broadway location in 1956. The elder Mr. Bass is still very much at it and is often seen keeping an eye on things near the checkout counter.

"I started working for my dad when I was fourteen. I got the dust in my blood and I never got it out," the son said.

The aggressive, energetic younger Mr. Bass has "the smell of success" about him, as one man put it. As he moves through the store with quick, small strides, his hands fly out to rearrange books, to pick one up and shelve it, to restack, to line books up on a table. When he speaks to an employee, it is usually a crisp order, delivered in the manner of a major addressing a corporal.

"You've got to hustle a little," Mr. Bass said. "You can't sit back and sell twenty-five dollars worth of books. You can't make a living out of that, as you once could.

"The pace that most of us were brought up in won't go anymore. It's an exacting business. There's a lot of action. I put in fifty-five hours a week and for a long time I didn't even have my own desk."

The Strand is stuffed to the ceiling with bargain books, out-of-print books, castoffs, general and scholarly stock, art books and, surprisingly, brand new books. An unmarked door at the side of the main floor leads down to, among other things, a particularly impressive collection of Americana, made up chiefly of new books purchased from publisher's overstocks. To a history buff it is a place of almost overwhelming temptation.

"We have about forty different categories of books," Mr. Bass said. "There's no other place in the world where you can come in and find as many different titles of books and the variety we offer, all for immediate sale." Prices run from twenty-five cents up to about $150, with most volumes going for well under five dollars. The stock is not made up of books that are mostly forlorn and dog-eared. Some are new, many are only slightly used, and a lot of Mr. Bass's books are formally dressed. They wear jackets.

In peak hours, there are sometimes 300 customers in the labyrinthine aisles in the store. "We get doctors, a lot of professional people, lots of students," Mr. Bass said. "Even at that, roughly fifty per cent of our business is mail order.

"Libraries are buying heavily. They have to fill their collections with out-of-print books. The largest sale I made this spring was $6,000.

"One of the biggest boosts we got was back when the Russians orbited their first Sputnik. Suddenly people were jolted and the idea got around that you've got to give the children a very good education. Librarians started to come round and really start looking for good, scholarly books—not just junk to fill their shelves.

"Another thing that has helped is the general affluence of the people. The increase in the price of new books has helped us immensely, too. The paperback revolution stimulated everything. It created an entirely new market for books. It's been a great, great boon to the whole business."

The bargain tables outside the Strand are a sort of trademark. "They used to pay the rent," Mr. Bass remarked. "You can't pay hardly anything out of them now." There are some bargain tables inside with diverse books—*The Complete Works of O. Henry; War and Peace* by Tolstoy; *The Goebbels Diaries 1942-1943; The Easy Chair,* graceful essays by Bernard DeVoto, going at ninety-seven cents each or three for $2.50. Another table has books at forty-eight cents each but you can beat the rate by buying five for two dollars.

Bass & Son boasts a stock of "5,000 new books at half price at all times." The store buys them from book reviewers, who get them from publishers as giveaways.

"They accumulate them until there's no space left in their apartments, then they call me in," Fred Bass said. "We pay them twenty-five cents on the dollar." For a $10 free book, the store pays $2.50. It sells the book for $5, which is fair to everybody—reviewer, store and customer—except possibly the publishers.

"A reviewer, a well-known man, will drive up and hand me over a load of books and, on our policy of cash, walk out with a check for $250-$300," Mr. Bass said. Some reviewers clear about $500 a month this way, which is more than enough to pay *their* rent.

"We get a lot of interesting people working for us—artists, poets, photographers. Working selling books, they don't feel they are sinning against their art," Mr. Bass said.

"That young man over there is Craig Anderson, Maxwell Anderson's son. Been here six months clerking.

"A guy came in a few weeks ago, dressed like a rabbinical student," he went on. "He had the coat and the side curls and the hat and he said to my father, 'I want to settle my account.'

" 'You owe us money? We'll get the card and you can pay,' my father said.

" 'It isn't that,' he said. 'I used to come in here and steal books. I stole a lot of books. Now I want to settle it.'

"They talked for a while and my father said, 'Give us $100.' But he wanted to give us $175, which is what he had with him, but my father said no, so we settled for the $100."

A thin, well-tailored young man with a crisp British accent went from store to store one afternoon, wheeling a shopping cart with twenty-eight books in it. No one wanted them, since they were volumes in high supply and low demand.

"Will you give me a dollar for the lot?" he finally asked one of the larger dealers.

"I'm sorry, no," the dealer said.

A moment later the same dealer offered to sell a customer 1,000 theological books at fifteen cents each, or 1,500 children's books at thirty-five cents each.

People are constantly walking in the doors with small batches of books to sell. "We have a good deal of dealing with boobs who don't know books," one dealer confided. "They want to buy a book for ten cents or sell you a book for $40."

Some dealers think that the grip of the electronic media on young people has hurt the book business and may eventually do it in. "I am in no sense a professional Jonah, but the situation is not very lively," said S. R. Shapiro, a canny and wonderfully articulate scholar and dealer who has an office, not a store, at 29 East Tenth Street and who specializes in books for libraries.

"Young people have been so conditioned by the lighted box that their attention span is oriented to it. They are not very friendly to the book," he said.

"While the printed book has lasted 500 years, there's no guarantee it will last another 500 years. It will last the century," Mr. Shapiro guessed.

Fred Bass sounded a hopeful note, even in the face of the closing of so many stores. "I think the business has a long way to grow," he said. "More and more people are reading and literate. We get a tremendous amount of young people, and they're coming in and buying with taste, good things."

Yet he also believes that "the printed book is becoming obsolete," and he has watched the increase of antique stores in the area.

"Someday, you'll have a telephone with a screen and you'll be able to dial a book," he said. "They'll put you in instant contact with thousands and thousands of books."

What then, he was asked.

"Then I go into the antique business—books will be antiques," Mr. Bass said.

Four Originals

The Man from I.Q. H.Q.

Dr. Hans Josef Eberstark, a man of immeasurably high intelligence, describes himself as "a member of the most democratic society in the world." He meant Mensa, a club that automatically bars exactly ninety-eight per cent of the world's population from its rolls.

Apart from that binge of exclusion, covering roughly 3,361,660,000 ineligibles, the club is democratic to a fault.

"There are absolutely no bars to admission," the thirty-seven-year-old Swiss linguist said, "except your score on an I.Q. test. If you're in the top two per cent, we want you."

With that single restriction, the international cerebral society is totally accepting. It will take in anybody of any age, race, nationality, religion, or social rank who can pay the dues ($15 a year in the United States).

Mensa will take in high school dropouts if they have intellectual genius. "There are intelligent people who drop out of school because they are so utterly bored by it," Dr. Eberstark explained.

The club's members are scattered in fifty-two countries. They include novelists, dishwashers, itinerant workers, corporation presidents, seamen, professors, students, researchers, a brewmaster, an oceanographer, a flavor chemist, the executive officer of a submarine and a four-year-old boy.

Dr. Eberstark, who speaks $16\frac{1}{2}$ languages by his own estimate (he counts Swiss-German as half a language), works as an international conference interpreter at Geneva. He flew into New York on the last stop of an eleven-city tour of the United States and Canada in what he called "a head-hunting expedition." He is a Viennese Jew who fled

Nazi persecution and was reared in Shanghai. His friends call him "a living computer," not without reason, as he was shortly to demonstrate.

"Give me a number," Dr. Eberstark said.

"Okay. 978510934724440."

"Give me more," he demanded.

"68391552."

"More," he said.

"3679841025."

Dr. Eberstark paused a minute. "978510934724440683915523679841025," he said, reeling them off with flawless precision.

"Now I'll give them to you backwards," he said, "52014875—ah—no—make it 897—6325519386044427-439015879."

Dr. Eberstark continued: "If I go to a restaurant I cannot be swindled by a waiter who is supposed to add twelve per cent to the bill," he said. "I'm not a very pleasant customer if you try to diddle me."

He did not memorize the digits singly, he said. "I sort of photograph them in my mind in groups of ten and sort of tape record them as a series of sounds. The tape recording is what I've just played back for you"—at forward and backward speeds.

"Klusio keflat hopyki njepl kufirts," he wrote on a slip of paper. "I transpose the numbers into phonetic groupings in a sort of numerical language I worked out just for fun."

An I.Q. of 130 on the Wechsler scale or 148 on the Cattell scale suffices for admission to Mensa. Dr. Eberstark's intelligence flies clear off the Cattell scale, which goes only to 161. His score is "161 plus."

Mensa is Latin for table. The society seeks to be a round table, or conversational forum, of the brightest people on earth.

"We are not a society of intellectual snobs. We don't sit around talking in six-syllable words," Dr. Eberstark said.

"You don't have to have a string of degrees to get in. It's not a matter of education but of raw intelligence."

The society, which was founded in England in 1945, is ready to accept members who cannot read or write. "When we expand into the under-developed countries we will have to include the illiterates who can pass an oral test," he said.

"Intelligence is not especially admired by people," he remarked. "Outside Mensa you have to be very careful not to win an argument and lose a friend. Inside Mensa we can be ourselves and that is a great relief. We have friends everywhere, and interesting friends.

"What is your birth date?" he asked.

"December 4, 1927."

"You were born on a Sunday," he said.

"The circumference of a circle divided by its diameter is an irrational number that goes out to infinity," Dr. Eberstark said. "It's been figured out to 100,000 digits, I think. I once memorized it out to 1,500 digits. 3,141592653589793-2389264338323,1415926535897932389626433832795028841971693993751058209749445923007—" and he went on and on and on.

Mr. Quickfingers

When he is on the concert stage, Louis Yelnick never wets his thumb or his forefinger. It would help mechanically, but it would be an unseemly breach of the best etiquette of his craft.

Mr. Yelnick is a professional page turner. He works single-mindedly at the discreet task of turning the music pages at just the right split-second for piano accompanists. His fee is a flat twenty-five dollars a concert, never more, never less. Concerts are not all equal in duration or in pace, but on the average it works out to about twenty-eight cents a turn.

A page turner's moment of truth is, obviously, the moment he turns the page. Mr. Yelnick's working position is a crouch that he calls "a half rise."

He does not come to a full standing position because that would draw too much attention to him—a page turner's art requires him to be as little noticed as possible—but he cannot remain seated because that would impede his performance.

A page turner's function, in Mr. Yelnick's broad view, takes in a range of supportive services, some of them precisely defined, others almost mystical in their effect.

Mr. Yelnick has it all worked out in a ritual that begins with the timing of his arrival at the concert hall, thirty minutes before the advertised hour. It mandates the brevity of his consultation with the pianist, dictates the manner of his walking on stage, the positioning of his chair, and it governs the mode and timing of his departure.

Most pianists use friends or students for page turning, usually paying them ten or fifteen dollars for the favor. "Sometimes we get ushers to turn the pages. They are musicians, of course," an assistant manager at Carnegie Hall said. "Or we'll go across the street and get a fellow who works in the record shop to do it." Mr. Yelnick regards all such arrangements as sub-professional. He claims to be, and no one seems to contradict him, "the only man in the concert field who hires out for a stated fee."

"Today I'm considered the best in the field," the monopolist asserted.

After ten years as a professional, Mr. Yelnick believes himself to have come to the height of his powers. "At forty-seven, my present age, I feel that I've reached full bloom," he said in an interview.

He does not minimize his stage role. "I can make or break a concert if I don't turn the page at the right time," he pointed out, not with any vaunted sense of power but with a cold eye for facts.

"The worst blunder I could make as a page turner is forgetting to turn the page at the right time or turning two pages at one time," he said. "I have never forgotten to turn the music. I have never turned two pages at one time." He avoids disaster by taking time to go over the music just before a concert "to make sure that one page is not stuck to another."

He did admit, however, that he was once a millisecond tardy in reaching for the page to be turned and, before he could do it, the pianist flipped it over.

Piano soloists, with very rare exceptions, play without music. Accompanists must play so many things that it is impractical to memorize them all. That is why a page turner works for pianists accompanying other soloists.

"When it's not a piano and a violin, it's a piano and a cello, or a piano and a singer," Mr. Yelnick said. "We people in the field usually say we turn for Heifetz," he explained. "You wouldn't name the accompanist."

Yet Mr. Yelnick relented on the point a little later and said:

"I've turned for Franz Rupp, the accompanist for Marian Anderson; I've turned for Brooks Smith, the accompanist to Yascha Heifetz; I've turned for John Wustman, Carroll Hollister and David Garvey. I've turned for twenty pianists."

In one way of looking at it, Mr. Yelnick is the third man in a duet. "I'm the man behind the man behind the man," he says.

As a boy, Louis Yelnick, who works by day as a sporting goods salesman for Macy's, had a large interest in music but no money. He could afford neither lessons nor concerts, so he picked his own way out on the piano keys and went to "as many free concerts as possible—museum concerts, concerts in the parks, band concerts."

"At one concert I noticed there was a page turner sitting next to the pianist," he said. "I was about eighteen at the time. I took note of this person, never having seen anything like it—sort of like being a caddy to a pianist," he said, mixing his two vocations in his speech. "I went to a few other concerts and kept noticing page turners."

The child is father of the man, and a dozen years ago Mr. Yelnick began borrowing classical music records from a library in Brooklyn along with the corresponding scores. "I would play these records in my den, and for hours on end I would follow the flow of the music with the score," he said.

That gave him training in turning pages until, he noticed, "I became quite proficient at it right in my own home." Mr. Yelnick soon started jotting down the pianists named in newspaper reviews, looking them up in phone books, and calling them.

"I contacted about fifty," he recalled. "Many said no. Psychologically, they would not want a person breathing down their necks.

"Between the two extremes—having a page turner breathe down your neck, or having your page drop on the floor—a page turner is less bothersome," Mr. Yelnick said, taking, for the moment, a rather low view of his craft.

"A pianist is sorely in need of a page turner. Many times the pianist will not look at the music, but he'll have his eyes toward heaven, or he'll have his eyes closed. I've even read reviews in the paper where the critic says the pianist would have been wiser if he had used a page turner. I think pianists are very silly for turning their own pages."

Not all pianists agree. Many turn their own pages with a lightning stab of a hand between notes.

Mr. Yelnick found that some pianists, to avoid turning pages, "buy several copies of a selection and Scotch-tape it together like an accordion and sort of spread it over their whole piano so they can follow it," he said.

Among the many nos to his early overtures, a few artists said yes. "My first concert was for an all-lady trio," Mr. Yelnick said. "It was at Carnegie Recital Hall in 1962. The Trio da Camera."

In the last decade, he said, "the places I've appeared in have included Alice Tully Hall, Town Hall, the Metropolitan Museum, the Brooklyn Academy of Music, the Pierpont Morgan Library and several others."

Mr. Yelnick's monopoly on his concert vocation has not given him a security complex. "Many times I've wondered if they'd ever get around to inventing some simple device, an automatic page turner, and put me out of business," he confessed.

The man nurtures his relations with his clients. "Once a year I send a card to all the pianists I've turned for, a New Year's card, and the writing on it says, 'I'm turning a new leaf.'" Mr. Yelnick liked that well enough to tell it three times and he thought it might make a good title for his autobiography, if he ever gets around to writing it.

He was asked if it would be possible for pictures to be made of him during a concert. "You can call the director of the concert," he said. "He might be delighted to have you take pictures—give it a little stigma."

On stage he does not wear a tuxedo. "I just dress in a dark business suit," he said. "I try to look as neat as possible. Polished shoes. I'll take along an extra shirt on my regular job, so I can change at the end of my working day. I have a locker there."

Mr. Yelnick arrives backstage, introduces himself briefly to the artist, checks on the program, looks at the music, unsticks any pages that are stuck together, "and then I retire to the corridor," he said. "An artist is on edge; he doesn't want any extraneous conversation.

"I usually question the pianist, to see if there are any cuts or repeats. Many times they delete a small section or sometimes they will repeat a section, and I must remember that.

"Some pianists tell you to wait until they nod, but most pianists tell me before the concert, 'Turn the music when you see fit.'

"The program is usually two sonatas and some individual pieces, and a sonata runs about eighteen to twenty-two minutes. The Kreutzer Sonata by Beethoven is really a 100-mile dash for me, it's so fast. I have to turn a page every thirty seconds, instead of maybe every minute and a half. I think they should have called it 'Sonata for Violin, Piano and Page Turner.'

"I use my thumb and next finger, and I pinch the pages in advance of the concert. I take the upper right hand corner of the music and I pinch it down, so it's a little easier to turn.

"Brand new crisp music is very bad for me. It won't lay flat. The pages pop up. A little breeze might turn the page or flip it back to the old page. I prefer the old, worn music. Pages that are sort of dog-eared do lay flat.

"I have to flatten out new music with the flat part of my elbow—never on the spot being played—to hold it down. There again I come in handy.

"As we're walking out on stage, I step out after the pianist, lagging a little bit behind. While they're taking their bows, I open the music for the first half of the program and set it on the music stand. That saves the artist from being encumbered with that.

"I have no negative feelings when I go out. I feel very relaxed. I'm the coolest person on the stage. If I thought it wouldn't offend the artists, I'd probably throw in a little witticism, but I try not to be too chummy.

"I sit at the pianist's left on a chair, not on the same bench—just a normal chair that doesn't swing or swivel. I angle the chair in such a way that my chair half faces the piano and half faces the pianist, in a sort of three-quarter turn.

"I'm five feet eleven inches, 160 pounds. You'd have to

really look at me from an unusual angle, because I'm positioned so the pianist blocks me out. My object is to be as quiet and inconspicuous as possible. The noise of a page turning can throw them off. Pianists are very, very sensitive to a sneeze or a cough or the rustle of a page. So I try to stifle a sneeze.

"Of course, I have to overlook some of their idiosyncrasies. They'll make a gurgling noise or breathe heavily or hum along with the music—all signs of nervousness."

Sometimes the pianists try to cramp Mr. Yelnick's style. "I sit about two feet away from the pianist. One pianist asked me not to sit too close to him—it would make him nervous—which was a very poor request because I have to be on top of the music."

There is no conversation between turner and player during a concert. About the only thing any artist ever says to him is, "Will you move back a little bit?" Mr. Yelnick said.

"I have to hang on every note that's being played," he went on. "I sort of lend a bodily attitude to the whole thing. Some pianists feel very good that somebody is right next to them to sort of mother them along. There's often a kind look by the pianist for my turning the page at the right time. There's a silent, thankful glance in my direction.

"I have had pianists who have darted angry looks at me for turning a little too late. There was one case where I had a little lapse of memory and the pianist gave me a dirty look because he had to turn his own page. The audience saw it and there was a buzz about it.

"Otherwise, I always turn at the right moment. I'm never late. My timing is perfect.

"I sit, but I half-rise about fifteen seconds before I actually turn the page. At the appropriate time, I pinch the upper right hand corner of the music page with my left hand. If I were to use my right hand, I'd be brushing across his face.

"I've already got the page off the surface. The top of the

page is slightly curled and already started, but the bottom is still intact. The page is half-turned already. The actual turn takes about a quarter of a second. It's just a fast whisk that does the trick.

"I do not wait too long. I always turn one or two measures in advance, because the artist has got it photographed in his mind already, the last two measures.

"The average piece is about eighteen minutes, with about eighteen turns. I would say I turn close to one hundred pages in an average concert.

"The artist comes off the stage wet. I always carry an extra, fresh handkerchief in my pocket so he can wipe his brow. It's just another little accommodation.

"After the concert is over, I've done everything but play it for him," Mr. Yelnick said, summing up his own contribution to the occasion.

"I go out to the wings and stay there for the second and third bow, because I don't share the applause. I have no desire to be in the limelight.

"Occasionally—and I underscore occasionally—I'm thanked by the artist. The average pianist doesn't find it necessary to thank me. Maybe one out of ten say, 'Thank you so much. You've been a great help. I don't know what I would have done without you.'

"After it's over, rather than get swallowed up in the crowd of well-wishers backstage, I simply leave, and they mail me my twenty-five dollar fee."

No one—no relative or friend—has ever gone to a concert to watch him turn, Mr. Yelnick said. No one has ever asked for his autograph.

"Occasionally," Mr. Yelnick said in a low-key tone, "while waiting on the subway platform, like at Lincoln Center, somebody may walk over and say, 'Weren't you on the stage tonight?'

"I say, 'Yes. I'm the one.' "

The Last of the Red Hot Principals

Abraham H. Lass has retired as the City's only "ragtime movie pianist high school principal." He has retired, that is, as principal of Abraham Lincoln High School in Brooklyn, but he remains, irrepressibly, a ragtime pianist.

Through half a century he has kept the skills fresh that enabled him to earn cash in his teen-age years by fast-pedaling and finger-sprinting on an upright piano in a "small, sour-smelling" silent film house on Sixteenth Avenue in Brooklyn. His keyboard style verges on parody in a record he cut for the Asch label called "Play Me A Movie."

As principal of the high school near Coney Island he had a flock of 4,100 students, about seventy per cent of them college bound, and once in a while he would take the stage at an assembly and knock them dead with his rinky-dink renditions. It took a hard student to hate a principal who would do that. Mr. Lass held the top job at Lincoln in the last fifteen years of a forty-year career in the City school system, running, he says, "from the Depression to the Revolution."

When Captain Joseph Mescall of the Coney Island precinct learned that Mr. Lass was retiring, a phrase leaped to his tongue that sums up a lot: "Well," the captain told Mr. Lass, "you're the last of the red hot principals."

Abraham Lass is, among other things, a collector of disparate identities. It would be possible for him to convene a Lass convention and, by erecting a series of mirrors, organize a discussion of great catholicity among his various selves.

The gavel, of course, would be controlled—and used with thumping authority—by former principal Lass, and he would deliver the keynote address, a rousing verbal assault on the present Board of Education.

The gavel would be necessary because Mr. Lass, the

newspaper columnist, would be likely to interrupt Mr. Lass, the world traveler, and because Mr. Lass, the philosopher of education, would rise on a point of personal privilege and demand that Mr. Lass, the recording artist, let him get a word in edgewise.

Mr. Lass, author or editor of seventeen books, would lead a seminar in *The American Experience in Short Stories* (the title of one of his books, with Professor Leonard Kriegel), describing the way the taking of the West, the small-town experience, the rise of cities and the Depression are all limned in short stories.

If Mr. Lass, the ragtime player, would stop playing the old songs, Mr. Lass, the raconteur and wit, would regale the convention with a string of lively anecdotes told with the sure timing of an actor.

It would be difficult to recount all the highlights of so rich a convention, but a Lass sampler could be compiled to suggest its breadth and tenor. It would include:

*A sad perception that "adolescence has become a kind of senescence," in which "the shadow of maturity falls too early over the young." Mr. Lass recalls that when he was a boy in Brooklyn "there were a few of the golden years of adolescence, maybe four or five of them, and you lived them with joy." The new generation "is not spending enough of its time being young," he says.

*Memories of decades in the City schools, including the time he taught *Hamlet* in a deliberate South Brooklyn accent to a class of not very bright students, supplying a simultaneous translation from the Elizabethan to the vernacular ("Polonius is trying to con Hamlet into this"). At the close of the term he asked a boy how he liked it. "It wasn't bad," the boy answered. "It was all full of quotations."

*A plea for the continuance of the merit system in school promotions. "I'm very glad for having paid my life back to this great, wounded City for having educated me," Mr. Lass said. "I don't believe it would have been possible for me to have gone as far in any other place—without knowing anybody, without influence and without any intervention. Maybe it's the old American dream that said if you worked hard and if you had patience, and if you could sort of stand the gaff, and if you did your best and stayed with it, the rewards would come, and this proved for me not to be a mirage."

To the Board of Education he applies a list of adjectives: "They are basically inept, irresponsible, uninformed ... also frightened, indecisive." He retired just after the system went into what seemed to him a steep and lamentable decline in which long-honored norms were overthrown. Mr. Lass maintained an unusually high degree of visibility as an educator and administrator by writing articles and essays for *The Saturday Review* and several other periodicals. His byline ran for years on an education column in the former *New York World-Telegram,* later in the *New York Post* and the *New York Herald Tribune.* This became the occasion of some jealousy among his colleagues. One day, as he stepped into a crowded elevator at the Board's headquarters, an executive loudly asked him who wrote his column for him.

"I'll tell you who writes it for me, Harry, if you'll tell me who reads it to you," Mr. Lass replied. There was no further static from that quarter.

Those who know him are aware of much of this, but few know that Mr. Lass is a large-scale collector of nostalgic Americana who owns a library of Tin Pan Alley sheet music. He collects old Valentine cards, painted postcards of handsome young women of the early twentieth century, and piano sheet music dating from 1840 to 1925. He finds time in the evenings to sit with his wife, Betty, and to go over these sometimes brittle bits of memorabilia.

"Whatever you collect says basically something about you," Mr. Lass remarked in his living room at 1384 East

Tenth Street. Both he and Mrs. Lass admit to a vague longing for the early years of this century, when life was lived in a quieter, surer America.

His record, "Play Me A Movie," recalls the music he played in the Eagle Theater in the 1920s. Most of it he composed in the flash of a moment's inspiration, and it is sweet and bittersweet, as are his own memories.

"I'm a product of another era," Mr. Lass said, moving from an easy chair to his piano bench. "I'm probably the only high school principal in America who played the piano in the silent movies." It was an art of a special kind. Scene changes required abrupt changes of keyboard pace and mood. A good player had to be a master of falling-over-a-cliff music, hanging-in-midair music, storm-at-sea music, lovers-kissing music, horror music and what was called "hurry music" to go with wild screen chases. Mr. Lass became adept at improvising them all.

He demonstrated that he could still play a good, impromptu score for Pathé News, circa 1922.

"There was always the horse race or the steeplechase," he said, his long fingers rippling along the keys. "And the strike picket line." He changed to deep, portentous chords.

"Then came the Paris fashions," he said, and one could almost hear the canaries twittering.

"The Eagle was in Borough Park, near Fortieth Street," he said. "I was sixteen years old and I played about three hours after school and on Saturdays. They paid me two dollars a day.

"I followed the screen action. The 'hurry music' could go with anything—cowboys, Indians, robbers, cops, any kind of chase. That, of course, changes very easily to the tornado scene."

Mr. Lass churned the piano keys into a dark fury.

For an "out into the storm" scene, in which a landlord evicted an impoverished widow from her flat, Mr. Lass played music that was stark, grave and tragic, but also tremulous. "I didn't have any sound effects," he explained. "I just had ten fingers."

The piano player sat about eight feet from the screen, to one side. "The first two years I knew him," Mrs. Lass said, "he had a permanent crook in his neck from looking up at the screen at such a sharp angle."

Mr. Lass set down some reminiscences about his ragpicking years on the Eagle's piano in these lines:

"I was a high school senior and I did a three-hour stint as relief pianist. I was relieved, in turn, by the full-time pro, a thin, dour, erratic pianist in his early thirties. He hated playing the piano, he hated the movies, and he hated the audiences, especially the kids. I loved them all. I loved playing for Douglas Fairbanks, Mary Pickford, Harold Lloyd, Charlie Chaplin, Buster Keaton, William S. Hart and Richard Barthelmess.

"The Eagle Theater was a compact, box-like affair. Up front, right under the small stage, I sat at the piano. Like most of the pianos in the old neighborhood houses, this one was an upright. Its guts and strings and hammers were exposed. When played it emitted the characteristically tinny, tinkly, nickelodeon sound.... Running like a leitmotif through every performance was the incessant cracking of Indian nuts (the popcorn of its day) between the teeth of myriad Indian nut addicts during the picture, and under foot as the audience left the theater.

"To heighten the dramatic effect of tender love scenes, or to provide live sound for Westerns or battle scenes, the older kids would fire off their then-popular, Kilgore repeating cap pistols. The younger kids, identifying with the hero as he was being stalked or about to be stabbed or jumped by the villain and his hirelings, would blurt such hysterical warnings as 'Look out! He's behind the door!'

"There were always kids reading aloud the florid,

polysyllabic subtitles to their parents or grandparents and when necessary (which was pretty often) supplying simultaneous translations in Italian, Yiddish and German.

"At critical points, the film almost invariably split. This set off an orgy of applause, howling, whistling, banging and floor-kicking. The audience seemed to enjoy these 'breaks' more than the picture. Periodically a man (usually the owner of the theater) would walk up and down the aisles with a Flit gun spraying a sickeningly sweet deodorant over the audience. The ventilation in the Eagle Theater left much to be desired. At about 5:00 in the afternoon, parents began wandering through the theater, anxiously calling in the darkness for Sam, Charlie and Harry, who had seen two performances and were on their third.

"When I got tired of playing—I usually played for about an hour-and-a-half at a stretch—I put a nickel into an automatic piano operated by leaking bellows, which at regular intervals asthmatically wheezed air instead of music. During a typical afternoon I supplied music for a cartoon, a serial, a comedy, a newsreel and a feature.

"As each scene flashed on the screen, I had to decide on the spot what music to play for what was probably about to happen, and for what actually did happen, which frequently wasn't exactly what I had anticipated. Fortunately, the subtitles and the fairly broad and obvious acting telegraphed enough clues to me so that I could hazard a reasonable guess about the kind of music that would back up the mood and the action and produce the satisfying, unifying, emotional effect that only music can produce.

"I had a number of things going for me in this game of match the music to the picture. My piano teacher, an old martinet, had given me an excellent grounding in the traditional classics and piano techniques. My musical memory was pretty good. I had a broad and varied popular and classical repertoire. I played easily, naturally and quite accurately by ear. I could, in addition, improvise and compose on the instant the music I thought would fit the shifting moods and scenes. So I improvised and composed my way through fires, terrestrial upheavals of all kinds—volcanic eruptions, rain and snow storms, typhoons, hurricanes—confrontations between the forces of good and evil—love scenes: young, tender, passionate, secret—humorous and tragic scenes, encounters with eccentric, lovable, sinister characters—breathless pursuits, escapes and rescues.

"Writing in *Harper's Bazaar* in 1946, Kurt Weill said: 'The silent movie needed music as a dry cereal needs cream.' I supplied that cream for four delicious years."

The educator's tastes remain as syncretic in the 1970s as they were in the 20s. Mr. Lass was sitting next to a book shelf with *Catch-22,* Fowler's *Modern English Usage,* the Bible, and *Some of the Best Jokes are Jewish.* On his piano the sheet music for "Snookey Ookums" lay next to a folio of piano music by Bach. He leafed through a stack of sheet music for some old popular songs. "It was a much simpler era," he reflected. "The pictures on the covers reflect the times, the customs, the dress.

"There were certain verities in life then. Today, policemen strike, firemen strike, school teachers strike. It's a different world."

"Abe, when I first knew you, I carried a parasol," Betty Lass said.

"When I was a little girl, Lord & Taylor's was on Grand Street," she mused. Her husband returned to the piano and she sang, very sweetly, hit songs from the years of their teenage romance.

"The past is elusive," Mr. Lass said. "You never really recapture it but you try. You try to clutch on to pieces of it in some form that is pleasant to you. Popular music is one of the most evocative forms of recall."

A school principal has an almost royal sway in his realm, and Mr. Lass's school was large enough to keep twelve secretaries busy on his staff.

A few weeks ago, he recalled, "I closed the door and walked out slowly to my car and turned the key in the lock and I said, 'Lass, remember this: you're not Principal Lass now, you're Mr. Lass' " and he drove home to his wife of forty years—and their half of the two-family house at 1384 East Tenth Street near Avenue N—sweethearts since the night he took her to their high school senior prom.

The Titan and the Tots

It was the meeting of the Titan with the Tots. The titan was Virgil Thomsom, the eminent composer and critic, and the tots were second grade children of P.S. 134 on the Lower East Side. Their common ground was music.

They met in the Henry Street Settlement Music School on Grand Street, where musically underprivileged children make music in a training program carried out in Mr. Thomson's name. Apart from that, they would receive no basic musical education, for P.S. 134 is one of the schools that have had it cut from the program for the sake of what is called economy.

The Virgil Thomson Music Fund, established in honor of the composer's seventy-fifth birthday, pays for an hour a week for 350 children in the second through fifth grades. The classes are designed to acquaint the children with the rudiments of music while giving them a taste of the pleasures of making music.

"I like the kiddies," Mr. Thomson said with an almost W. C. Fields-like relish. A moment earlier he had reflected on the wisdom of certain nannies who had learned to "tranquilize" squalling infants by popping their heads into the oven for just a bit of gas.

Mr. Thomson, rotund, baldish, gray-eyed, looked very

trim in a vested suit and easily conveyed the impression of a man who is ready for anything.

When a seven-year-old in a green sweater twisted in his first-row seat and pointed his forefinger at Mr. Thomson in the back row and said, "Pshoo!" Mr. Thomson coolly raised his hand, cocked his forefinger, levelled it at the lad and returned fire.

The fare to which he was treated by the nineteen children in the class was on the rarified level of "Cat's in the buttermilk, lapping up the cream" and "I'll play on my sticks—clicka, clicka/click, click, click."

They were led by a nun in secular clothes with an uncosmeticized face who had a round-O way of pronouncing every syllable ("Let's hear the first row sing *hell-O, hell-O*") and a gentle manner. She worked every second against a general undercurrent of restlessness and disquiet.

The children were equipped with triangles, rhythm sticks, bells, maracas, tiny tambourines, bongos and congas, mostly for keeping the beat. "Got to keep them terribly busy," Mr. Thomson remarked.

The nun, full of a long-practiced tolerance for childish ways, was aided by the children's regular teacher, a sterner-visaged young woman who sat facing her charges, seeking to maintain discipline with a series of non-approbative facial expressions.

"Let's get our quar-*ter* notes," the nun said exactly. "All right, Carmen, let's play. Now, Vance—that's enough."

It was no insult that Mr. Thomson fell to drowsing, his chin dropping to his chest, for he had been known to do just that at the opera and symphony, thereby getting a good rest before writing brilliant reviews of performances he had partly missed. He was the music critic of the *New York Herald Tribune* from 1940 to 1954. The composer was born in Kansas City, Missouri, on November 25, 1896. He graduated from Harvard in 1922 and went off to Paris for a long stretch before taking up residence in New York.

"They're full of energy, and they're clean," Mr. Thomson

said after the class. "As children go, I thought they were extremely well-behaved." Teaching them music, he said, was a "correct sociological enterprise."

It was at the right age, too, he remarked. "I don't think anybody can ever learn to make a snare drum roll after twelve." He curled his pudgy fingers and ran them through swift gestures illustrating the snare drum and the kettle drum roll.

Mr. Thomson sat for a while in the office of Bertram M. Beck, executive director of the settlement, in a brick-faced building that went up in 1820. A portrait of Beethoven, tight-lipped, gazed down from the wall.

Of Mr. Beck, he said: "The essence of tact is to know how people want to be approached. I don't have it. He has. He wrote me the most perfectly elegant letter." For all its elegance, the letter proposed that money donated to the settlement for a production of one of Mr. Thomson's operas be used instead for training children.

"The opera went beyond their resources, musical or financial," the composer said. Did he accept the use now being made? "Matter of fact, I prefer it," he said. "To have my name attached to a serious musical program in a proper slum music school pleases me very much. I've great respect for these New York settlement houses."

Of his interest in settlement programs and old jazz halls and a score of other things far from the velvet ropes of Lincoln Center, Mr. Thomson said, "I've spent my life connecting with off-center things, because I don't like establishment things. I was born in a Confederate family and I am always agin' the government, or anybody who thinks he's running me like a government.

"I've known this place for thirty or forty years. Henry Street has always been very prominent in the artistic settlement world and in a way, you know, the lower the slum, the brighter the people you deal with. I like the people who run the settlement and who they run it for."

As for the economic emergency that has squeezed music out of some public schools, Mr. Thomson said, "It all comes from paying the help. In earlier times, when we had good hotel service and good household service, nobody earned any money, really, except the people who had it. Now everybody's getting paid. It's bursting the economy at the seams. I'm all for it."

He told Mr. Beck he was delighted that the settlement had established a fund in his name "to tide the schools over 'til they can get back to music education—if and when."

The City's population is musically sophisticated, able to turn out 90,000 hearers for a symphony concert in Central Park, Mr. Thomson observed, noting that, "Music appreciation has been taught for fifty years now in our high schools and colleges, and taught not merely on the rave level but on the technical and analytic level. There's nothing equivalent to it in the world—in Europe, South America, Asia, or the islands of the sea.

"New York is probably at the top in its general level and spread of musical sophistication, with its Jewish population, the old Germans, the Italians. The only people who don't patronize music are the Irish and the Poles—their priests won't let 'em buy tickets."

Mr. Thomson said it was clear that "this country has the highest music consumption in the world in every form, from the latest pop to the finest chamber music and jazz, which is just a highly specialized form of chamber music. Jazz is not commercial, it never has been really; rock is commercial." He spoke a bit about the old "jazz spots" and "jazz dives" like the Savoy Ballroom and the Five Spot on Lafayette Street where a patron heard "proper jazz."

"There's a curious sociological circumstance in that, right along with the enormous public appetite for music, there is technological unemployment, with the currency of the gramophone and all that."

The result is more and more of less and less—"a broader

and broader distribution of music, and a smaller amount of professional employment and performance opportunities for musicians."

He spoke of records with "one part missing," called Music Minus One. "If you play viola, you get the one that is missing the viola. You put it on and play with full orchestral accompaniment. There's also Sans Voce—without the voice. Saves on hiring accompanists."

On the way to the subway with his friend, Samuel Lurie, Mr. Thomson came to a difficult crossing with six lanes of traffic feeding from three directions.

"Can we cross?" Samuel Lurie asked.

"We can always cross," Mr. Thomson said. He stepped off the curb and walked straight out into the traffic against the light, alone. By his stance in the midst of the maelstrom, he made it plain that he expected traffic to rearrange itself around him. Without faltering or paying the slightest attention to any of them, he was soon the object of startled avoidance by fast-moving taxis and trucks.

As he made his stubby-legged way toward the opposite curb, his form was screened from view at times by big trucks sweeping just behind him. Mr. Lurie seemed to hold his breath on the doubt that this friend could avoid being flattened, but Mr. Thomson might as well have been walking on a prairie. His time had not come and he seemed to know it.

The critic went down into the Sixth Avenue subway and headed for his suite at the renowned Chelsea Hotel on Twenty-third Street—a clear case of a landmark going to a landmark.

Port City

Pier 39

The sun had barely come up even with the rooftops. It glanced in through a window and laid a streak across the desk of the boss of the pier—across the pipe rack, the steel in-box, a copy of the New Testament and some papers.

Outside the waters of the harbor were burning gold and it seemed that the sleek ship, now being nudged into place at the dock, might melt away. It was 7:07 A.M.

Captain Russell W. Neitz tilted forward in his chair, stood, stepped quickly across the mirror-polished terrazzo floor, brushed a curtain aside and gazed out.

The *Savannah Maru,* a graceful Japanese freighter, 511 feet long, was almost in place far down the long pier. A small party stood on the stringpiece to welcome her to Brooklyn—two men forward and two men aft to tie her fast.

A day of din and scurry had begun with the docking of the freighter at the Northeast Marine Terminal and Stevedoring Corporation's Pier 39, and it continued long after darkness had settled over the harbor.

Soon more than 230 men would be crawling over the ship and the pier to dig out the many layers of cargo and to operate the six cranes fixed to the structure of the freighter.

They would find it laden with treasures from the mysterious Orient—watch bands, plastic flowers, umbrella handles, pencil sharpeners, cameras, a consignment of plastic Ten Commandments bracelets and hundreds of other things.

Ships have been docking in New York for centuries and men have been unloading them as long, but life on a pier has changed enormously. Mechanization, employment stabilization and the coming of the computer have brought a shift that old-timers regard with wonder.

Casual labor hired by the day in rough shape-ups is out. The longshoremen at the pier are mostly hired by the year now and they enjoy a guaranteed annual wage of $12,300.

Pier 39 sits at the entrance to Gowanus Bay, a busy pier in a booming port city. An average of three ships a week dock there. Nine longshore gangs of eighteen men each work there all year. The pier's payroll alone runs over $4 million a year.

The pier needed extra labor for the day, so Thomas Costa, the hiring agent, made one of his last trips over to the hiring hall two blocks to the north on Thirty-seventh Street. He hired forty-one longshoremen, and twenty laborers to help load trucks.

The hiring of additional labor for the pier will not much longer be done by picking men up at the hiring hall. All Mr. Costa will have to do is to punch a request for additional hands on a computer keyboard the evening before. The system, already installed, links the pier with the Waterfront Commission's hiring halls.

"We tried it one day," Dominick Viola, the terminal superintendent, said. "We asked the computer for twenty men the afternoon before and, the next morning, nobody showed up. So they asked us to hold off until they iron some of the lumps out of it."

At 8:45 A.M. all the men stood at the head of the pier. Mr. Costa took attendance, checking off the absentees on blue sheets. Then he went upstairs and punched all the absentees' numbers into the computer.

"The regular men have a guaranteed wage, but they have to show up," somebody said. "If they show up and there's no work, they get paid."

Twenty barn-size doors of the pier shed—large enough for

an armory—were opened toward the *Savannah Maru*. Crewmen on the ship pushed buttons that automatically slid open the hatch covers over the cargo.

The pier shed's smooth cement floor stretches 1,050 feet to the pier's end, and the ship's cargo would be spread over nearly all of its surface and piled almost to the roof.

Angelo Maisto, a longshoreman, swung up into the high seat of one of the ship's cranes. He seemed secure against a biting wind in five layers of warm clothing—three zippered jackets interleaved with overalls and a wool shirt.

He would work only one hour at the crane's controls, a critical spot. Then he would work an hour on the deck and take an hour off before returning to his perch.

"Any mistake you make, you could kill a lot of men," Mr. Maisto said.

"If you pick up more than the crane can take, you'll spill it on a gang. So you check the weight."

"How?"

"It's in the hands," he said, rippling his fingers. "You judge it by the feel of the levers."

If a load feels too heavy, Mr. Maisto shouts down to the men working in the hold, who lighten it before he lifts it up over the railing and deposits it on the pier.

Later, eight fork-lift machines were scooped up from the edge of the pier and hoisted into the ship's deep holds. The freighter had 4,400 tons to unload before sailing for ports to the south.

There were 980 separate bills of lading for New York, and their variety was suggested by the mixed assortment of bales, boxes, cartons, crates, skids and metal containers jammed into the holds.

The clerks in the freight department had typed up all the bills and had them mimeographed and bound as a thick book. But the exact contents of the shipments were carefully omitted. On one page, the book listed simply: "77 drums . . . 110 pails . . . 600 bags . . . 2 cases . . . 100 bundles . . . 99 coils . . . 415 paper bags."

The anonymity of the merchandise helps protect the more valuable items from shrinkage by theft.

A cargo net, which looks like a hair net for a giantess, can lift twenty refrigerator-size cartons in a jumble and set them down in a gentle spill—not, however, if they contain refrigerators.

There were a few cargo containers, which look like railroad boxcars, aboard. Their size did not imply their weight. "A 20-foot container can have up to twenty-three tons in it—if it's stuffed with ball bearings," a dock hand said. "But if it's silk shirts, it'll only go five tons."

Whenever a cargo container thudded down on the stringpiece, a motorized monster called a hydraulic top loader would roar over, sink its teeth into the top and lift the whole thing up, with no underneath support, and bear it away.

With eighty pieces of power equipment on the pier, the scene suggested a battlefield for dinosaurs. The roar and clatter of motors and of wooden pallets striking the cement thundered in the steel pier shed.

The fork-lift vehicles, called "hi-los" by the men, ran at times in herd formations. They accelerated in bursts up to twenty miles an hour and zig-zagged wildly among the stacks of merchandise.

"It's changed," an old dock hand said. "It used to be hand trucks, dollies and muscle—real muscle. Now everything is mechanization. It used to be iron men and wooden ships. Now it's iron ships and wooden men."

He did not spit nails, and the characterization may have been overstated. The dock workers, men who wear hooks in their rear pockets, did not look as though they had gone soft.

Pete Spano, the head foreman of the longshore gangs, paced back and forth on the ship, his eyes searching the holds.

When he saw something he didn't like, he forced air through his upper teeth in a piercing whistle, a signal to the men in the hold to look up.

"Frankee!" he bellowed, his forehead creased with a frown, his right hand waving in an admonitory gesture. "Take the top one off! Reverse the load!"

That was not quite all there was to it, for the foreman's command of profanity would qualify him for an earned doctorate in advanced reprehension.

A cube made up of 125 small cardboard cartons, held together by straps, had been placed *under* a heavier cube of twelve large cartons. The smaller cartons looked loose enough to give way under the larger ones during the lift.

Each withdrawal from a hold is called a draft. "There are a million ways of lifting it out," Mr. Spano said, explaining that the men suit the method to the cargo. One rule is that "boxes go with boxes, bales with bales, cartons with cartons."

Mr. Spano's main aim is to "make sure the hook never stops." Every time a load is set down on the pier, the gangs have got to move it out of the way to make room for the next draft. So, if the hoisting hook stays in constant motion, the cargo moves.

Mr. Spano knows a little Japanese. He called out "ha-no-nay!" That means "Hey you! Listen up! Let's go!" another man said.

At 11:05, the ship crane over the number three aft hold broke. Within minutes seven Japanese were working on it.

Mr. Spano, a leather-lunged shouter, has a voice that cuts through a wintry wind, but if a man is out of range, a series of signals convey his message. His two hands wrapped around his neck mean "no more choke"—a reference to a method of lifting cargo.

At times, Mr. Spano was like a symphony orchestra conductor, signalling his choices of cargo-handling methods to men in different sections of the hold.

"There's a million and one ways to get hurt," said Peter Kiplock, safety director in the terminal. "We try to get the men to wear safety shoes. We can't make them, but if a man brings in a copy of the purchase order for steel-tipped shoes, we put $3.50 into every pair.

"There are over fifty kinds of safety shoes—even hush puppies. You'd never guess.

"About four months ago, we had a safety meeting all on safety shoes. One guy there, after the meeting, he bought a pair the next day. Two days later a piece of pipe, weighing approximately a ton—dropped on his toe.

"His toes were bruised, but without that shoe he wouldn't have had any toes left. He has his five toes and he's still working."

Sister Henrica, a nun who covered the whole Brooklyn waterfront, begging for charity, for forty years recently retired, depriving Dominick Viola of the terminal staff of weekly proof that longshoremen are "the softest touch in the world."

"They'd always get a chair for her. Never let her go around," he said. "They'd take her basket and one of the men would go around with it. 'Too heavy with a quarter—much lighter with a dollar,' he'd say. 'You want me to hurt my arm?'"

Usually the basket would pile up with bills and Sister Henrica would leave relaxed and enriched for her cause.

"As rough as they may be speaking, if they see a woman on the pier, they won't let a word out of their mouths," Mr. Viola said.

With all the care in the world, some cargo gets damaged in transfer—dented or split open or torn. It is carted into a separate area on the pier that is "like a hospital for damaged cartons," Mr. Kiplock said. It is a big, wire-fenced cage.

The deft surgeons there use tape, wire, nails and boards to bind up the wounds. In the afternoon three crates with fractured slats were treated and released.

Trucks come to the pier on a schedule of definite appointments—at 8:00 A.M. or 10:00 A.M. or 1:00 P.M.—as many as 350 in a day.

Every truck stops at the little scale house and is weighed in on a scale that runs up to 100,000 pounds.

"The manifest shows what the cargo they pick up should weigh," somebody explained. "If a truck is supposed to have 10,000 pounds and it weighs 12,000 pounds on the way out, we want to know what the extra 2,000 pounds is. Sometimes we have to stop a truck and take a look. Sometimes it's an honest mistake."

The pier has a staff of thirty-five regular checkers, and no trucker puts on any cargo unless a checker is standing beside him.

Checkers used to be picked from among the longshoremen by a simple method. If a man wanted to be a checker and happened to know how to read and write, he'd get the job. But literacy has gone way up and it's not that simple anymore.

Dutch Carlson, a checker with nearly thirty years on the waterfront, finds that he has to read figures in several languages and in gibberish. The Germans make certain figures distinctively and the Japanese have some special touches, and sometimes a scrawl looks like a three or five or maybe an eight.

The men dropped work for coffee at 10:00 A.M. and 2:30 P.M. and they broke for lunch at 11:55. A few, who live nearby, drove home; a few went to their cars to eat; a few went out to Eddie the Pizza King's place or to the truck parked just outside the gate with coffee and sandwiches. Most of the men had brought lunches from home. They made seats and tables out of cargo cartons and spread their hero sandwiches and beer.

At 5:00, the men went on overtime and they all worked until 9:00 P.M., as Mr. Spano kept the hooks in ceaseless motion. Thomas Martinez, pier superintendent for the

Mitsui-O.S.K. Line, which owns the freighter, announced that the gang foremen were invited aboard the *Savannah Maru* for sake and sukiyaki at 1:00 P.M. on the third day in port, by which time all the luster pearls and brass swivels and hurricane lanterns and canned smoked baby clams in cottonseed oil and hamster cages and beaded handbags and yarn and zigzag sewing machine parts had been dug out of what had seemed to be bottomless holds.

Storm Rescue at False Hook

Fifty-two men scrambled down rope ladders from the stricken tanker *Chelwood Beacon* early yesterday and late Sunday and leaped to rescue craft below. They were plucked to safety by men on two small vessels that heaved violently in the waves of the storm-churned Atlantic. A Coast Guard official described the rescue operation as one of the most "daring and expert feats of seamanship" ever seen around New York harbor. No one was lost and the several injuries were quickly treated.

Southwest winds sent awesome twenty-five-foot-high wall waves crashing into the rescue scene. A Coast Guard cutter constantly circled the stricken tanker in a wide arc to break the effect of the waves. It was an attempt to "cut the sea back a little bit," a Coast Guard man said.

All fifty-two hands were safely and comfortably settled in transient rooms in Manhattan after a night-long ordeal that might easily have led to tragedy if the delicate maneuvers of the rescue had gone wrong at any point. But the British tanker, heavy with a full load of crude oil, remained the prisoner of a treacherous shoal known to mariners as False Hook. It sits in the waters off Sandy Hook close to the entrance to New York harbor. The tanker ran aground there Sunday.

Some thought the *Chelwood Beacon* had been driven far out of its deep channel by raging winds; others believed that buoys marking the way had been swept out of alignment, creating a false path to potential disaster. A special harbor pilot, with an intimate knowledge of the shapes and contours of the harbor and its underwater terrain, had already boarded the tanker to help guide her to an oil dock at Port Reading, New Jersey.

A motorboat launch called the *Narrows,* manned by two New York harbor pilots, carried out the first part of the rescue under extraordinary hazards. The Coast Guard cutter, *Yeaton,* came in to the Battery late yesterday morning with the last twelve survivors after twenty-three straight hours of emergency duty.

In the furious, sleet-thick gales of Sunday afternoon, the 634-foot-long "baby supertanker" got out of the safe channel leading into the harbor and ran aground. The ship lay first in an east-west position, but waves and winds beat on the helpless craft and twisted her around ninety degrees to a north-south position. The tanker, which needed thirty-three feet of clearance below, was grounded in water only twenty-four feet deep. Oil leaked from a crack in her hull. There was danger that the crack would open further and split the ship.

Three tugs and a cutter stood by her through the desperate night. But the tugs could not haul or yank the tanker off the shoal. The cutter *Yeaton* did not attempt to stay close enough to take men aboard, because her skipper feared that he would knife the cutter's sharp bow into the tanker's hull. Indeed, at one point, the two bows banged each other with a metallic ring.

Jacob's rope ladders hung over the tanker's port side. Men clustered near them on the red deck, waiting to go down. Southwest winds hurled wall waves into the area, and the cutter *Yeaton* circled the tanker in a feeble attempt to reduce their power. The little motor launch *Scotland* worked in close, seeking to hug the tanker amidships, but it kept thrusting upward and then sliding down in successive waves and troughs. Only two men were on the launch, the operator and a deck hand, as its bow heaved in gales of up to 45 knots. One man was at the helm. The other stood ready to try to grab men hanging from the ladders.

For the escaping crewmen the question was when to let go of the ladders and trust themselvses to outstretched arms below. Spaces opened and closed suddenly between the tanker and the launch, leaving a gap of dark and violent water into which a man could drop, easily to be lost, if he were not trapped between grinding hulls.

It was extremely difficult to bind the launch close to the tanker. When the launch did come in tight, the operator left the helm and dashed back to help at the ladders, then dashed back to the helm, holding her as steady as he could. In this way, in pass after pass, thirty-nine men were taken aboard. The launch is a satellite craft of the 168-foot *New Jersey*, the boat that carries harbor pilots near their points of rendezvous with ships coming into the harbor.

The crewmen, Asians, Latin Americans and Europeans, came on soaked in brine and were soon transferred to the *New Jersey*, which afforded them a bit of cheering warmth and carried them into a Staten Island dock. Thirteen men—including a pilot, eight officers and three crewmen and the master, Captain Peter Jones—remained on the bleeding tanker.

The cutter *Yeaton*'s adventures had started about noon Sunday when it went to help a 487-foot Norwegian freighter, *Dyvi Atlantic,* whose anchor could not hold her steady in Gravesend Bay under the furious winds. "It was like an ant going out to rescue a big cat," a Coast Guard man observed. The heavy freighter was loaded with Volkswagens. After the freighter was taken in tow, the cutter sped to the oil tanker, grounded a mile and a half off Sandy Hook, about fifteen miles south of Manhattan.

At 8:00 A.M. yesterday, after the tanker's master had decided that the risk of losing lives was too great to warrant keeping anyone on board, the cutter began to move in to grab the remaining men from the ladders. It was "damn tough," said Lieutenant James G. Heydenreich, commander of the *Yeaton*. Eight men scrambled onto the cutter on the first approach before waves rebuffed its careful advance, but the cutter pressed in close again and the last five men dropped to safety.

Nearly fifty newsmen waited at the Battery, as the men came in at 11:15 A.M. They were dressed in khakis, foul weather gear, pea coats, fur parkas, and officers' topcoats with brass buttons, and they had been directed to say nothing. They were loaded into two station wagons and wheeled off to an unnamed hotel. The fear was that early statements might reflect on legal obligations later in a damaging way.

The Coast Guard Merchant Marine Investigation Office opened a preliminary inquiry into the cause of the grounding at False Hook. A survey party went to the abandoned tanker to seek to determine the best way to free her, but no decision was made last night on whether to drain off enough of her 30,000 tons of heavy, black Venezuelan crude oil to let the tanker float off the shoal at high tide, or to use tugs to nudge and tow her into deeper waters. (The tanker remained grounded at False Hook for several days but was finally reboarded, pumped out, and hauled in for repairs.)

Going Home

William Baur had a gift to give—his most productive years—and he gave them all to India. He was a very young man when he left his home at Webster Groves, Missouri, and traveled 10,000 miles to Madaya Pradesh, taking his bride of just one week.

Yesterday, after forty years of missionary service, the couple came home. When they arrived their four children and ten grandchildren (including three they had never seen) staged a "grand welcome" for them on the West Forty-sixth Street pier. The children waved bright red banners showing their names in large block letters: Kristy, Freddie, Kathy, Bruce, Lisa, David, Jeany, Debbie, Jimmy and Kimmy. Their ages ran from two to twelve years.

A green picket fence keeps passengers in the Customs area twenty-five feet away from greeters. The children were mostly too short to see their grandparents over the fence, so they wedged their noses and chins tight between the pickets and gave them grinning, one-eyed stares.

Behind them, their parents held aloft a six-foot scroll of white sheeting marked, "Welcome Home Baurs."

After the shouting and waving and fluttering of banners was over, the first generation had two hours in which to gaze fondly over the divide at the second and third generations.

"After forty years, we're retiring—at least from India," Mr. Baur said. The couple had packed their whole store of worldly goods, including many Indian objects, in fifteen wooden crates, black metal trunks and barrels, and it all had to be assembled for inspection.

For sixteen of their years overseas, the Baurs directed a leprosarium in which 600 lepers dwelled, at Raipur in central India. The couple lived in a small house across the road. Three of their four children were born in India. One came during a brief furlough in this country.

The Baurs' honeymoon missionary trek carried them from wheat fields in the heartland of America to "the rice bowl" of central India—a broad stretch of flatlands in the state of Madaya Pradesh rising to green hills in the distance. Mr. Baur, now sixty-four, was twenty-four when he left for India.

"It was his decision. I just decided to go along," Alby Baur said yesterday, smiling at her husband.

Why should a newly married man from Webster Groves, Missouri, leave the privileged life of the United States to go almost "half-way around the world" to a people he had never seen, accepting far leaner circumstances and family dislocations?

For Mr. Baur, there was the influence of the home in which he was reared and that mysterious heart-whisper that missionaries know as the "call."

"I think it was the good Christian home in which I was brought up," Mr. Baur said, "where from childhood on we had family prayers morning and evening, and we were told about the needs across the world in various countries and the possibilities of service."

His father was a professor of church history at the Eden Theological Seminary. The entire seminary, including family quarters, was housed in a five-story, 1884 brick building that stood in the middle of a twenty-acre campus near some cow barns at Wellston, Missouri.

"I had six sisters," Mr. Baur said, "and as those young theologues came through the seminary where my father taught, they naturally got acquainted with these young girls and as they became of age, one after the other, the six of them, they all married ministers."

Of the professor's four sons, three became ministers, and one became a physician and finally went into psychiatry.

"He wanted to find out what was wrong with the whole family, and finally he wound up feeling that he was the oddball," Mr. Baur said, his blue eyes twinkling with merriment.

Of the Baurs' four children, one boy became a minister and one girl married a minister. Another daughter is a nurse, and a son does social work with children from broken homes in Chicago.

Mr. Baur went out as a missionary of the Evangelical Church, but mergers have turned him into a member of the United Church of Christ. For a while he made evangelistic tours, and Mrs. Baur ran a boys' school and worked with women evangelists.

Through all the years, right to the last, the couple ate rice and curry at noontime. They saw famine, illiteracy, illness and superstitions afflict the people.

"Sometimes what seems the hopelessness of the situation" discouraged the couple. They faced eighty-five per cent illiteracy. They saw thousands of cattle roaming freely while people went hungry. If the temperature in the hottest part of the hot season was "only 110 degrees we thought we were having a cool spell, but it was dry heat."

"If we had to do it again, knowing all that we do now, we would do the same thing," Mr. Baur said. "It's a matter of doing the work that you're called to do. It helps you to get over a lot of rough spots, knowing that you're called."

The Baurs will drive all the way home to Missouri in a Volkswagen. They expect to "find some niche—probably some small church out in the country."

"Grandmother wants to get acquainted with her grandchildren," Mr. Baur said. "All things come to those who wait, and we've waited for this for forty years."

The Baurs' older son, the Reverend William L. Baur, will leave next month for Raipur, India, with his wife and three children. He will work in hospital administration, only sixteen miles from where his parents lived and worked so long in the vineyard of the Lord.

Portrait of a River

River-watching along the eastern edge of Manhattan can be a desultory pleasure these autumn days, especially toward evening when the sky is changing and the wind coming off the water is often strong and cool.

It can be instructive, too. The East River is a heavily traveled avenue of commerce and recreation whose traffic continues twenty-four hours a day. It bears everything from tiny outboard craft that seem to be lost in the foam of their own spray to giant tankers that move like sliding screens across the face of the opposite shore.

At 7:22 the other night, what looked like a camera tripod forty feet high, with a crow's nest at the top and a ladder running up to it, came sailing gaily up the river, mounted on a barge. Sharing the barge was a barn-like wooden structure painted brilliant orange. The whole rig, pushed by a mustard yellow tug, lent the river a carnival touch.

It was one of seven diesel derricks operated by the New Haven Railroad in the harbor. The derrick's cables lift huge chunks of equipment—steam boilers or lathes—from freight cars on sidings at the water and swing them onto barges or into the mouths of freighters.

A moment later there was a spectacle. A massive ship, the *World Explorer,* came north. Its rust-splotched black hull is 560 feet long. The ship entered the narrow west channel that runs between Welfare Island and Manhattan. Its smokestack, streaked red-white-and-blue, passed within 200 feet of apartment house windows that come flush to the river line at Fifty-third Street.

Bug-sized cabin cruisers bounce up the river, dodging out of the way of oncoming barges.

Those who watch the river patiently will see fireboats, garbage scows, submarines, Coast Guard cutters, cruise liners, yachts, sturdy tugs, stone scows, tankers, seaplanes, and freight car floats carving wide Vs in the silver blue water.

It is said of Captain Joseph H. Miller of the Circle Line that he knows every ripple in the river. He has been a pilot here for forty-two years and he has been sailing longer than that. He says he has navigated around Manhattan Island thousands of times in his day, and he would like to go on doing it forever.

Captain Miller is a big man with blue eyes and a memory filled with harbor lore. He wheeled his 600-passenger liner, formerly a Coast Guard cutter, around the Battery and nosed into the East River. He feels a loneliness in the harbor.

"This used to be some port," he said wistfully. "To me, it's like a ghost port now. There used to be five different ferry runs in the East River. They're all gone now. Tunnels killed them."

He recalled the night liners that used to sail from East River piers and take passengers east to Connecticut, Boston, New Hampshire and Maine and south to Savannah, Georgia.

"The Old Dominion Line ran to Savannah," he said. "The Vermont Line, as they called it, she'd run up east, clear to Maine, I think. Every night you'd see those boats heading out. They're all gone now."

"I was born upstate," he said, passing under the Brooklyn Bridge. "Orphaned at thirteen years old. Left school, worked in a brick yard. Worked so hard I used to cry sometimes.

"I was sitting on the end of the pier one day in Kingston. The Cornell Steamboat Company used to come in there with towboats, barges and scows. I said to the mate, 'Gee, mister, I'd like to work on one of these things.'

"He said, 'What would you like to do?'

"I said, 'It wouldn't make any difference, long as I could get on one.'

"He said, 'Come with me, son,' and he took me up to the captain. The captain said, 'Get your clothes and be here in the morning,' and let me tell you I was there!

"I was a deck hand. Twenty-five dollars a month pay. Lived on the boat. We used to have thirty-five to forty boats in a tow—ice barges, brick scows, coal boats. At night you'd look back at the tow, and each one of the boats had a little kerosene lantern up on a pole, and you'd look back and see all those lamps, and it looked like you were towing an island.

"I started in this business when I was fifteen years old, and I was twenty-three when they made me captain of the tug, *Lewis Pulver*. I put in thirty-three years with Moran Towing company. I'm in my twelfth season with Circle Line now, and I've never tired of it. I've been around this island 8,000 times, and I like it every time."

"My son's a skipper, too," the captain said, telling of Edmond, who is six feet seven, and who broke in with his father as mate and then became a captain with the line.

His sightseeing liner is a 165-foot-long former Coast Guard cutter with Sperry Electric Steering. "This is a picnic now," he said, disengaging his wheel and giving it a spin to show how easily it went round. "I used to take a pen knife and scrape the callouses off the palms of my hands from the wear on the wheel. You had ropes that went down and you had to pull on the wheel. You'd put your foot up on it, too.

"This run has increased tremendously," Captain Miller said. "It started with one little boat, the *Islander*. The six o'clock run, the last of the day, used to be our weak run. Now sometimes you have to use an extra boat. People have caught on that it's the twilight ride. You get the sunset over Jersey and the Palisades.

"Another thing that's increased tremendously is private motor boats and yachts on week-ends. Some of them don't know where they're going. They cut right across your bow. If they are close enough, I step out and shout at them: 'What if your motor cuts out on you? Then what?'"

Though it is sister to the North River and helps give Manhattan its extraordinarily good harbor and docking situation, the two rivers are not the same in mood or temperament.

The North River is expansive, relatively placid, easy to get along with. Seamen like her.

To the casual eye, the East River presents much the same face. But those who know her say she is turbulent, exacting, full of hidden faults. Mariners are wary of her.

"The thing most people never see about the East River is the bottom," said Captain Grover Sanschagrin of the towboat *Teresa Moran*.

"I went over it once with a depth recorder which makes a graph, and if you did that, you'd think you were in the Grand Canyon. It's nothing but jagged peaks and deep holes. Looks like a saw tooth. It drops off into holes of fifty to sixty feet and shoots right back up. It's rather frightening.

"That's why it's so full of whirlpools and eddies. You'll see a big bubble of water, boiling like a pot, maybe over a fifty-foot area. When the ship hits it, she has a tendency to slide to one side or the other, because it's a force of water working against her."

Except when he goes aboard a dirty freighter as a harbor pilot, Captain Sanschagrin wears a business suit with a handkerchief showing in his pocket and a tie held with a silver clasp. His tug is not as small as it looks when it's towing a big passenger liner. It's 111 feet long, has two decks, a wheelhouse above them, a galley and a handsome interior of polished wood.

A river is not necessarily as wide as it looks, he remarked. "You can have a wide river that has a wide channel" for ships, he said, "but you can have a wide river with a narrow channel.

"The North River is wide and the channel goes clear across. The channel *is* the river. About the only hazard you have over there is traffic, but you can go around.

"The East River has more turns in it, bends in the channel. The current is stronger and the channel is narrower."

The North River is like a broad avenue, smoothly paved. The East River is more like a narrow side street, clogged with traffic and badly pitted. "The East River demands closer attention and more wheeling, to keep her on her heading," the captain said. "To a layman, it's like trying to steer a car on a very bumpy road, with holes in it."

There are no dangerous shoals or rocks in the North River, but the East River has them. It also has islands and it has Hell Gate, the tight, treacherous channel between Astoria, Queens, and Wards Island (opposite 101st Street to 115th Street in Harlem), where sharp rocks and strong tidal currents have snatched at literally hundreds of vessels and doomed them. Some gougings have been made in the infamous pass for greater safety. It seems to have an appropriate name for its hazards, but some trace it to the Dutch term *hellegat,* meaning beautiful pass. There was a time, of course, when there were only meadows and woods running along the river's edge.

"Navigating a heavy tanker through Hell Gate keeps you on your toes," Captain Sanschagrin said. "The same tanker going up the North River is nothing." His father was a canaler, captain of two barges that worked the Erie and the Champlain canals. "When most boys played with little cars and trucks, I played with little barges and tugs," he recalled.

As a captain here since 1944, he admitted to a longing to sail the great sea beyond the harbor. He pilots the big ocean liners in New York harbor, getting on and off just at the harbor entrance.

"Sometimes I wish I could just stay on," he said. "It's a big temptation not to hide somewhere. I've never made a trip on a passenger ship, never in my life been past the point where Ambrose Light used to be."

The East River is not really a river at all. It is a strait. It is under the exclusive management of the Atlantic Ocean. It runs in two directions. During flood tide the salt water runs up the strait. During ebb tide it runs down.

"Now don't call it an estuary," Captain Miller had warned. "It's a strait. I settled that a long time ago by looking it up in the dictionary. It connects Long Island Sound with New York Bay." A "strait" is a passage that links two large bodies of water. An "estuary" is the lower part of a river, where its current flows into the tide.

"Where does the East River end?" one old harbor hand asked rhetorically. "It has no source," he said. "It is just a wash of the Atlantic Ocean running around some islands."

"The river starts at the tip of Manhattan," Captain Richard W. Young of the Coast Guard said, sending ripples through his pencil line mustache as he spoke. "It's fourteen miles long. The Throg's Neck Bridge draws a very neat line between the river and Long Island Sound.

"Because the strait is a narrow opening between two masses of water, the shift in tides creates more current," he said. Captain Miller had a vivid image for it:

"A terrific strength of tide runs between Welfare Island and the Manhattan shore, because the channel is narrower there," he said. "It's like water running out of a soda water bottle—as it gets to the neck it comes with more force."

The velocity of the current, only 1 knot at Throg's Neck (a knot is one nautical mile an hour) goes as high as 4.6 knots at Hell Gate.

It is a peculiarity of Manhattan that it has two rivers running more or less parallel and one of them is called the East River, while the other is called the North River, a bit of geographical anarchy. The North, or the Hudson River, is ruled by the ocean tides for a very long distance, though less rudely than its sister.

"The North River gives you about thirty minutes of slack water," Captain Sanschagrin said. "You get a high water slack and a low water slack—no motion of water. In the East River, four minutes is all you have of slack water, both tides."

The main East River channel is forty feet deep from the Battery to about the Williamsburg Bridge (which connects to Delancey Street on the Lower East Side). The channel is thirty-five feet deep from there to Long Island Sound. It varies from 1,000 feet to 550 feet in width.

Welfare Island begins at about Fifty-first Street and runs to Eighty-sixth Street, a long and slender loaf of land sitting in the middle of the river. The Queensboro Bridge arches over it.

Because the margin of safety is small, ships sometimes work out cautious ways of approach. Some tankers have to short-load to reduce their draft and come in less than fully loaded because they would otherwise need a channel closer to fifty feet deep. Some deep-draft vessels wait until absolutely "tip top high tide" before venturing into the shallow channel.

The American Merchant Marine Institute has complained about "numerous rock shoals existing at a depth of less than thirty-five feet, mean low water, in the area south of Belmont Island," which is opposite East Forty-third Street. That small island has a bell and a green flashing light just ahead of it to deflect mariners from a collision course.

The shoals are not marked by aids to navigation. Buoys get dragged off position by scows and barges. There are places north of the United Nations where small waves dash up against narrow outcroppings of rock standing about three feet out of the water, with strings of gulls sometimes perching on them.

About 22,940,000 tons of cargo are brought into the East River and unloaded in a year, according to the Army Corps of Engineers. About 15.2 million tons of that is oil, Arabs permitting, for terminals on the river. Close to 610,000 tons of sugar comes in, and more than one hundred other products—bananas, dried milk, tobacco, rice, aluminum, lumber, ore among them. Some 2,950 self-propelling tankers enter the river in a year, and 73,100 rail freight cars are shuttled over it. They bear the signatures of the Erie Lackawanna, Lehigh Valley, Jersey Central, Chesapeake & Ohio, Penn Central and other lines.

Gazing across to the Queens shore from Manhattan, the eye falls on signs for Sunshine Biscuits, the Sternberger Warehouse, Paragon Fuel Oil Burners, Adam Metal Supply, the Schwartz Chemical Company. There are cranes; clusters of tall cement storage-silos; dingy factories—soot-blacked brick piles with giant smokestacks.

The East River was once the maritime center of a young, expanding nation—its port to the world. A little over a century ago, down where the Fulton Fish Market stands, the slender bowsprits of Yankee clipper ships reached half way across South Street when they docked. Big wooden wagon wheels rumbled over cobblestones in the busy cargo and passenger center. Lately the section has been lined with old piers, many unused and condemned, some with hulking sheds of corrugated metal gone to rust. One bears the faded emblem of the Peninsular and Occidental Steamship Company.

The only square-rigged sailing vessels that rode those waters for decades were the ghost ships of some men's nostalgic imaginations. Yet if the architects of the South Street Seaport have their way, scenes out of the 1850s will fill the eye at that very spot for decades to come.

The Seaport planners have worked unceasingly to save a three-block section of the old waterfront—a series of 160-year-old low brick buildings on Fulton, South, Front and Beekman Streets—by restoring the facades to their first condition and recreating the former maritime scenes, complete with a square rigger, fishing craft and coastal trading schooners. When they began, the first floors in the houses were mainly wholesale stalls in the City's antique and brawling fish market. The upper floors were mostly empty.

Peter Stanford, a tall, urbane Harvard graduate who is the full-time president of the body, was standing at the corner of South and Fulton Streets, drawing on a pipe. "The era of the square riggers, which is just below the horizon of our lifetimes, was in full flower here," he said. "The last stronghold of that era was right here, from 1860 to 1910.

"These buildings were all standing here when the *Flying Cloud* set sail from Maiden Lane on June 2, 1851—it was at 2:00 P.M.—for her record-breaking voyage to San Francisco, then just a bunch of shacks on a muddy hillside. It took eighty-nine days. That was the height of the clipper ship era.

"It's a kind of miracle that these buildings have survived here," he said. The pungency of fish seems to have been the preservative.

"Possibly because it smells so bad people stayed away from here," said William C. Shopsin, an architectural consultant. "Thanks to the fish market, some of the best examples of Federal commercial architecture of the early nineteenth century remain intact.

"This is one part of the City where you still get the feeling of the scale of a past age. The charm of these buildings is in their street facades—the pitched roofs, the narrow fronts, the brick chimneys and walls."

Schermerhorn Row, a relic of the gas-lit era, faces Fulton Street between South Street and Front Street, a line of four- to six-story brick buildings, graceful and dignified in the Federal style. They were built in 1811 and 1812. James G.

Van Derpool, former president of the Municipal Art Society, called them "The finest surviving examples of their kind in America."

The corner building is the one in which Sweet's and Sloppy Louie's, two plain but usually excellent seafood restaurants do business (Sweet's on the second floor at 2 Fulton Street, Sloppy Louie's around the corner on the street floor at 92 South Street). It was rebuilt upward in 1870 as a waterfront hotel. The newer brick on top, not as well laid as the earlier, quite plainly shows the change. Some of the windows are a little lopsided now. "That's because they're sagging with age," Mr. Stanford said.

He strolled two blocks north to 118 South Street, where Meyers Hotel, a five-story house whose bricks have the dull rosy cast of great age, is still doing business. It has a splendid carved wood bar on the first floor, but otherwise it suggests a seaman's flophouse. "Looks like a bit of a dive now, but it's magnificent structurally," he said. "It was a bloody fashionable resort for the people of the gilded age."

If Mr. Stanford did not exist, a short story writer for *The New Yorker* would have had to invent him. His credentials and background have just that blend of formality and ease that makes for rich characterization: Harvard B.A. in history, 1949; Cambridge M.A. in English, 1951; former copy editor for Alfred A. Knopf; a random scholar and sometime ad man (he wrote the Beefeater Gin ads of a few years ago that were so irreproachably dry and witty); a writer for yachting magazines and a trans-Atlantic voyager under sail; a savorer of naval history.

When the Seaport idea had begun to entice him, his work for Compton Advertising may have shown a little slack, for, as he tells it: "My boss said, 'Look here, Stanford. It's either Compton or the Seaport.' So I thought, 'Well, here goes nothing.'"

He occupied an office over an old curio shop at 16 Fulton

Street and before long found himself in possession of a $6 million plan—and a $50,000-a-year budget. He had to do a good deal of skillful wheedling and coaxing among the rich and the influential. Seagulls often screeched outside his window and sometimes when he wanted to call an important person, Mr. Stanford would wait until the seagulls came near to supply authentic background to his own velvetly urgent depiction of the Seaport idea. On drafty days he would light his pipe by touching a roll of newspaper to the face of the electric heater near his desk and bringing it up flaming.

"There used to be a wonderful variety of traffics here that have vanished," Mr. Stanford said, mentioning "tallow merchants, coopers and riggers, sailmakers, grog shops, cargo agents and brokers." The Seaport, a two-acre historical enclave, is bringing them back in its storefront exhibits.

"Some of the early builders of clipper ships had their offices here," Mr. Shopsin said, "and a lot of the coffee grinding and tea trade was in here and the spice merchants"—sources of splendid aromas.

In working to set up "a living museum" of the quaint old New York Seaport, with indoor and outdoor as well as on-the-water displays appropriate to the years when church spires, not skyscrapers, dominated the Manhattan skyline, Mr. Stanford ran into serious obstacles, including the faintheartedness or disinterest of certain public officials. It was a constant encouragement to him to remember that San Francisco's museum of old wooden ships in the Hyde Street lagoon began back in 1949 with a letter to the editor and no cash. In much less than two decades, $20 million had been spent on a mixture of historical, commercial and park exhibits there.

"The waterfront is potentially, by its history and by its physical extent, one of our major resources, and it is without question the single most under-used resource in this City,"

Mr. Stanford said. "We've cut ourselves off from the water by expressways and fences. The waterfront is an assemblage of crumbling piers used as a dumping ground for old police cars. It is used as a transportation alley when it should be used as our front doorstep."

Across the river, the view from the Brooklyn and Queens side takes in the spectacular sweep of the Manhattan skyline. In the early morning, the glass-slab face of the United Nations Secretariat can catch the whole ball of the fiery sun and throw it back east.

Front row bench seats for the changing panorama of the river are available, just above the United Nations site, to those who walk to the dead end of East Fifty-first Street and take the stairway down to a narrow foot bridge that crosses, through treetops, to the river's edge.

Six persons, including a young couple seeking the romantic ambiance of twilight, occupied the eight benches north of the steps the other evening, when a helicopter came skimming low over the water and flew underneath the Queensboro Bridge.

Near sunset, the clouds, the long bridges, the tops of some of the structures on the Queens shore, and the bridges of ships are brushed with rose, while the grayish water turns slowly to ink.

An old workhorse of a towboat plowed the water, having no hint of glamour. Close behind it came a fabulous sight: a graceful, newly painted ocean-going yacht, pale, blue and white, with three deck levels. It looked like a vision at dusk. Yachts from Long Island Sound use the river as an exit to the Atlantic for coastal voyages running south to Florida and the Caribbean.

The Canal to Nowhere

The Gowanus Canal, a richly aromatic avenue of steadily declining commerce, slices more than a mile into Brooklyn from Gowanus Bay, earning some gratitude and a great deal of enmity from those who dwell, by choice or by lot, in areas steeped in its flavors.

The few commercial users who linger on its banks regard the canal as a lifeline of supply. Its residential neighbors sustain the relationship of enemies to the canal, often with scalding fervor. "Stinking ditch" is among the more elegant insults they employ, though there are those who hope it can be reclaimed from industrial ugliness and made sublime.

"Clean it up or fill it in," is the popular local formula for dealing with the alliaceous trench.

To call the Gowanus a waterway is to affirm the fact that the fluid that sloshes in it is composed partly of water, but it is to overlook the fact that it does not freeze in the bitterest weather. The Gowanus used to freeze at times in winter and tugs had to break the channel clear. Now, its antagonists suspect, the chemicals in it act as their own antifreeze.

No odes are written, no hymns sung, to the canal, but in the "Trilogy of Gowanus Creek" William Henry Hale wrote:

"Hail to Gowanus Creek peacefully slumbering/Girt round by forest and greensward so fair/Waken! For destiny hails thee deliverer!/Thou must the triumph of liberty share!"

The Gowanus creek was widened and deepened to a canal in the last century, when sewers began to be emptied into it, and it is girt round today by anything but forest and greensward fair.

Its shores are improved chiefly by heaps of gravel, oil depots, working or abandoned factories, trailer vans, and a

mulligan stew of industrial rubble mixing old bedsprings with rusted auto hulks.

Once it teemed with oysters. Old World visitors recorded in 1679 that "Gouanes oysters are the best . . . large and full, some of them not less than a foot long."

By the values that informed the industrial age, the Gowanus did, indeed, "awaken" from its long, primeval nap to take on the characteristics—the brick and brawn and steamwhistle commotion—of commercial expansion.

That upbeat began to subside after World War II, and now the Gowanus is a lonely and little used outlet to the harbor. Its soup-thick surface glides back and forth with the tides and is only rarely churned by barge and tug. It has the color of true jade for much of its length and would look as serene as porcelain but for one fact: the Gowanus—there is no clearer term for it—burps.

The thick sludge at its bottom forms and releases bubbles of noxious gas in the summer. The bubbles rise to the surface and burst. The canal's whole surface is continually agitated by these eruptions. The effect is that of a fistful of pebbles flung by a boy. At any glance there are ten thousand widening circles in the water, crossing and recrossing to make endless chains of rings.

Few men know the rippled complexion of the canal, or its idiosyncrasies, and the tragedies it sometimes discloses, better than Pete Hall, the mate on the tug *Gowanus*.

His right to that knowledge goes back before his birth. His father was marine engineer on the tug *Taurus* with the same company—The Gowanus Towing Company, now in its 101st year.

"He took me down here for sailing when I was thirteen years old," Pete said. "Then when I was sixteen, he got me a steady job here. My brother, Jimmy, he was fireman. I've never been off to no place else."

Pete has never had a layoff in thirty-five years with the

company. "Four more years, I'll be fifty-five, and I'm going to retire," he said. "Traffic isn't what it was," he's quick to say.

According to Vic Peters, who despatches the company's two tugs, old timers liked to boast that "more tonnage went up the Gowanus than went up the Mississippi in a year."

At the height of its trade, the company had seventeen boats, mostly 200-horsepower small tugs, working in the canal. Now its two tugs do a few canal jobs but they roam all over the harbor, too.

The mate ducked out of the sun into the galley under the wheelhouse and flung his cap on the bench behind the big green table where the captain and his three-man crew relax between assignments.

"We had nine steamboats before the war—the *Americus, Victorius, Hesperus, Taurus, Gowanus*— and I worked on every one of them," Pete said. "The names were left from World War I when they all had names ending with U.S. to be patriotic.

"We used to start up the canal about 7:00 in the morning, with two loaded coal barges, and we'd drop one off at a yard and go on up with the other one, and we wouldn't get back 'til late in the afternoon because of the congestion in the canal."

City policemen used to be posted at the canal entrance to direct traffic in and out and be sure that access was left for fireboats.

"Years ago we had three traffic cops, then it went to two, then it went to one," the skipper said. Now that one is gone.

Captain Leo Fontaine is a big, affable man with a deep voice and a sun-browned neck spiraling out of his bleached tee shirt. He's had forty-four years in the business, he said.

"Fifty years ago there was fifty to sixty customers on this canal," he said. "Now there's three."

"Up where the gas house was, mothers would take their kids down on a cold winter's morning and have the kids inhale the fumes—supposed to be wonderful for whooping cough." the skipper said. "That was the old-fashioned parent's remedy. The kids' faces was red as apples.

"It was good for these people had asthma, too," he appended.

He and the mate remembered brickyards, grain depots, cement yards, a brewery, a paint factory, a jute factory and other installations that crowded both sides of the canal. "The International Salt Company used to be here, too," the captain said.

"We picked up a lot of dead bodies in the canal," Pete said. "You gotta tie a rope around them—that's the law—and pull 'em to the dock and call the harbor police. You're not supposed to touch 'em with a pipe pole. The police take 'em on their boat.

"You fall in that canal and if you're not saved right away, because there's so much oil and chemicals and junk in there—you get that into your lungs and you're a goner."

The canal sometimes gives off the odor of ripe cheese left out too long at room temperature.

"They're building apartments all around it and they want a beautiful smell," Pete said. "They want to build a marina and use it for small pleasure boats."

Pat Brandon, the deck hand, sat in the doorsill between the deck and the galley and gazed out at the low water.

"It's dead," he said. "You gotta go up there on a high tide. We take loaded barges up there. At low tide they could hit bottom."

Hitting bottom is no cinch along this vile Nile because of its resistance to objects hitting the top. Paper cups and other items of debris do not float in the syrupy Gowanus, they rest on top of it.

With the full glare of the midday sun upon the canal, the eye can penetrate the water to a depth of approximately one millimeter.

Just beyond the Third Street Bridge, there is an eerie sight—three abandoned and half-sunk tugs, blackened by the scummy deposits of years, slanting up out of the ooze. At high tide, only one can be seen.

The canal turns from green to black near the Union Street Bridge and comes to a dead end just short of Butler Street, a blunt arrow pointing to downtown Brooklyn.

The Bayside Fuel Oil Depot and Premium Coal and Oil stand opposite T. E. Conklin Brass and Copper in the final stretch. The canal is about 1.2 miles long, about 100 feet wide, and 12 or 13 feet deep at high water, the captain and the despatcher estimated.

"All the companies on the canal agreed to dredge it, but nobody's getting the money up, and it's filling in and filling in and filling in, and pretty soon they'll have to close it," Captain Fontaine said.

"We work by the tide," Pete said. "If high tide's at 2:00 in the morning, we go out. We work twelve, fourteen, maybe twenty hours. It's tide work."

Before long, Pete expects to see himself in the movies. A film company hired the tug for an hour for a scene in a motion picture.

"There's this gang of gangsters in their fancy car and they're racing to get over the bridge before we get there, but we give three blasts on the whistle and the bridge opens, and the car stalls on the bridge, and the gangsters are shaking their fists at me, and I wave back," Pete said.

"The movie director says, 'Don't look at the camera.' I asked the assistant director, 'How did we do?' He said, 'You did beautiful.'"

The Seafarer

William Willis, an aged wanderer over trackless oceans, has returned from his latest agonizing adventure in solitude, looking like a man who had spent a few days in Miami Beach.

The seventy-three-year-old mariner had lain almost helpless in the bottom of a tiny cat-yawl, drifting back and forth in the Atlantic, covering 1,750 miles in sixty days, alone against the sea while a hernia stabbed his abdomen with knife-twist pain.

He looked remarkably hale. "Well, plenty of fresh air," he shrugged.

He is a lean man (five feet seven inches and 138 pounds) with arms as tough as hawsers, eyes small and sharp as an eagle's. He has wild, wiry eyebrows and a white mustache and beard on a bronze-red face. He left New York in his $11\frac{1}{2}$ foot yawl, the size of a Central Park rowboat. He trusted the winds to drive him to Plymouth, England, in forty-five to seventy days.

He was 850 miles east northeast of the City Monday night when a Coast Guard Albatross seaplane brightened the night with flares, and the cutter *Ingham* plucked him from the ocean. Back from the sea for rest and medical care, he relaxed in an armchair in his small suite in the Oliver Cromwell Hotel, just off Central Park West at Seventy-second Street.

Twelve years ago, when he was only sixty-one, Mr. Willis drifted on a frail balsa raft from Peru to Pago Pago in Samoa with a cat and a parrot. The two-part, 9,800-mile Pacific voyage ended at Tully, Australia. The call of the sea came when he was only four years old at Hamburg, Germany, where he remembered "wandering down to the harbor, getting into the boats and being chased out."

"Once I got out," he remembered, "and the harbor police caught me because I was drifting down the (Elbe) river, and my mother said to me, 'Ah! You were born with an angel on each shoulder.'"

Mr. Willis is a seafarer of few comforts, but one he cherished failed him this time: "A transmitter was sent me from Marconi International—Lord Nelson himself sent it from London—a survival emergency transmitter," he said. "I had it lashed on deck and it never worked. It was absolutely dead." Lord Nelson, he reported, is chairman of the British Electric Company.

The loss of the transmitter was a critical one. When the hernia put him in "agony" after three weeks, he had no touch with other human beings. His sextant allowed him to measure "the exact height of the stars, the planets, the moon and the sun—all the celestial bodies—above the horizon." That fixed his latitude and longitude. A transistor radio brought in Government time signals "that give you the tick of the second twenty-four hours a day."

His rations had a John-the-Baptist-like severity. He lived on four teaspoonsful of dry whole wheat flour three times a day. He packed the flour in small wax-lined paper bags obtained from the Kiehl pharmacy on the Lower East Side.

"There's no element for the human body that is not contained in this," he said, shaking a box of flour in the air. He drank three medium tins of evaporated milk a day, but not with the flour. "If you mix it with liquid, you get very little good out of it," he said.

He also carried "a little honey and a little olive oil," his wife, Teddy, said. As on previous voyages, he took "no water—not a drop," Mr. Willis said. He believed it was the first time anyone had ventured to cross the Atlantic in a boat without shelter. He carried a zippered kit that allowed him to take his "blood pressure, pulse and urinalysis every day."

As a fifteen-year-old, he went to sea "as a deck boy on a

big, four-masted bark, a 3,000-ton sailing ship, one of the last of her kind, and we sailed from Hamburg to the Gulf of California in 168 days, with coke from the Ruhr for copper smelters."

He jumped ship at Galveston, Texas, when he was eighteen and began loading ships, "carrying 300-pound sacks, the hardest labor on the face of the earth." He had ten years of it and then he fell to wandering on land, "working in forests, woods, mines, harvest fields, oil fields—building oil derricks in Oklahoma, working only a day if I wanted to.

"It must be born in me to see other places, other people," he went on, "to seek solitude at times. I've lived an unimpeded life, never any constriction on me. I could quit any time I wanted."

In his days of pain, he "saw a few ships in the distance, but they didn't stop.

"By luck, the *Sapphire Gladys* came straight out of the mists, right at me, and still she passed by. I'd been waiting for weeks, and I knew I was really cooked. Then she swung round." The American freighter radioed the Coast Guard.

He said he would go out again, with his wife's consent.

"I'm asserting myself," Mrs. Willis said quietly. "This last time it was too much to take," and Mr. Willis nodded and muttered something about it not being "worth breaking up my marriage."

(Later, the old man felt the sea calling and he set out again, alone, and that was the last anyone knew of him. That time the sea swallowed him up.)

In Cold Blood

In Cold Blood

As zoological parks search for rare animals, and museums of natural history search for rare fossils, the New York Blood Center searches the world for rare blood.

It finds it at times among the Cakchiquel Indians of Guatemala, the Cashinauas of Peru, or Pygmies in equatorial Africa, and sometimes it finds rare blood running in the veins of a donor who drops in off the street to give a pint.

When that happens, the pint is flash-frozen and slipped into a deep freeze unit to be stored for a hospital emergency requiring that kind of blood.

The New York Blood Center stocks "samples of blood from all over the world, all the races of man," according to Dr. Aaron Kellner, head of the center for the Community Blood Council of Greater New York.

It keeps them in a kind of "library" of rare bloods, which is as hushed as a rare manuscript room but cooler, since the blood must be kept in refrigeration. Samples can be withdrawn from cold storage at any time and thawed for immediate "reference" or study by blood specialists.

The center has a catalogue of "300 known rare blood donors." It draws blood from some 300,000 donors, most of whom have sturdy blood of no particular distinction. It does not know the exact figure because there are 4,600 donor groups with widely varying memberships.

From all sources, the center processes about 38,000 gallons a year, over two-thirds of the whole blood used by 282 hospitals in the metropolitan area. The people who run it would be happier if that figure rose to 50,000 gallons—for there are still times when a patient lies in a hospital holding tenuously to life, waiting for enough blood, of the kind he must have, to help him survive.

And there are times—especially in "seasons of drought"—when the center lies perilously close to running dry. "We were down to eighty-five pints one morning at the end of August," a staff member said.

As the main source of blood supply for hospitals in twenty-three counties in New York and northern New Jersey, the center finds so narrow a margin rather harrowing. It aims to have 5,000 pints on hand—about four days' supply—for current needs. Most of the time it has a two or three day supply in stock.

"The metropolitan New York area uses more blood than any comparable area in the world—more than London, more than Tokyo," Dr. Kellner said. In addition to the local needs of its immense population, people from every state and several nations come to the City for surgery.

The true aristocrats of blood are not found in any Social Register. Contrary to a popular notion, there are not several types of human blood, there are scores of basic types, and there is blood of so rare a vintage that only one person in one million has it. That person is just as likely to be an oil truck delivery driver as a member of the Racquet & Tennis Club.

The center, a few yards east of Second Avenue at 310 East Sixty-seventh Street, presents a plain brick face of 1929 trade school architecture (it was formerly the Voorhees Technical Institute).

Behind that bland, three-story facade, like a diamond cached in a peanut shell, are eighty-five laboratories of brilliant modernity. Most of them are the size and shape of a railroad car cut in half, and they lie off long corridors that slice through four acres of floor space.

The center operates round-the-clock every day in the year, rallying to the blood needs of the hospitals, sometimes with a breathless urgency that requires police cars to race through the empty night.

At 11:15 A.M. the other day Mrs. Norma McPartland stepped into the center, reclined on a kind of contour lounge and gave a pint. She was replacing some of the blood supplied to her husband for open heart surgery a few days earlier.

When she left half an hour later, she did not guess how far her blood would go.

A phone call had come from Misercordia Hospital in the Bronx at 9:30 A.M. A month-old girl with thrombocytopenia, a form of leukemia, required three pints of blood.

By 2:00 P.M. a mobile unit from the center reached the hospital. Within the hour some of Mrs. McPartland's blood was given to the infant, along with some of the blood given by two policemen, John Langheto and Eugene Fernan, regular donors.

By 3:15 P.M., a patient at another hospital had received part of Mrs. McPartland's blood, and before the supply is exhausted, three more will have had a share in it.

In all, five recipients will have Mrs. McPartland's blood flowing in their veins, out of her one pint.

It is not Mrs. McPartland's whole blood that was used this way. The pint she gave was swiftly divided into fractions—not into simple fluid fractions but into its component parts. Particular parts then go to particular people.

It would not do for the patients to look too closely at the blood components given them. Some of Mrs. McPartland's blood, when it was broken down, looked like ginger ale and some of it looked like weak cranberry juice.

Used in this way, a donated pint goes farther, and it is safer for recipients.

"For a long time, blood was considered a single material," said a doctor who was overseeing the processing of blood into components.

"Most blood transfusions were in the form of whole blood." Dr. Kellner said. "But most people don't need whole blood. They need a portion of it." When a donation is split up among five or six patients, each one gets only the material he actually needs.

"The unit of whole blood—that's pretty horse and buggy now," said Virginia Jefferson, executive associate at the center.

"It neglects the essential fact that blood is a mixture of a great many things," a clinical specialist explained. "There are three different kinds of cells—red, white and platelets—each with a different function—and there are vital proteins, more than one hundred of them.

"There are proteins that combat infection, proteins that affect the fluid balance in the whole body, coagulation proteins, and many more.

"Would you be surprised if I told you there are one hundred different—I should say, well over one hundred different—blood types?" he asked, not pausing to check the effect of this statistic, which, as it turned out, proved to be wildly conservative.

"In 1899 the first four blood types, now known as major types, were discovered—A, AB, O, and B. So to start with, you have four major groups, and each one has a positive and a negative."

In a tour of the center, a stop was made in front of a bulletin board with rows and rows of small tags hanging on hooks. Each tag was marked with an alphabetical symbol.

"These are all the antigens in blood," said Mary Walker, a laboratory supervisor. "They are always being discovered." She pointed to a tag bearing the letter A, representing the first of the antigens, discovered by Dr. Karl Landsteiner in 1900.

"There are 200 antigens, and you either have each one in your blood or you don't," she said. Their presence or absence in a person's blood is tested by serums. There are antigens named "Goo" and "Job."

"Antigens is just a fancy word for blood group factors," Dr. Kellner said. "When I say that you are Rh positive, I mean your red blood cells have the Rh factor, or antigen.

"Look at the word: Anti-gen. It means capable of generating antibodies.

"If I inject an antigen into myself—any old antigen, in smallpox, typhoid or yellow fever vaccine—the body responds to that antigen by specific antibodies. That becomes my defense against that disease."

At this point, Dr. Kellner lifted the discussion of blood types up a few astronomical notches.

"The fact is, every human being, except for identical twins, has a separate blood type of his own," he said. "Blood is more distinctive than fingerprints because there are more variables in blood than in fingerprints. Because there are so many antigens, and so many possible combinations of them, no two people share exactly the same combination of blood group factors. There are trillions—there are literally trillions—of possible combinations."

"About ten minutes ago a pint of blood came in from Chile," Miss Walker said. "It's from a young woman. She's a VEL negative. She lacks the VEL factor and practically everyone has it.

"A Dr. Montegaro in Chile sent samples to a man he knew in New Jersey, Dr. Philip Levine of Ortho Diagnostics in New Brunswick. He put her in touch with us. This is the fifth pint we've received from her."

The young woman's blood, which is rated "extremely

rare," is frozen and stored at the center, which is keeping it for her in case she has an emergency need for it. (After the plasma and red blood cells are separated, the frozen red cells can be kept for at least five years.)

Braniff Airlines flies the blood to New York without charge, and a driver from the center picks it up. "The airlines are tremendous. They're wonderful. The farther you have to send blood, or go to get it, the easier it is. The hard place to get it to is New Jersey. The bus lines aren't very eager," Miss Walker said.

The center enrolls among its rare blood donors anyone whose overall blood type occurs only once among 250 people.

A staff associate brings the exactness of the connoisseur to the question and insists on making a distinction between "the hard to get and the truly rare."

The scale of rarity starts low—blood that one person in ten has is considered rather special—and runs on up to the one out of one million figure. The associate thinks that "One in 20,000" is a good place to draw the line.

Because of their proximity to the needle, personnel at the center tend to give blood fairly often, especially when they learn of pressing need. "My blood is not very rare, but it is just odd enough to be needed once in a while," one staffer said, a self-admitted non-donor before he became a professional blood banker.

"I had to take a government physical a few weeks ago, and the guy took one look at my arm, and I had to take out my identification card to show him I wasn't a mainliner."

When a request for rare blood comes from some distant place, say Mexico City, the center can often get it there in twelve hours. Blood types are classified by computer. That is why it can be almost instantly discovered whether the needed blood is in stock or, if not, exactly who has it. The automatic bloodhound also tells where he can be found—by name, address and telephone number.

Since blood must be broken down into its components very soon after it is drawn from the donor, the center only uses blood collected in Manhattan and the Bronx for that purpose. It tried motorcycles and helicopters in the race to get blood to the center in time from more distant points in Brooklyn and Queens, without much success.

A silvery chain hangs in a long corridor—the trigger for a high-pressure shower that may be used by persons who have all their clothes on. It is near laboratories in which spilled acid could require immediate and powerful drenching. It has rarely been used for that purpose, but now and then school kids have given it a tug and got themselves a good dousing for the effort.

The walk-in refrigerator in one hall is occupied by a young woman in a red-quilted suit, whose job is labelling bags of plasma (the liquid portion of the blood as opposed to the cell structures). It is a job that has to be done in the cold, and it involves sorting out orders for delivery the next morning to hospitals.

"You know how blood used to come in a kind of pint bottle," Dr. Kellner said, spreading out on his desk an assortment of plastic bags strung together "by tubing which is known in the trade as spaghetti."

"Blood banking used to be conceived as a very simplistic operation. The bank was a kind of collection and delivery service. It would collect from the donors, do some simple processing and deliver it to the hospitals.

"We have more than 500 people on our staff, and close to a third of them are in blood research."

"Even the processing is getting more complex," Dr. Kellner said, picking up the first of the plastic bags. "When you give a pint, the red cells go into this bag," he said, giving it a pinch. The platelets (essential to clotting) go into the second bag. The plasma in the third bag is quick-frozen and then thawed overnight. In this process, anti-hemophiliac factors known as cryoprecipitate become solidified.

"It floats around and you can separate it just like you get cream from milk," he said.

"You get half an ounce to an ounce of cryoprecipitate, used in treating hemophilia." He picked up a fourth bag. "We've still got plasma left and this plasma can be further fractionated into albumen, gamma globulin and other things."

The separation of the red cells, white cells and platelets is done by spinning the blood at high speed. "Because they have different weights, the heavier things fall out. The lighter things will float up," Dr. Kellner said.

"Platelets are one of our most important products," a staff man said. "They can only be kept a few hours, so you have a race against the clock to process them and get them to a hospital." Platelets—a light pink residue when they are separated—are used in open heart surgery and cancer treatment.

"We also stock a product, fresh frozen plasma, used especially for shock and severe burn cases," he said. "I've seen it used hundreds of times for auto crash victims."

"Blood transfusions can be hazardous, it's not like taking an aspirin off the shelf," Dr. Kellner said. "The transmission of disease by blood transfusion is a very real hazard in every transfusion."

Some individuals, aware of that, use the center very much as they would a savings bank, coming in every once in a while to make a deposit of blood. One man banked his own blood, by freezing, for several months in anticipation of surgery. He had the assurance that his own blood was compatible and free of any traces of disease. The rule of thumb is that the safest blood you can get is your own.

"Some patients with hemophilia have had heart attacks from their hearts' having to receive so much fluid. They couldn't pump it all," Dr. Kellner said. "That's why it's bad medicine to give people whole blood if they don't need it. They may get something beyond what they need and it may do them harm. It's like going into a butcher shop. You only want three pork chops, and they give you the whole hog."

"You're bleeding beautifully, sir," a nurse purred to a middle-aged man whose arm was being tapped in the donor's section, which is open every day of the year (no appointment necessary). A West Side receiving station is also in operation at 150 Amsterdam Avenue and another has been opened downtown in the World Trade Center.

Sometimes a bus load of donors pulls up in front and thirty or more people troop in to contribute. There is a club in Queens that has no other organizing principle; it is a social activity centered on giving blood.

Not everyone who comes in with blood to spare is permitted to give. "If a drop of your blood floats in a tube filled with copper sulphate, it means it's too light in hemoglobin to give right now," an attendant said. "When the drop of blood sinks to the bottom, you're it."

Most of the blood, eighty per cent, is collected by mobile units which set up temporary stations in offices and other places convenient to donors. The center wishes that were not the case. It cannot make the blood go as far when it collects it at outside points and processes it later.

It is possible at the center for a donor to give his blood and have it too. The nurse takes a pint, passes it through a small window into an adjacent laboratory, which immediately separates the plasma from the red cells, extracts the platelets—and sends all the red cells back through the window. The nurse then pumps them right back into the donor.

"Blood is a very perishable commodity," Dr. Kellner said, drawing on his pipe. "We have been working very hard to make it last forever."

The shelf life of whole blood is twenty-one days. Beyond that the red cells do not have enough vitality left to be helpful to a patient.

"A red cell in the body lasts for 120 days," a physician explained. "In three weeks outside, the red cells are equal to 119 days old. They're old in the senile sense and they don't function."

"Now we have the frozen process. It's so simple and so beautiful," Dr. Kellner said.

In the cryobiology laboratory a vat of liquid nitrogen "that is so cold it is hot" is ready to freeze blood at the command of Dr. Arthur W. Rowe, the originator of the quick-freeze process.

"We freeze red cells—about one-half of the pint," he said. "When Dr. Allen in the laboratories picks up a rare blood on the analyzer—where they screen for rare bloods—it is sent over to us for freezing."

The doctor used a pair of long-handled tongs to pick up a pan-like container filled with freshly siphoned red cells. He plunged it into a vat, which immediately went into an angry boil. The cells were flash-frozen at minus 320 degrees Farenheit.

"Once it's down at this temperature the storage life is very long. We have transfused two-year-old blood, and it's as good as fresh." The blood is frozen in pellets that look like grains of wet sand. The container is thawed on demand and used within twenty-four hours.

There is no other way that the woman from Chile, whose blood is so rare, could have a supply against emergencies.

"It used to be that when a doctor needed a rare blood for a patient, it precipitated a pretty mad scramble," Dr. Kellner said. "He'd be on the phone calling all his friends, hunting for donors." Now the center may have the rare blood waiting in the deep freeze.

"The old tyranny of twenty-one days robbed us of thousands of pints of blood needed for transfusions every year," Dr. Rowe said. Until salvaging methods were devised to save parts of it, blood that was not frozen but kept for early use, still had to be thrown out after twenty-one days. Collections are now controlled through electronic guidance that matches current demand to supply. That keeps waste to a minimum—a little more than one-half of one per cent.

The center was formed to end the chaos in the collection and distribution of blood in the City. Blood was once handled by over 150 agencies, and there were no central records.

To have reached an annual budget of about $8.5 million and a staff roster of over 500, the center has had to grow with astonishing speed. There was nothing remotely like it here in 1961 when Mrs. Jefferson took a leave of absence as president and executive director of the Milwaukee Blood Center, and came here to see what she could do about "the blood mess."

She took a two-room suite on the twelfth floor of the New Weston Hotel and set up shop with a couple of filing cabinets and a part-time secretary. "She *was* the blood center," a staff physician said. Mrs. Jefferson had known Dr. Kellner since the early 1950s. He become involved in the preliminary work on a voluntary basis.

"We started here in this place with four walls—nothing—and three people," Dr. Kellner recalled. Their plan got a terrific boost when the National Heart Institute came across with a $10 million grant stretching over a seven year period into the 1970s. The center does not go to the general public for funds; only for blood.

"What we need in this joint is blood," Mrs. Jefferson said in her blunt, gravelly, good gal manner.

"In spring, the blood flows freely—you know, the sap

rises," Dr. Kellner said. "In the summer and at Christmas time, it drops to half of what it is the rest of the year. July is the low."

"We're dealing with life-and-death situations every day," an aide remarked, "and the need for blood is great in the summer and at Christmas, when the accident rate goes up on highways and in homes."

"What we need is people who will donate annually—just as they go to a dentist—a pint a year," he said.

One of the center's physicians apologized for sounding perhaps too worked up about his cause. "My wife insists that blood banking is in the blood," he said quite matter of factly.

Enrolled donors secure for themselves a guaranteed supply for future emergencies. Non-donors must pay twenty-five to sixty-five dollars a pint at hospitals. Or they must find friends to match the blood they are given, pint for pint. A young mother in Manhattan, who needed one hundred pints for hemorrhaging, got a hospital bill for $2,500 for the blood.

Large-scale research, involving a check on 90,000 people a year, is going on to determine the characteristics of people who have or who carry hepatitis—a person doesn't have to have it to carry it—and to classify them by income, education level, religion, ethnic background and so on. This may help to check the communication of that disease.

The center sometimes has to counteract "certain ethnic superstitions" about blood, since there is "no distinction whatever" between the blood of the various races, and it is not necessary for a recipient to know whether he is getting the blood of a white, black, yellow or red man. "What about blue blood?" a boy asked a staff member one day after hearing this verdict.

The life-sustaining role of blood and its universality are far from novel discoveries; these very facts are asserted in ancient scriptures. "The life of the flesh is in the blood," the third book of Moses says in Leviticus 17:11. The other fact is as plainly stated in Acts 17:26, which says that God "has made of one blood all nations of men to dwell on all the face of the earth."

The center has forged an alliance with anthropologists who go to the remote corners of earth. It gives them test tubes and syringes and gets them to send back samples of fine, exotic bloods.

Under One Sky

Explaining the Weatherman

Late one winter, when climatological events here went spectacularly counter to prediction (there were, on one occasion, 13.5 inches of snow where merely "flurries" had been foreseen), an opportune elaboration of a classic wheeze won quick favor in the taverns and parlors of the city:

"Everybody talks about the weather bureau, but nobody ever does anything about it."

"Weather Bureau Goofs Again," the perceptive critic at the afternoon newspaper wrote.

In the face of this acclaim, my friend Hugo (it is not his real name), who as meteorologist in the New York City office weighs the portents for nearly a tenth of the nation's population, exhibits a half-smiling placidity of a sort to make the Mona Lisa seem a paradigm of excitation. "I live with it," he says.

A few years ago, when he was in the office at Albany, Hugo got a phone call from a man who shouted simply, "I hate you, I hate you, I hate you."

The public supposes that a forecaster deals with a set of formal situations that have only to be carefully observed to be correctly assessed. A patch of cloud here, it is thought, and a bit of wind there add up inevitably to a spot of misery tomorrow. The fact is they do not. Weather maps, like fingerprints, are different each from all the others. The map at 9:00 A.M.—with rain over Poughkeepsie and high pressure in Vermont—may by 11:00 A.M. have dissolved into one of half a thousand different patterns. Prediction, therefore, is largely a subjective process of mediation among possibilities.

The forecaster must take into his accounting the actions of

a dozen observable influences (wind direction and velocity, temperature, humidity, air pressure, cloud formations, etc.) none of which behave in systematic, readily definable ways. Beyond these, there are perhaps hundreds of weather-governing factors unknown to man. Meteorologists have only the dimmest notion, for instance, of what drives the winds from west to east across the country.

The best a forecaster can do is to say that, on balance, it looks a great deal like rain. The day may dawn as bright and clear as a pony of Windex, and he knows that it may. Infinitely more than the public, he is aware that every weather situation presents a range of possibilities, from which he must select, using the best method he knows, what he believes to be the foremost probability.

He brings to the task the sum of his knowledge, the weight of his experience and the burden of his fears. If he is having a bad streak, he may—like a manager juggling the lineup experimentally—put his thoughts in a mental dice cage, rattle them around and see what comes up. After a bad snow, the use of the word snow in any context sends the copy editors of the smaller and louder newspapers on the double to their pencil boxes to plot the blacking of the front pages with gleeful warnings of catastrophe: "MORE SNOW ON WAY!" The "more" may be only a predicted mild reprise, but it sells papers. When a forecaster has come up against this situation half a dozen times, he learns that a little lie may convey the truth better than the truth itself.

Forecasting is not in the truest sense a science, though it is on the way to becoming one. At the moment it is a partly scientific, partly intuitive process founded on laws, conjectures and superstitions. Hugo, for instance, may, in the space of twenty minutes obtain meteorological data from instruments of the greatest delicacy and then go up on the roof and determine whether or not it is snowing by holding the sleeve of his coat to the sky.

He is perfectly willing to admit that a man with intermittent arthritis may have as good an index to the likelihood of rain as the government's forecasters. And though he does not subscribe in full to the doctrine that because—

> *Last night the sun went pale to bed*
> *The moon in haloes hid her head.*
> *Loud quacked the ducks, the peacocks cried*
> *The distant hills were looking nigh.*
> *Restless were the snorting swine,*
> *The busy flies disturbed the kine....*

—that because of this it is necessarily going to rain, he is by no means ready to deny categorically that it is so. If at some time it should be indisputably demonstrated that the behavior of ducks and swine at twilight is a foresign of the morrow's weather, Hugo would be among the first to campaign for the establishment of an official pig and peacock observation station.

Some years ago, Ernest J. Christie, former head of the office here, broke the bands of the literary conventions that had long held government forecasters to the sort of language one associates with an assignment upon wages. He told his little band of temperature clerks to start putting the Byronic flourish into their prose. If "bountiful and bonny" is the phrase for a summer's day, he told them, go ahead and use it. This worked a minor revolution in the weather bureau. A few of the Civil Service boys began taking as fierce a pride in their style as their content.

Christie was a tremendously earnest little man who courted celebrity in the Federal bureaucracy by his determination to enlarge the boundaries of public weather service. He became the father of the fixed frequency forecast, by which anyone with ten thousand dollars worth of special equipment was able to tune in the forecast at any hour of the day. WNYC-FM spared Christie a couple of thousand cycles at the top of its spectrum for which it hadn't much use because noise broadcast at that frequency is inaudible to human beings.

A few years ago, through a minor typographical slip, a weather forecast printed at the top of page one seemed to be venturing beyond its authorized scope. The forecast, as it appeared, read: "Fair today, war tomorrow."

It was, of course, and happily enough at that, wrong as usual.

Rainbow Rain

A man in a polka-dot suit stood in haze-filtered sun at the corner of First Avenue and Thirty-ninth Street the other day, deploring the capricious winds.

Nick Cozeres, a painter who has been doing steeplejack jobs for forty-two of his sixty-three years, never knows when a sudden shift of winds will force him to knock off painting the exterior of three 460-foot Con Edison smokestacks.

He and the other steeplejacks can work only when the wind is blowing toward the East River. Otherwise objects below get a paint shower. Sedans as far west as Second Avenue might be finely flecked with windblown dye.

The great stacks rise at the river, just south of the United Nations, from the old brick generating station that squats on First Avenue from Thirty-eighth to Fortieth Streets. They are being done over in a barbershop motif—red, white and what the utility described as a "sort of powder blue." The motif has carried over to Mr. Cozeres' splattered clothing.

The stacks were soot-gray until three weeks ago when ten men started going up their sides in electrically powered buckets called "spiders," stroking the curved steel plates with $4\frac{1}{2}$-inch brushes.

The painting crew has one member who does nothing but walk around on the ground, observing the wind and

watching for tinctured drizzle. At first hint of the dread phenomenon, he dashes to the platform near the stacks' base and calls off the crew. The men descend to the street and quickly clean spots while the paint is still wet. Until the wind is right again, they must be content with daubing around the base.

The job is being done by a crew from the Gerben Contracting Company, partly for esthetics and partly for airplane safety. The Federal Aviation Agency says that objects that stand above the tops of buildings must be marked with horizontal stripes or checkerboard designs in white and a shade of red called "international orange" that has very high visibility. Increasing helicopter traffic here has made this necessary.

The stacks are thirty-one feet in diameter at the base, tapering to twenty-one feet at the tops. The color scheme is blue halfway to the tops, succeeded by wide bands of white and red.

The spiders from which the men work are metal platforms three by two feet with pipe railings three feet high. The men push buttons to make their spiders go up or down. They run on single cables powered by electric motors. All ten buckets are tied together with a "bracelet" of rope for maximum safety.

While the high-flying painters work above him, the sentinel on the ground watches constantly for the faintest sign of rainbow fallout.

Ichthyological Armageddon

The shaggy green hills around the boat lake in Van Cortlandt Park looked down upon a curious scene: men with test tubes standing on the shore putting filmy green water through an elaborate series of tests. The big park in the Bronx, clothed in the light green loveliness of May, had been giving off a reek of dead fish in its south central sector. The margin of the lake was lined with dead perch and assorted other fish from thumb-length size to eleven inches long.

The men were from the closest thing the city has to a homicide bureau for fish—the laboratory division of the Department of Water Supply, Gas and Electricity. They stood at the site of what looked like an ichthyological Armageddon.

It was the third year in a row that fish had died en masse at the lake. The problem has perplexed and troubled several city departments. Morris Ribner, senior bacteriologist in the laboratory's mobile unit, had the basic facts: driving rain and flash floods in the Bronx Thursday evening; on Friday several thousand dead fish on the small lake's shores.

Over the weekend the toll rose until the perimeter was crowded with dead perch, crayfish, tadpoles, snails, goldfish, catfish and carp swaying limply in the wavelets at the shore. It was Mr. Ribner's job, using instruments and bottles stored in the back of an olive-green station wagon, to try to find out what had killed the fish.

"Last year, we found that the fish weren't getting enough oxygen," a member of the unit said.

"The worst is over," said John Walsh, an assistant. "When you see the dead fish, the lake water is probably already getting better. It's like measles. You don't know when you have them at first, but when you see the manifestation, you're already getting better."

A Parks Department official, who had conferred with experts from the State Conservation Department, said it appeared that the flash floods had loaded the lake with silt, washed down from hills and banks around the lake. The silt caused heavy sedimentation and also hung suspended in the water, preventing the fish from getting oxygen, he said.

Assisted by Edward De Marco, the two men from the mobile unit made eight tests—for temperature, odor, specific conductivity of electricity, acidity or alkalinity, dissolved oxygen content, carbon dioxide, bacteria and toxicity. They scooped up samples of muck, slime, residue, kerosene slick, fermentation, protozoa, algae, molds, fungi, and anaerobic (oxygenless) bacteria.

There was plenty of science at the fish-kill, but it was no help to the fish. The Parks Department man described the victims as "salvage fish, yellow perch and guppies mainly, of small value," except, of course, to other perch and other guppies. "The Conservation Department will restock the lake soon," he said. "Next we'll net the dead ones up from rowboats and take them to the incinerator."

Mr. Ribner dumped six guppies from a Mason jar into a two-quart bottle filled with lake water.

Two hours later he looked in. "Well, the male is chasing that female; if he's thinking about her he's not worried about the water," he reasoned.

He rowed out to the middle of the lake and he also walked along the shore, taking samples. Later, he said the smaller lake on the golf course and the boat lake were fed by the same source and that both had received the same flood waters. But only the fish in the boat lake had died.

Mr. Ribner said he thought that decayed plant life and pollutants from the heavily vegetated bird sanctuary had been washed into the boat lake. He also suspected that fungicide spray used on the golf course just above the lake had been drained into it.

"You have to be a detective," he said.

Dr. Ross F. Nigrelli, of the New York Aquarium at Coney

Island, said it was likely that the fish had not died of poison or disease but of suffocation.

"With the rise in temperature and increasing daylight, you get a very dense growth of algae that is photosynthesizing," he said. "They produce considerable amounts of oxygen by day. But at night they utilize the oxygen, depleting the water of it, and they produce carbon dioxide, putting excess amounts of it into the environment. This prevents oxygen from being taken up by the gills, causing anoxia, or suffocation."

Whatever the cause, it was clear that city life can be perilous for fish, as it sometimes is for humans.

There was a stagnant-looking, filmy, brownish-green scum on the lake yesterday; occasionally it was broken by the snout of a fish apparently coming up for air. The Water Supply man said there was "nothing polluted about the lake at all."

The air was another matter. "I came here for fresh air and look what I get," said a housewife who was pushing a baby stroller in the fish-ripe breeze.

Silent Jungle

The Hall of Primates at the American Museum of Natural History has a cast of ninety-seven characters who look healthier now than they did when they had been dead a shorter time. The mounted specimens in the old hall had begun to look like the underprivileged creatures of some arboreal tenement—dusty, cracked and threadbare. In a four-year recess before they were put into the new hall, the plaster-filled chimpanzees and wire-frame gorillas were

patched and dry cleaned. Now they are back behind plate glass, frozen in jungle attitudes that often convey a sense of mid-air motion, as with those who appear to be leaping from tree limbs.

Most of the specimens have real skin and hair stretched over molds or frames, but some have wax faces and false teeth. The display also includes a dozen skeletons, some doing a weird dance with arms upraised.

The primates are arranged in what is said to be their probable order of development. It begins with what a museum man called "the lowly tree shrew" (it isn't a shrew and it doesn't live in trees and it may not, in fact, even be a primate) and traces the alleged line through lemurs, lorises, tarsiers, monkeys and apes to "the highly complex creature, man."

This journey is said to have begun before the Eocene period 60 million years ago, but it can be seen virtually at a glance in the museum display. Some of the larger primates are shown in approximations of natural settings. In one case, an orangutan peers from behind a fig tree in Borneo. The smallest living primate, the mouse lemur, weighs forty grams and could snuggle comfortably in a man's hand.

Meshie, a female chimpanzee from Cameroon, was once the pet of a staff anatomist. She rode a tricycle, used the elevator and ate in the museum cafeteria. Now, mounted, she sits hunched on a log in a glass case and gazes out with one hand set at her chin.

"Now there's a peculiar animal," Dr. Sydney Anderson said in his slow, midwestern drawl, pointing in at the aye-aye. The curator is a native Kansan and he designed the present hall. The aye-aye has a set of teeth like a rodent's and a third toe far slimmer than its four other toes. (Nearly all primates have five toes or fingers and are skilled at grasping things.) The lean digit is used for "scratching and combing hair and fishing grub worms out of tree trunks," Dr. Anderson explained.

For a while he had planned to use "some beautiful models of American Indians" to illustrate man, but it was feared that Indians might think they had been considered closer to apes than other men. Dr. Anderson then thought of having a wax model made of himself for the display. "But that would not of course eliminate another risk," he said. "The risk that some viewer might infer that we have implied that a curator is the highest form of animate life."

Call It What You Like, It's Still "Grant's Tomb"

People who visit the memorial to General Ulysses S. Grant on Riverside Drive at 122nd Street quite regularly report to the guards that when they look down over the circular parapet on the entrance level they see General Grant in his tomb.

That requires exceptionally piercing vision, since the general's dust lies in a lead-sealed coffin, which is covered by a cedar box, which is covered by a nine-ton sarcophagus of red Wisconsin granite that is also sealed with lead.

However, the guards think they know the reason for the reports. The red Wisconsin granite was chosen for its resemblance to mahogany and its surface is always kept dusted and brightly polished. It is a reflecting surface, and what the visitors see down there is the reflection of some other visitor's form.

That accounts for about ninety per cent of the reports. The guards have no glib explanation for those who not only see old General Grant down there but also his sword. They are awed into respectful silence by those who insist they see General Grant, with sword, sitting on his *horse*.

Whatever they think they see, it must add a touch of vivid drama to a visit to the somber, soundless interior of the mausoleum.

A series of deliberate, sometimes subtle changes—a few already made, others shortly to come—are slowly altering the character of the monument, through which more than eighteen million visitors have passed since it was opened in April 1897. The changes include the removal of a chain that had barred the public from the lower crypt all this century. Allowing visitors to use cameras in the high-domed monument is another departure.

Most people call it "Grant's Tomb." That makes members of the National Park Service wince. It was originally called the Grant Monument. "Grant's Tomb" has never been its name, except by popular usage, since the common people somtimes have a directness about appellation that escapes official namers, or strikes them as being a little too homely.

"It's the Grant Memorial," a member of the service said. "We're trying to get away from 'Grant's Tomb.'" These men prefer the full official name, the General Grant National Memorial. The service gave it that name when it took custody of the building in 1959, but almost fifteen years have passed and it has been hard to win even a small degree of public acceptance for the longer name.

"A changeover like this is very slow in coming," said Jerry Wagers, chief of historical interpretation for the service here. "But all the guidebooks and the tour people are very careful to use our terminology now." This is important to the service because the difference between the terms "tomb" and "national memorial" reflects the difference in the old and the new concepts of the structure's basic purpose.

General Grant, who died in 1885, had asked to be buried in New York City. The family obeyed his wish, and the body of the Union commander was first placed in a temporary vault, made of 1,000 bricks, in Riverside Park. The general's final illness (cancer of the throat) had occupied the front pages of the papers for months before he died at Mount McGregor in the Adirondacks on July 23. He devoted his waning energies to writing his two-volume Memoirs, recognized as classics of their kind, finishing them days before death.

Earlier, he had been under care in the City. Once or twice in those final months a regiment on parade stopped in front of his house, and General Grant came to a window overlooking the street to take their salute.

The stately funeral procession from City Hall to Riverside Park on August 8 was said to be the most solemn and imposing spectacle the City had ever seen. The body of the soldier-president, a man who had been summoned to war from a position as a clerk in the family store in Galena, Illinois, and whose life had been a spectacular series of alternating failures and triumphs, was borne to a plain mound of brick and iron in a commanding site in the park, not far from where the present structure stands.

The Grant Memorial Association, formed by the City's leading citizens, issued a call "To the People of the United States," inviting them to participate in the creation of a national memorial as the voluntary gift of the people. A competition for the design was announced and models and drawings came in.

By the time the association was incorporated in February, 1886, $115,000 had been received, but donations dwindled to a trickle. After a harrowing series of disagreements and delays, 90,000 donors had finally contributed $400,000 to build a structure designed by John H. Duncan, and all but $38,000 of the sum was raised by popular subscription in the City. Much of the rest came from Brooklyn, then a neighbor city under its own sovereignty, with the rest of the country paying some heed but very little cash.

The Duncan design emphasized strength, simplicity and dignity. The tendency among memorial designers to go to the grandiose or the absurd being what it was, *The Times* surveyed the winning plan and editorially breathed a sigh of relief that "it will not be ridiculous." Ground was broken on April 27, 1891, and the tomb was opened exactly six years later.

The association had custody of the monument and paid for its staff, upkeep and repairs. The direct responsibility fell into the hands of George D. Burnside, the tomb's construction superintendent, whose sense of paternal status enabled him to turn the job into a minor dynasty. "He put most of his life into the tomb," a member of the park service said.

Burnside was in charge until 1940. ("I figure it's my destiny," he once said, chewing on a stubby, black cigar.) His son, George C. Burnside, long his father's assistant, took over and did not retire until December 30, 1965, giving the family a linear identity with the memorial from its inception until a little after the centennial observance of the Civil War had passed.

The Burnsides greeted the public, enforced the rules (no smoking, no photographs, and gentlemen remove their hats) and were allowed half the profits from booklets and postcards they sold to visitors. The younger Burnside was once stoned by unruly youths he tried to evict from the tomb.

The elder man was loquacious on the history of the monument, which was so wound up with his own history that he could not extricate them if he had wanted to, and it was hard at times for visitors to know whether they were hearing his life story or an account of the tomb. Mr. Burnside may have come to look upon the tomb in roughly the way the owners of historic manors open for public inspection look upon them in England, as public assets held in family trust.

The wishes of the general's survivors were followed and, from the start, the gray granite monument, which sits on a bluff overlooking the Hudson River on Morningside Heights, was kept as a tomb in the strictest sense of the term. It was a matter of some dispute and delicacy a few years ago when a telephone, with a muted bell, was finally installed inside the structure for the staff. Indeed, so scrupulously was the character of the monument enforced as a tomb that it was not until recently that a small toilet was installed behind the outer wall of the crypt, relieving—to say the least—a sixty-five-year-old complaint by tomb personnel.

Until quite lately, the whole focus of the building has been on the massive twin sarcophagi of the victorious Union commander and of his wife, Julia Dent Grant, beneath the dome in the sunken crypt. The Duncan interior is a solemn marble hall of simple grandeur—a public setting for the granite slabs on which the names of the nation's eighteenth president and wife are cut. (A minor oddity is that the top of Mrs. Grant's sarcophagus, sealed after her death in 1902, is half an inch higher than that of her husband. Another is that the principal marble used in the interior of Grant's Tomb is Lee marble.)

Because of this emphasis, there was virtually nothing in the great hall to relate Grant to the travail and glory of his time: the period of the Civil War and Reconstruction, 1861 to 1876. For many decades there seemed no need for such expository details. Those who entered the tomb through the twin bronze doors—each sixteen feet high and weighing 2,700 pounds—often brought their own clear memories of the time.

Old Union Army veterans would come in and walk slowly over to the parapet and stand there very straight and gaze down for a long time. Sometimes a few tears would slip from their eyes. No one had to remind them of Shiloh and Appomattox and Vicksburg.

For them the hall was filled with the fire and thunder of the Civil War as they stood in its deep quiet. They had known the smoke of that war and the drums. The faraway look in their gaze mirrored old battlefields.

In 1934, on the 112th anniversary of Grant's birth on

April 27, 1822, a group of the general's old war comrades, now very aged, came in and stood in the hall. In 1892, when the cornerstone was laid for the tomb, a fourteen-year-old boy, Ben S. Rosenberg, sang the National Anthem. As recently as 1961, he made a contribution toward the cost of completing the memorial.

The burial place of General Grant stood unfinished for more than 60 years—and it is unfinished still. A peculiarity of the original search for a design was that architects were asked if their plans were suitable to being built in sections, as funds came in, so that at the completion of each section the monument would not look incomplete. The essential Duncan structure is, of course, all there, but significant details of ornamentation are lacking. A splendid, terraced approach from the river was drawn but never started. "The original design was never fully executed, but it's as finished as it will ever be," a member of the park service said.

Four years after it opened, the memorial settled in its sandy base and cracks were torn in its walls, giving rise for a time to fears for its "collapse or ruin." The files of the association, rich with the history of the effort to create the memorial, were devoured in the Equitable Building fire in early 1912. According to Thomas M. Pitkin, a supervising park historian who made a study of the structure's past, only a few scattered documents survive.

Several drives to finish the monument were announced but they kept smacking into unforeseen obstructions, like World War I and the stock market crash. A considerable refurbishing was carried out in 1938, in time for World's Fair throngs.

Visitors to the tomb were counted at 457,018 in 1898, the first full year of operation. By 1906, the number reached a peak of 607,484 and then it began to slide until, in 1933, only 95,584 persons came. The tally began moving upward again to 250,000, before settling into a pattern of about 125,000 annual visitors in the early 1970s.

The greater the distance from the Civil War, the more severe the burden of maintenance became. Roof repairs amounting to only $1,600 in 1953 produced a serious deficit, and the association began talking about turning the edifice over to the Federal government. The park service took custody on May 1, 1959.

Even after the last hoary remnants of the Grand Army of the Republic had passed from the scene, the sons of Union Army veterans—men who had heard of the war first-hand from those who had been in it—would come in; but they, too, withered, grew scarce and have since been gathered to their fathers.

Now that the generations who knew the Civil War by direct experience or by family recall are gone, there is to be "a shift in emphasis at the memorial away from the mortuary to the interpretive," Mr. Wagers said. "We want to tell the story in terms of human relationships," he remarked while inspecting the structure.

A first step in that direction was taken when three mosaic murals of marble and glass—showing Grant at Chattanooga and Vicksburg and meeting his defeated adversary, General Robert E. Lee of the Confederacy, at Appomattox—were unveiled in crescent-shaped recesses high on the interior walls.

It is 150 feet from the base of the crypt to the top of the dome, and there is a graceful balcony high in the dome, 120 feet above the crypt, that has been closed to visitors since 1900. The tomb has nine amber, leaded stained glass windows: three face north, three face east, three face west, but none face south.

Regimental and battle flags of Civil War units—flimsy, tattered, terribly frail—were displayed in octagonal, dome-topped glass cases. "Some will just turn to dust at a touch," a tomb attendant half whispered.

The flags have since been removed. In their place, in trophy rooms just beyond Egyptian arches, there are more directly instructive exhibits with photographs and texts, though it is doubtful that they are more evocative than those faded battle flags.

Some thought has been given to the possibility of using taperecorded narration to help visitors get a sense of the times as they stroll through the hall. It has been found, however, that "acoustics in the rotunda are terrible." Now there is thought of using an earphone system, but that is not likely to come before the nation's bicentennial in 1976.

Since before the turn of the century, a heavy bronze chain had blocked public access to the stairways that led down into the open crypt. Those dim stairways became the repository for cleaning equipment and other items that needed to be stored. The chain was removed only on anniversary dates to permit veterans or patriotic groups to lay wreaths there. But now the chain is down and walk-in visitors may go below whenever they wish to.

"We think it improves the quality and immediacy of the visit," Mr. Wagers said. Some had feared that "small boys would be jumping over the lower parapet to clamber onto the granite slabs," but small boys appear to be quite subdued by the sight of the great sarcophagi.

The small, glass-walled office the Burnsides once used is gone and, instead, the tomb staff uses a nineteen-foot-high round office, windowless and tubular, like the base of a missile silo. It is in the southeast corner. One difficulty they must reckon with is graffiti. It takes solvent, acids and a power-driven wire brush to efface scrawlings made in lipstick, crayon, liquid markers or with sharp stones.

Soon the soot-blackened interior dome will be cleaned and painted and the City will floodlight the exterior at night. (Explaining the way the Federal and City governments divide certain housekeeping functions, a staff member said, "We haul up the flag, but they repair the ropes.")

The memorial is open from 9:00 to 5:00 seven days a week from April 15 to November 1—it is closed on Mondays and Tuesdays the rest of the year—with James Henry, Frank Lebeda or Al James always on duty as guards and guides, genial custodians of inconsistent ghosts.

The Secret Hodgepodge:
One Mask, Many Faces

The Metropolitan Museum of Art, that gray eminence on Fifth Avenue, is a congress of buildings that runs from very old to very new. On the journey, it has stopped off at a great many way stations in between.

As seen from any vantage on Fifth Avenue, the museum's 1,000-foot neoclassic facade—it is 999 feet to be exact—presents a severely handsome unity of monumental proportions.

The two-section wing that stretches north of the main entrance is so exactly duplicated by the newer wing that stretches south of it that Arthur F. Klein, supervisor of plans and construction for the Metropolitan, said, "It looks like they just flopped the building over, and got on the south what they had on the north."

The building's limestone face, which covers an almost five-foot thickness of bricks, is monolithic in its aspect. But behind that stern facade, admired for its dignity and grandeur, there is bunched a rather haphazard collection of buildings—seventeen in all—that take up seven acres of ground and offer, on their several levels, more than seventeen acres of floor space.

With one stroll around the entire museum, the image of unity dissolves, and the reality of disparity appears.

Cross purposes and contradictions abound in the various forms of the exterior that can be seen from the west, the north and the south in Central Park. There are, for instance, exactly four and one-third arches in the north-rear face of the museum. The fifth arch is abruptly cut off by the wall of another kind of building that is set into it at right angles.

Nevertheless, inside, these structures seem to flow together with a reasonable sense of ease, especially in the public galleries. Their disharmony is sometimes more apparent in the non-public service and storage areas—rather like a marriage that seems all smooth to public view but is a crabbed alliance in private.

An old section of the Croton Aqueduct curves through a subbasement. It has been sealed off to make a waterproof storage vault. The columns on the floor above it are irregularly situated because they follow the long curve of the aqueduct below, into whose wall footings they are securely set.

Mr. Klein put on a pedometer one day to measure his daily rounds in the museum and was mildly astonished to find that he had paced off more than fourteen miles.

"The museum in itself is a whole history of American architecture," remarked Arthur Rosenblatt, the museum's administrator for architecture and planning. "The best firms, the giants of American architecture in their day, had their hands in the place. If you study it, it records every style." Among them Mr. Rosenblatt designated one as "1938 W.P.A. modern" and Mr. Klein pegged another as "nondescript."

There are some who think of the Metropolitan as a kind of American Museum of Architectural History.

The structural variety has been obscured because Richard Morris Hunt came along and, in 1902, plunked a new building out on Fifth Avenue that was just wide enough to hide all the other buildings, which date from 1880 onward and are set more deeply into Central Park.

"Hunt just tried to erase the memory of Calvert Vaux and the succeeding architects," said Mr. Rosenblatt. He made a good job of it at that, for when McKim, Mead and White added the north and south wings on Fifth Avenue—from 1911 to 1926—they followed Hunt's lead in many exact details, so that the whole front face of the museum grew according to Hunt's style.

Seeing the vastness of the museum today, it is a little hard for New Yorkers to grasp that the Metropolitan Museum of Art was born in exceedingly humble, rented quarters.

Its first home, at 681 Fifth Avenue near Fifty-third Street, was a four-story brownstone—plain-faced, almost homely. Two lanterns at the base of an eleven-step stoop, and two columns at its top, were the only touches of ornamentation. As the American counterpart of some of the venerable institutions of Europe, it bore roughly the relationship of a tool shed to a manor.

It had housed Dodworth's Dancing Academy before it was rented out, at $9,000 a year, to the fledgling museum. The house included a stable, which the trustees planned to let as a small source of revenue. On February 20, 1872, the place was opened to the public. "The hanging committee have worked like beavers," John Taylor Jonston wrote of the preparations.

Henry James called it "the charming little academy in the Fifth Avenue," and while its collection might not do much to edify those who had beheld Europe's treasures, it would be "a source of profit to students debarred from European opportunities," James thought.

After some fifteen months there, the museum packed its belongings and moved downtown to the old Douglas Mansion on West Fourteenth Street near Seventh Avenue. It was officially described as "a large building, measuring seventy-five feet front by eighty-five feet deep" with "five times as much wall-space available." It could be swallowed whole by just one of the European paintings galleries in the present museum.

The square, rather squat mansion was an adaptable place.

At other times in its eclectic history, it served as a bedding and furniture mart, a bowling alley and as the training school of the Salvation Army.

The move had been forced by the prodigious diggings of one Emanuele Pietro Paolo Maria Luigi Palma de Cesnola, an immensely energetic Italian soldier who pried open 8,000 tombs of Phoenician, Assyrian, Greek and Egyptian origin on Cyprus, seized their treasures, and parlayed the feat into a job as the first full-time director of the museum. Roughly 10,000 of these relics were brought to the Metropolitan.

The museum opened on Fourteenth Street in the spring of 1873 and remained there while its own building was going up on what was to become its permanent site. Its first Central Park structure was opened on March 30, 1880.

The wings of the Calvert Vaux-Jacob Wrey Mould design were clipped even before construction began, so the first unit was built with pop-out walls showing the outlines of many corridors into non-existent wings.

The cavernous first unit with its ornate cast-iron arches under a glass roof suggested a public arena for circuses. James Jackson Jarves pronounced it "fit only for a winter-garden or a railway depot."

In 1888 a wing sprouted to the south designed by Theodore Weston and, in 1894, another unfurled to the north designed by Arthur L. T. Tuckerman. Hunt's neoclassic structure, which today houses the Great Hall and includes the main entrance (now with an air-curtain that can withstand a sixty-mile gale), appeared in 1902.

The hall has been restored by Kevin Roche to the solemn beauty of its original design. Mr. Roche also designed the new entrance and wider stairs and added two front plazas with twin, one hundred-spout wall-of-water fountains. The effect seems to be somewhat out of scale, even for the Metropolitan, and, hard as it must have been to do, it makes the entrance look vacantly formal, massively powerless and bland.

In approaching the museum, to operate on it architecturally, Mr. Roche saw it as "an assemblage of partially completed buildings by different architects in different styles," and he noted that "in almost all cases these parts of buildings were parts of master plans, but in no case were any of them completed."

McKim, Mead and White's north and south wings filled out the museum's tract from Eightieth to Eighty-fourth Streets on the Avenue. The modern glass face of the Thomas J. Watson Library was wedged in between the Hunt and Vaux complexes in 1964, and other structures of various shapes and sizes have been stuck in, bringing the number to seventeen.

A Many-Fingered Voice

Among the people who hear with their eyes, it is sometimes said that Bernard Bragg has "a golden voice, in his hands."

In the art of painting thoughts in the air with signs, some possess a more elegant diction than others.

David Hays, the producing director of The National Theater of the Deaf, was reflecting on this the other day, amid preparations for another European tour. The troupe's members will take the first steps in Sweden toward the creation of a Swedish theater of the deaf. It would be the third such company on a professional level. The other is in Moscow.

"Our view is that social good will come if it is absolutely competitive, non-condescending theater," Mr. Hays said in his office on Broadway near Sixty-first Street. It is on that principle that the theater here has worked. The National Theater of the Deaf enjoys its own private full-employment

economy, with every actor in it engaged in some phase of its work on a virtually uninterrupted basis.

Body language is nothing novel to these masters of eloquent mime. "These people have a really superb theatrical medium of their own," Mr. Hays said. "From the time they were kids they had to depend on acting skills to get their ideas across.

"There's more variety in signing than in speaking, because the whole physical being of the actor expresses his intent in his action. The whole body legitimately becomes a part of the word. You can do this language right from your toes.

"The facial expressions that go with the signs do a great deal to inflect the words, of course."

There are deaf actors whose fingers trace thoughts with the delicacy of ballet. There is a liquidity of motion, a symmetry, a grace, and a special power of emphasis in their signs.

Some deaf actors are able to create patterns that go beyond meaning to impart artistry and emotional color to what they say with signs. That is why Mr. Bragg, a member of the company, is said to possess "a golden voice."

Signs can be "much stronger emotionally than speech." Mr. Hays said, because they are subject to almost an infinity of gradations and because the entire body is in them.

"We find the attention span of even little children is stretched way beyond what their teachers have thought to be the limit," he said. "On our stage, just by saying the words you have action, due to our method of delivering the word."

He made his point graphic by slowing his speech and carefully illustrating each word or thought in signs, gaining an evident increase in clarity and emphasis. "Unfortunately, my hands are not lovely," Mr. Hays apologized.

Signing is not fingerspelling. Any English word can be fingerspelled, with a handshape for each letter. A double letter is simply held slightly longer, or moved to indicate the doubling. When a skilled user goes at top speed, the "hearer" does not see the individual letters; the entire word is suddenly perceived in the air.

Onstage, actors avoid fingerspelling. It is not as broad or as colorful as signing: the use of one or two-handed symbols, each standing for an entire word or idea. Signing is, in the director's phrase, "the beautiful visual language of the deaf."

It is, he said, "a language with all the color of the dance."

The deaf have no physical deficiency in their vocal chords. What is lacking is an ability to imitate heard language. "Imagine how difficult it would be," Mr. Hays said, "to draw a fire engine if you had never seen one, and if you couldn't see the markings your pencil was making as you drew."

One of the ideas behind the theater is "to show the world that deaf people are handsome and skillful and vivacious, and deserve better jobs and a better image."

There are fourteen actors in the troupe, of which three are hearing and eleven are deaf. To meet the national demand for performances, the company is often split into two Little Theaters that travel widely, acting in schools, colleges and theaters.

The main company, formed under the aegis of the Eugene O'Neill Theater Center, has made two major stands on Broadway. Since the work began in 1967, it has played more than 900 performances in 34 states, Canada and Europe. The troupe operates under five grants, with basic support coming from the Federal Department of Health, Education and Welfare.

"But the tours all have to break even," Mr. Hays said. "The H.E.W. money covers rehearsals and staging costs. Once we get into our bus and truck, we are free of financial support." From that point on, the company must earn its way on box office receipts. Almost everywhere, the deaf actors are enthusiastically received. They can see and to some extent feel that audience response, but they never hear the laughter and applause.

Performances are visual and verbal. They are based, not on mime creations, but on great works of spoken language. A hearing actor usually presents the spoken word, which gives audiences the experience of hearing the word and seeing the word at the same time.

A brochure sent ahead of the company says, "You will be amazed at how much you understand when the spoken word, by our speaking player, joins the visual word. Each will seem clearer and richer."

Geoffrey Moorhouse, writing in *The Manchester Guardian,* reproved London stage critics for missing "a highly professional performance from somewhere in the same league as Marcel Marceau," and he credited the troupe with owning "a colossal vocabulary of grace and waver." He watched, with growing wonder, a "speechless version of 'A Child's Christmas in Wales,' a virtuoso performance by Bernard Bragg."

It was Dylan Thomas "not with a voice rich as a Christmas pudding but Dylan Thomas with the movements of a clown playing on thistledown," he wrote.

On the European swing, the troupe will do several works in its repertory, including the Dylan Thomas piece, e. e. cummings' "who knows if the moon's" and four fables by James Thurber, including "The Moth and the Star" and "The Fairly Intelligent Fly."

In the latter, a fly in the air figures it's safe to land wherever he sees a lot of flies, so he lands on a strip of flypaper. In Thurber's "The Unicorn in the Garden," a husband bored with the monotony of his marriage tells his wife he has seen a unicorn with a golden horn in the garden.

She calls him a booby and says he should be in the booby hatch. His insistence on the apparition leads her to summon a psychiatrist, a policeman and a straitjacket. When help arrives, she tells them the story, which her husband denies with round-eyed innocence.

She is clearly mad, so they carry her off with her hands tied behind her back. Thurber's moral: "Never count your boobies before they're hatched."

The Red Riding Hood story is played straight until the end, when instead of being eaten up, the girl shoots the wolf dead, proving, as the narrator says, that "it's not so easy to fool little girls nowadays as it used to be."

There is an "almost mystical" quality to communication among the deaf, Mr. Hays said, and that is why "they have very little trouble understanding each other across foreign boundaries.

"They develop such a charade-like capacity for communication, that they can come to understand each other very quickly. That makes them better tourists than most people. They have ways of making their wants known in other countries that you and I don't have."

Their handicap is not always apparent, because "deafness is invisible," he said.

I Heard Them Singing

They were a choir of the deaf. They sang to a piano accompaniment they could not hear. The mind knew all that as fact, but still the ear did not detect the secret of their inner silence.

It had required, a teacher said, a "tremendously special effort" of practice and rehearsal. The twenty high school students sang "Happy Birthday" at the one hundredth anniversary party of the Lexington School for the Deaf.

To hear a choir of the deaf sing is to listen to a miracle of melody synchronized with a prodigy of diction. They sang in perfect unison with nearly perfect clarity.

But it was not the exactness of their diction that was to be wondered at so much as variations in pitch, the musical fidelity and true tone of their voices. They were born to silence, yet they sang.

When the spring term is over, the school will close its gingerbread castle on Lexington Avenue between Sixty-seventh and Sixty-eighth Streets. It will move out of the five-story Victorian relic to open a $9 million, electronic-age campus on 7½ acres in Jackson Heights, Queens, with facilities for 370 students.

A blue birthday cake with four tiers was rolled onto the stage. Dr. Edwin Neis, a seventy-seventy-year-old graduate in the class of 1905 who practiced dentistry here for fifty-one years, clasped his blue-veined hand over the tiny fist of four-year-old Gina Marciona. Together they wielded a silver trowel and put a deep incision into the cake.

Dr. Neis, a bald and bespectacled man with a white mustache over a benign smile, wore a clerical collar and dark suit. He is retired as a dentist but remains active as an ordained Episcopal clergyman ministering to the deaf. He speaks but he does not hear.

Gina, a pupil, stood on top of a box in her starched smock dress, holding a bouquet of pink carnations.

For a century, the school has been conferring the gift of speech on those who cannot acquire it by the normal method, imitation of sounds. Nearly 10,000 graduates have "gone out into life, searching for, and achieving in large measure, first class citizenship, in actuality not in myth," said Dr. Clarence D. O'Connor, superintendent of the school for the last thirty-six years. He has lived on the premises all that time.

He told of those who were "keeping important and well-paying jobs, buying their own homes and paying taxes" on paychecks earned in printing, architectural drafting, photography, computer programming, bookkeeping, and machine shop work.

One graduate took honors at Princeton and is lip-reading through graduate studies in Christ Church College at Oxford. The school says it was the first in the nation to teach speech and lip reading to the deaf.

Dr. O'Connor, a small, dapper, elderly man, told an audience of parents and pupils that the school had begun, in a sense, in a class of six children conducted in a home here before the end of the Civil War.

It was later formally organized on Fourteenth Street by Mr. and Mrs. Isaac Rosenfeld, who had a deaf child, Hannah. In 1870 it rented three houses for $7,500 a year on what would later become the Astor Hotel site in Times Square, training thirteen students.

It was called the Instititution for the Improved Instruction of Deaf Mutes until 1938. The school moved into the red brick building on Lexington Avenue in 1881. "Sometimes I check my own shape in the early morning and find the building in better shape than I'm in, and I haven't been here one hundred years," Dr. O'Connor quipped.

Children, he said, are "brought here practically in arms." The 270 students in forty classrooms, about half of them residents, pay no tuition. Their ages run from eleven months to twenty years. Most of them go out as "intellectually equipped, economically independent and emotionally secure individuals," A. Piza Mendes, a trustee since 1921, said.

There is a rule against sign language or fingerspelling in the school. Speech is the goal because "a deaf person who is oral functions in both societies—that of the deaf and of the hearing," a teacher said. "I don't say they never do it. I just say we don't allow it. It's quite a strain to sit through a whole school-day lip reading."

The youngest children are slowly "made aware of the world of sound" and they become accustomed to some of the equipment that helps them to learn language and speech first, and then reading, writing and arithmetic.

At the new campus, deaf children will be taken in "from age zero" for the infants-and-baby program, with school enrollment starting at age three and continuing through senior high, except that apt students will frequently be graduated, according to a recently instituted policy, into regular schools as soon as they are ready. They will continue their studies in the hearing world in which they must ultimately work. Indeed, one pupil made the switch at five years old.

Letter to McNulty

Dear McNulty:

The St. Patrick's Day parade here, in spite of fables contrary, is a thing of great propriety. I wanted you to know that. It came smartly up Fifth Avenue yesterday, throbbing to the music of one hundred bands, and there wasn't a truncheon in it. There was a mace or two, but they appeared to be of a severely ceremonial character.

The weather had evidently been ordered by Saint Patrick himself. It was a brilliant day—clear, cold, breeze-whipped. Benign winds swept even trifling clouds away, and the sky had been painted a brilliant blue. It was a day for marching indeed, McNulty, but it wasn't much of a day for standing tall in your shoes and watching. Those who couldn't get into it, stood on the sidelines, marching in place.

If a man had attempted a census of dimples he would have been swamped. The Avenue was dappled with dimples. Some boys showed by their smiles that they found trudging up the

Avenue with so many pretty ankles just ahead no great hardship at all.

It was a day with alchemy in it. Silver batons thrown into the air became brilliant streaks of sun, but they turned silver again in the hands of strutting majorettes. And why does the brass bowl of a tuba reflect everything upside down, reversing earth and sky?

The sun was high to their backs and the wind was fast in their faces and 100,000 sons and daughters of Eire matched strides with their shadows for fifty-two blocks—winsome girls and handsome boys and men as stalwart as oaks.

Drum thunder rolled in the Avenue. Glockenspiel mallets beat out a tinkling affirmation, "It's A Great Day for the Irish," and this time the claim was not made hollow by bitter winds and swirling snow, or hail. I've seen the time, McNulty, when polar bears might reasonably have balked at the working conditions on St. Patrick's Day.

The Mayor told friends that he had ordered a warm day but was turned down, as usual, by the Board of Estimate.

The forces of nature have conspired against us some years, McNulty. I still haven't dried out entirely from the year of the soak—a drenching mist that could be more easily felt than seen. They are normally men of awful caution, but that year none of the proud eminences near the Mayor would accept the shelter of umbrellas, lest they be photographed flinching from punishment.

They stood there, grinning, while the bare branches of trees overhead gathered the mists, fused them into drops and loosed a shower whenever the winds stirred. They had their reward though. Fifth Avenue runs level almost to the south end of Central Park, then rises. So, seen from the stand half a mile away, the marching battalions came like a vision out of the fog on that rise.

I've seen the time when snow thickened the air all morning so when the parade got off, store awnings were heaped with white. Some sagged a bit and boys who leaped up to punch them brought small blizzards down. Those days it was our fortitude, not our fortune, that went on display.

It doesn't make any difference, of course. The parade officials never flinch. When the Irish are set to honor St. Patrick on his day, no howling threat of a blizzard, no northeast gusts as sharp as knives, no sub-freezing cold will do to stop them. They come out to march, McNulty.

A college Air Force R.O.T.C. unit sounded off in lusty unison stepping in perfect cadence—big boys blue. Their polished shoes caught the sun on every upstep. Sidewalk bootblacks who set up shop on the cross streets where the units form do a sweet business putting a last minute gleam on marchers' shoes.

At Forty-fourth Street, close to where the parade begins, a man in a green hat had the temerity to hold up a big sign proclaiming, "Saint Patrick was a Baptist."

"Tell me, how was he a Baptist? Tell me that?" a ruddy-faced man demanded.

The parade was under Irish management—Cumann-na-mBan, Clan-na-Gael, the Ancient Order of Hibernians and others—but it proved to be a mobilization of Irishmen of Irish, Spanish, French, Italian, Chinese and African extraction. Saint Patrick's Day brings out the Irish in a great many people.

An Asian diplomat who crossed Fifth Avenue during the procession offered the sum of his impression. "This certainly is an unusual outpouring of a folk ethic," he said.

The surnames of one typical rank of marchers ran this way: Mennit, Campagna, Neill, Goldner, Gillespie, Corbo, Cotteta, de Prophets, Caughlin, Carney, Hall and Janelli. But the parade was Irish-true in spirit and Irish-happy in heart, and Irish-blithe in style, and—well—only Italian in part.

Sean McGonigal led the St. Columcille's Pipe Band of Kearny, New Jersey, in what he certified were "Molly

Darlin' " and "The Wearing o' the Green." There were about 115 bands in all, scattering notes into the air. At times they came so closely spaced that the strains of "America"—which, heaven help us, McNulty, is "God Save the Queen"—were all twined together with those of "Harrigan" in a symphony of discords.

There was no want of bagpipes, of which Samuel Butler once rightly said, and he should have said it twice, that they "make a viler noise than swine in windy weather when they whine." They gave out with "Scotland the Brave" and "Highland Laddie" and the customary questions about kilts were shouted from the sidelines.

Cardinal Dougherty High School boys struggled past Sixty-eighth Street against sudden bursts of wind that kept threatening to pin their banner to the pavement. There were a great many people who marched in perpetual jeopardy of losing their headgear because of that wind. It was a good thing yesterday to have a hat one size too small, or failing that, a head one size too big.

As usual, every honest effort was made to keep the spectacle free of gimmickry and folly. Parade officers inspect the units before they march and cull persons dressed in inordinately loud or comic greens. If these do not retire voluntarily, they are assisted to the sidewalk by as many policemen as are necessary to persuade them of the folly of their ways.

Once, four well-dressed men came out of the crowd a few blocks up the line and attempted to unfurl a banner demanding "Civil rights for Northern Ireland." This occurred in full view of the dignitaries who stood in front of the great bronze doors at St. Patrick's Cathedral. The partisans were quickly set upon by twenty policemen who rushed out and gave them the hearty heave, with the spectators nearby crying encouragement—"Hit them boys!" "Knock their heads!" and the like. It was clear that few Irishmen objected, on principle, to a bit of a fracas for the sake of peace.

Brendan Behan, the playwright, was barred outright as obstreperous. He did not take this altogether kindly and said some colorful things.

"I suppose there are some prudish people in America just like everywhere," he said. "They want to look like Queen Victoria's husband. If someone drank a glass of Irish whiskey or stout, it would do a lot a good for the old country. Rather than hang shamrocks around your ears."

It was the 1,500th anniversary of the death of St. Patrick according to responsible reckoning, and many there were who came to do reverence to "the saint who brought to our mountains the gift of God's faith, the sweet light of His love," as someone has written. McNulty, your heart would have been done good to have been there.

St. Patrick's Day is not the day he was born, but the day he died. The heroes of earth are remembered on their birthdays, but celestial heroes on the day of their decease, for then it is that they enter life eternal.

The Cardinal stood on the steps of the cathedral and took off his biretta every time the flag came by, which was often. He has staying powers the politicians lack. He was there when the first man in the first battalion came by, and five hours later, when the last sturdy youth in the sixtieth battalion passed, there he was on the steps, still smiling.

In the cathedral, the Reverend Francis X. Duffy called forth the semblance of St. Patrick and closed with an old Irish blessing:

"May the blessed sunlight shine on you and warm your heart until it glows like a great peat fire, so that the stranger may come and warm himself at it, and also a friend. And may the light shine out of the two eyes of you, like a candle set in two windows of the house, bidding the wanderer to come in out of the storm, and may the blessing of the rain be on you—the soft, sweet rain.

"And may the blessing of the earth be on you—the great, round earth; may you ever have a kindly greeting from them you pass as you are going along the roads. May the earth be soft under you when you rest upon it, tired at the end of the day, and may it rest easy over you when, at the last, you lay out under it. May it rest so lightly over you that your soul may be out from under it quickly—and up and off and on its way to God."

The parade's caboose battalion crosses the finish line near 6:00 P.M. and dissolves into convivial disarray, and spectators dwindle with the colder drafts of dusk. Let me tell you, at the march's long end, shivering men turned toward reputable places, blue-lipped, for a cup of hot broth.

Orders went out for all groups to march sixteen abreast. Twelve abreast was the rule until two years ago. A wider parade is a shorter parade, the committee has found.

You should have seen them, McNulty, coming on 100,000 strong. Wasn't it Sean O'Casey who set down somewhere the words ". . . your name will be a banner and a shout"?

Well, that is what happened to the Irish yesterday. Their name became a banner and a shout.

The Sweet Sell

Coconut Keynote

The Association of Philippine Coconut Desiccators convened a two-day symposium, a kind of coconut convention, in the Plaza Hotel yesterday. Even before the keynote speaker rose, the delegates were rallied to their theme by a preliminary exhorter who urged them to "think coconut."

Before an hour had passed they were treated to a review of some of the great figures in the century-old development of the product—Henry Vavasseur, Robert Heinekey Buxton, Percy V. Appleby, Wyndham Stopford and Howard Hick among them—men who have been enrolled in the pantheon of the desiccated coconut.

The word des-ic-cate (des e kat) v.t. is defined as to "to dry thoroughly; dry up." A desiccator is defined as "one who, or that which desiccates." A desiccator can therefore be a person or a thing.

To reduce the matter to its simplest essentials, the sponsoring group is an association of persons—desiccators—who use things—machines called desiccators—to dry up—that is, to desiccate—coconut meat.

The dried meat can then be shipped in its light, fluffy form, flaked or shredded, with great ease and at much lower cost than whole coconuts. The product is an essential ingredient of such good things as cookies, cakes, candy bars and coconut custard pies. The delegates were treated to something a little more exotic—coconut soup—at their banquet.

The man who thought it up confided privately that he can put out an entire seven-course dinner based on coconuts—"from soup to nuts"—but he said this went beyond the tolerance of the Hotel Plaza kitchen for desiccated coconut as a universal ingredient.

The delegates came out of the numbing blasts of Fifth Avenue into the gilded elegance of the Savoy Room where, under a crystal chandelier and in front of a blue banner blazoned "COCONUT IN THE 70s," speaker after speaker took the rostrum.

They heard warming words of welcome by Conrado Escudero, the association's representative here.

"Ladies and gentlemen, esteemed colleagues of the coconut community," he began, and soon his words were euphoric.

"Imagine yourselves," he suggested, "in a tropical setting wherein as far as your eyes can see, endless rows of coconuts are sweeping from one direction to the other, palm leaves swaying breezily, while hanging above, gently, are bunches of ready-to-fall fresh coconuts."

Mr. Escudero closed with the injunction to "think coconut." He was presumably indulging the hope that the man who thinks coconut will soon talk coconut and eventually eat coconut, and that, of course, is where the money is.

The keynote speaker was Andrew M. Hay, a former British Army Intelligence officer and former president of the British-American Chamber of Commerce and a Chevalier of the Confrerie des Chevaliers du Tastevin.

Mr. Hay—tall, trim-waisted, straight-backed, ruddy faced—brought a distinguished mien to the rostrum. He is president of Calvert, Vavasseur & Co. and also of Red V Coconut Products Inc. of Manila, both dedicated to the desiccated nut meat. His topic was the "History and Future of Desiccated Coconut."

His hour-long address, a good start on a book on the subject, reflected a third-generation command of his matter and a capacity to see shredded coconut against a backdrop of tariff disputes, wars, the rise of industrialization, and vast economic shifts.

His grandfather, Robert Heinekey Buxton, was the man "to whom it occurred that the shipment of coconuts in their whole form around half of the world was a wasteful and expensive method of acquiring shredded coconut for use in candy factories," Mr. Hay declared. Desiccation came of his discontent.

In a low-keyed British accent Mr. Hay began, "I have been graciously invited by the Association of Philippine Coconut Desiccators to talk about the past and the future of desiccated coconut. To talk of the past is perhaps the easiest part of the assignment, not least because I have the rare, if not unique, peculiarity—distinction would be, I think, too strong a word for such a minor discipline—of being probably the only man who can come before you whose family have been intimately connected in an entrepreneurial capacity with this industry for three generations."

Mr. Hay traced the effect of the industrial revolution in England on distant coconut plantations lying under the sun between the Tropics of Cancer and Capricorn: factory work led to wages for the masses and wages to "the possibility of small luxuries," thereby creating an enormous demand for candy.

A candy-making industry rose to fill that demand. It was soon "searching for inexpensive ingredients with a wide popular flavor appeal," and coconuts neatly filled that bill.

Even today, he said, desiccated coconut is a bargain among nuts, favorably set in relation to "pecans selling at $1.80 per pound, walnuts at $1.15, almonds at $1.13, Brazils at 74¢, cashews at 85¢ and even the humble peanut at 42¢ per pound"—while coconut comes at 25¢ a pound.

He decried the imposition by the United States of an import duty of two cents a pound on coconut, and warned that promoting coconut among calorie-conscious Americans required unflagging vigor since "our product is used primarily in baked goods, pies, candy and ice cream—not any of them part of a reducing diet."

After fourteen years of cultivation without fruit, a mature tree starts to produce about sixty coconuts a year.

It takes about 7,000 coconuts to make one ton of desiccated coconut, and the toothsome product—which some promoters have called "angel flakes"—is shipped to consumer nations in one hundred-pound paper sacks. The United States is consuming about 92 million pounds of desiccated coconut shipped from the Philippines in a year.

There was a display at the rear of the hall of spearmint-flavored coconut and peppermint, lemon, chocolate, pineapple and cinammon-flavored coconut, and long-thread, rice-cut and nugget coconut, not to mention confetti coconut (tiny flakes of brightly colored coconut meat for cupcake toppings).

Present were coconut brokers, processors, shippers, insurers, research and development people, and college professors and medical personnel interested in the nutritional, allergenic and economic properties of the product.

"Are there any manufacturers here?" an incorrigibly ignorant bystander asked.

"No," a desiccator replied evenly. "You see, the *tree* is the manufacturer."

Cheese

The State of Wisconsin wants us all to eat more cheese. It wants that because eating cheese is good for us, and very good for the State of Wisconsin, whose economy bobs on a sea of curdled milk.

To get our minds off other distractions and on the central thing—cheese—the state and its dairy industry threw an informative, and decidedly toothsome, party in the Regent Room of the New York Hilton.

"Mention my name from Sheboygan," said a hearty receptionist in a white knitted frock, without giving her name. She applied a gummed Wisconsin Cheese Festival label to the breast pocket which, when it was peeled off two lip-smacking hours later, took the surface threads of the garment along with it.

A slim cheese lover named John, among the 425 invited guests, confessed that he hoped to be greeted at the door by the cheese queen. He pointed to a five-foot-three-inch coed who was wearing a gown of pale green gossamer under a sash identifying her as "Alice in Dairyland." But a chunky individual, built on the lines of an upended loaf of processed American cheese, blocked the way.

He had a broad, healthy, reddish face and he stuck out his hand and said he was with the Wisconsin Department of Agriculture. He seemed to know a great deal about cheese, none of which he was disposed to conceal.

"We had a fondue party for the entire city of Pittsburgh in September," he said, "on the mall outside the Gateway Center. That's what we wanted to do here, but it's the wrong weather.

"We have no fight with New York cheese, but we happen to make half—well, almost half, like forty-eight or forty-nine per cent—of the nation's cheese."

"Cheese made in Wisconsin could cover the United States

to a depth of three inches, including the Grand Canyon," offered Milton Mayer, a sales executive, evidently a man of prodigious imagination.

Alice in Dairyland's dimples seemed to exert a magnetic force upon the men entering the room. The diamonds in her tiara may have been suspect, but those in her eyes were not, and she gave her name as Susan Masterson, a twenty-year-old University of Wisconsin junior who is taking a year out to tour the country.

"She's a state employee," the chunky man said. "She just talks about cheeses here, but in other places she's talking turkeys or apples."

In the room itself a forest of toothpicks, each stabbing a sample-sized bite of cheese, lay on a huge horseshoe buffet. Brokers' and manufacturers' displays lined the walls.

"We can't show our non-Wisconsin cheeses," said Bill Dorman of the cheese-famed Dormans, "but we sell a sliced port salut that we can adjust to local tastes. Most people like it a little milder, but out in San Francisco they like a little more bite to it."

Herbert Schevitz of Hoffman's of Wisconsin and Moonachie, New Jersey, was holding a "mini-wheel of Swiss with mini-eyes."

"We don't call them holes, we call them eyes," he said. "The mini-Swiss has very tiny eyes. If you make a Swiss and it doesn't have eyes, you call it blind. You never market it."

The chunky man raved about a "flaming chocolate cheese sauce—no, I'm serious, you take chocolate sauce and blend it with club cheese and add a little crème de cacao and a pinch of cinnamon, brandy or cognac, set it aflame and pour it over ice cream."

He paid lyric tribute to "cheese fudge, made of club cheese and powdered cocoa."

He is probably way ahead of his time. In a consumer survey, ninety-five per cent of cheese users confessed to using cheese in sandwiches, while only 6.8 per cent admitted to using cheese in salads; a scant 3.5 per cent owned up to using it in spaghetti or macaroni; and 1.6 per cent associated cheese with vegetables.

The American public has a good deal to learn about cheese, starting apparently at macaroni, which is a kindergarten lesson. At this rate, a student can work his way up to cheese over broccoli by about the second year of college, leaving the more sophisticated uses, like cheese fudge, for the masters or doctoral programs.

Cheese goes well with fruit or wine, of course, but not just any cheese with any fruit or wine: camembert goes nicely with plums, grapes or fresh pineapple; provolone with pears; brie with strawberries or peaches; edam with honeydew melon and—pay strict attention now—parmesan with cantaloupe. Whether Neufchâtel wine goes well with Neufchâtel cheese in anything but a kind of crazy rhyme scheme nobody seemed to be quite sure.

Joe Bree, a cheese salesman with the L. D. Schreiber Cheese Company of Green Bay, Wisconsin, had clear blue eyes and a grip as sure as a vise. His company's American cheese comes off rollers in long ribbons, not loaves, he said, "and it's sliced by computer, which adjusts itself and readjusts itself continually to the weight."

The Roger Stanley little orchestra was off in a corner playing "On Wisconsin" about as militantly as a piano, a bass and a violin can.

The eye, and very often the fingers, were drawn to rows and rows of cheeses: natural caraway, baby muenster, smoked Swiss, part-skim mozzarella, jack cheese, provolone, ricotta, parmesan, mild cheddar and cheeseburger slices. One company had smuggled in a row of New York State cheddar among the Wisconsin cheeses.

In the early days, back in the 1850s and 60s, before Wisconsin had become established in the trade, cheese made there and shipped to places like Chicago was often sold as "New York Factory" or "Excelsior, New York" cheese. The deception was practiced by dealers, not the manufacturers, who usually shipped their product unmarked. Standards began to be set in 1872, and it has been a long time since Wisconsin cheese was smuggled to midwest consumers as the authentic article from New York.

The cows in Wisconsin turn out better than 18 billion pounds of milk a year, and from it cheese makers produce 586 million pounds of American cheese, 21 million pounds of munster-type cheese (supermarket lingo for muenster) and 20 million pounds of malted milk powder, which is enough malted milk powder to make a milk shake the size of Lake Erie, to be served with a generous wedge of cheese-covered Ohio.

"The market for cheese is simply immense," a skilled informant said. "The total cheese market is 2 billion, some odd hundred million pounds of cheese. The rate of consumption in this country used to be $5\frac{1}{2}$ to 6 pounds per person per year. Today it's like $13\frac{1}{2}$ pounds."

Basically, cheese is the solid portion (curd) of milk separated by bacteria from the liquid portion (whey)— precisely the stuff Little Miss Muffet was trying to choke down when she dreamed up her famous excuse not to have to finish it.

The custard-like curd is molded into slabs, which are turned until they shrink to one-third their size. The slabs are chopped into pieces and a small amount of salt is added to spark up flavor. The last step is curing, the duration of which determines flavor. From the same milk, treated with different enzymes, brick, blue, muenster, Swiss, limburger and cheddar cheese all proceed.

Aging cheese can take anywhere from days to months to years. A good deal of cheese is aged in caves, which are falsely suspected by the uninformed of being natural cheese mines. ("We've just struck a good vein of blue cheese, Harry, but we'll have to get it out of here before it turns lousy. Send another crew in.")

The Purity Cheese Company of Mayville, Wisconsin, bills itself as the "World's Largest Specialty Cheese Maker."

"We make more packages of cheeses per day than any other company in the world," the agent said proudly.

"How many packages of cheese a day do you make?" he was asked.

"We won't say that," he smiled.

One company sponsored a cheese-opinion poll, in which 1,229 persons were asked, "Do you like cheese?" 1,150 said, "Yes." Twenty said, "No." And fifty-nine said things like "Hop off!" or had not yet formed any opinion.

Cheese did handsomely well in the cheese-makers' poll, as any poll taker knows it better had, if the results are not to be suppressed. (One sound way of taking a poll like this is to stand in front of a Cheese of All Nations shop, stepping over to people who come out carrying bags containing at least three pounds and asking brightly, "Do you like cheese?" This weights the sample in the right direction.)

In the poll, 99.3 per cent of the respondents could identify American cheese; 79 per cent recognized roquefort; 26 per cent gruyere, and only 4.6 per cent kuminost.

A brochure given out at the festival said of a cheese buffet: "Your favorite flower arrangements add accents of festive color, candles evoke intimacy, and soft music makes the good taste of cheese and wine linger on." Exactly how soft music works to make the flavor linger longer is a mystery the cheese people celebrate but cannot explain.

The brochure says that at a White Wine Buffet the guests will "experience mingled mild and nutlike flavors, and reminisce life's deeper meanings." But at a Red Wine Buffet, "hearty tastes bring out the storytellers, and rolls of laughter." Put out the wrong bottle and you may get yocks where you wanted philosophy.

An English gourmet, Ernest Oldmeadow, once summed it all up pretty well when he said, "The only way to learn about cheese is to eat it." A good many guests were taking

Oldmeadow's route at the festival, acquiring facts by taste and knowledge by digestion.

A plump, elderly lady, jeweled to bedazzle a count and with blond hair, went from tray to tray, piling samples on a plate.

"I've got pucker-mouth," a man complained who had apparently tried a few too many varieties of cheeses.

One of the better cheese collectors had picked up eleven packages and was balancing them on two piles as he walked around. Some small slices and wedges had dropped to the floor and were ground under heel, creating a rather arresting design of smears on the carpet. It is a good idea at a cheese party to serve samples over linoleum, preferably in a marbled pattern.

The champion cheese sampler of the evening was Hy Simon, a photographer. "Don't get a hernia," a friend was saying to him as he stuffed a shopping bag with packaged cheeses and then jammed a few more wedges in.

At the bottom of the moving stairway, on the way out, the bag burst and the cheese spilled out over the terrazzo floor as from a cornucopia. Mr. Simon abandoned the pile and dashed off, returning later with two shopping bags, each of which he came close to filling from the spill.

The Return of a Big Loser

Reading time: 3 minutes, 57 seconds

It was the party of the hour. It was held last night, but its hour was about 1934, and it seemed that everybody who was once anybody was there.

The place was the Rainbow Room at the top of Rockefeller Center, and the purpose was to introduce the new-old *Liberty* magazine, which you are not going to be able to purchase for five cents.

It will go on the newsstands as "the nostalgia magazine," a quarterly, at seventy-five cents a copy, with the same old formula that lost millions for a succession of five publishers in the good old days from 1924 to 1950.

The new version is a sort of old-time capsule. It will publish "only the great old stories of the past," reprinted from photographic plates of the original magazine pages. "There's nothing new in it but the ads," one of the owners gloated, and they will be mixed with old ads, too.

In fondly recalling the past, the revived *Liberty* will enable us all to relive the wonderful years that brought us the Depression and the War and Prohibition. "It's all part of the nostalgia craze," said publisher Leonard Mogel.

This time around, its owners hope, the chronic money loser will turn a pretty profit. After all, as Mr. Mogel put it at the party, "there's no typesetting, no royalties or authors' fees." The whole editorial process requires the use of a still camera and a half gallon of developing fluid.

"*Liberty* Lives!" the magazine proclaims. Though the articles include the best, and some of the very worst, of the old *Liberty*, the revived version is printed on higher quality paper.

Some 850 people had crowded into the Rainbow Room by 6:00, a good many of whom did not appear to need old magazine articles to remind them of former days. They wore the faces of yesteryear.

"Whaddya mean 'what's new?' " a blonde of advanced middle years in flapper style dress (the invitations had suggested old clothes) bawled at a man who had the temerity to pose that question.

Alice Faye of the silver screen was there, still blonde and blue-eyed and slimmer than many had remembered her. Hildegarde came, as did Benny Goodman and Toots Shor and Patsy Kelly and Ruby Keeler and Thelma Carpenter and Connee Boswell. The Jimmy and Marion McPartland All-Stars puffed out gusts of pure Dixieland.

The Rainbow Room belonged to the *Liberty* era. It was opened in 1933, a mirrored chamber where ghosts still do the charleston, the lindy and the jitterbug. If the perfume of nostalgia had got any thicker in the room, there might have been a few asphyxiations.

The new *Liberty* leads off with an editorial by Bernarr Macfadden dated August 5, 1933, in which he attempted to rout the Depression with exclamation marks. "The Depression is Staggering," the editorial is titled, and its first line is, "Hurrah for President Roosevelt!" There were other "hurrahs" and an exhortation, "So do your part, dear reader—and then some!"

"It takes four hours, five minutes and eleven seconds to read this issue, not including the advertising," said Mr. Mogel, who had apparently added up the figures, based on *Liberty*'s peculiar habit of posting an exact reading time at the head of every article.

The issue resuscitates a short story by Mackinlay Kantor ("A Man Who Had No Eyes," reading time "5 minutes 2 seconds"), a series of predictions by H. G. Wells in 1931 ("What Will This World Be Like Fifty Years From Now?" reading time 11 minutes, 15 seconds) that, fortunately for us all, still has about eight years to run.

Benito Mussolini returns to give us his benign and stolid counsel on "Church, State and Sex" (reading time 10 minutes, 40 seconds, and not worth it) and there are articles by Adela Rogers St. Johns, Cornelius Vanderbilt, Jr., George Bernard Shaw, Leon Trotsky and Shirley Temple.

Mahatma Gandhi lets us in on "My Sex Life," a series of revelations about as prurient as a cup of hot Postum. ("In my dwelling I sleep at night surrounded by women, for they feel safe with me in every respect," he boasts.) Robert Benchley announces his co-discovery of Vitamin F, the vitamin responsible for the secretions of the salivary glands and the tear ducts. "Naturally, a diet consisting entirely of Guiana hen and wild Irish rice is terribly, terribly short on Vitamin F with the result that the natives are scarcely able to lick their lips, much less a long envelope," Benchley warns in a field report.

Liberty magazine was founded in 1924 by the late Joseph M. Patterson, publisher of the *New York Daily News* and Colonel Robert Rutherford McCormick, publisher of the Chicago *Tribune*. Its circulation reached 2,415,000 by 1930, but *Liberty* never caught up with *The Saturday Evening Post* and it never turned a dime for its founders, both hugely successful newspaper publishers. The chronic, year-in, year-out money loser cost them $14 million before they cheerfully traded it in for Macfadden's doomed tabloid, *The Detroit Mirror*.

At the end, *Liberty* fell into the hands of one Osborne S. Bond, the business manager of the *Elks* magazine. It lay dormant from June 16, 1950, until the hour when Mr. Mogel and others thought they spied gold deep in the played-out prose mine, and began the process of dredging it up.

Espousing the pleasures of life as seen in a rear-view mirror, Matty Simmons, the new editor, said, "I feel very strongly that we're living in the biggest period of nostalgia that this country has ever gone through, and there's good reason for it. Today and tomorrow look so miserable that it's much more pleasant to look at yesterday. I'm not a fortune-teller, but I can't foresee any quick solution to all our problems, and until there is one, people are going to go on looking fondly back at yesterday."

"We can go on for one hundred years," Mr. Mogel said. Mr. Simmons thought that too modest. "With 17,000 articles, we can run forever," he said.

The path to Hildegarde was blocked by a massive encumbrance. "I'm the champ-peen of the world," boomed Minnesota Fats, the pool genius. "I can tell you every pool room from here to Zanzibar." He said this with an evident sincerity that sent one immediately in the opposite direction to make an emergency phone call.

Before the party was over, Lillian Roth, star of long ago, was introduced, and Alice Faye received the "Film Star to Remember" plaque. Miss Faye appeared in movies from the early 1930s through the middle 1940s, starring beside such actors as Jack Oakie, Don Ameche, Warner Baxter, Al Jolson, Fred Allen, Dick Powell and Gregory Ratoff. She crooned her way through "Tin Pan Alley," "Little Old New York," "Hollywood Cavalcade" and "Alexander's Ragtime Band."

Alice Leppert was her real name and they were telling the story of her rise from a New York tenement to the top of the Hollywood heap in some of the gushiest pulp magazines of the 1930s, and a thriller it was.

Her early circumstances seemed to have "dedicated her to the most mundane of roles on life's stage," but she sought a more fabulous place for herself—not clerking from 9:00 to 5:00 in some five-and-dime—but as a star of the world of make-believe. There was real stuff in Alice Leppert, "good American stuff, warm and with a courage and a will-to-live-and-get-there as firm and sure as stainless steel," as Gordon Ardley wrote.

Sweet Alice wanted out of the dreary cycle of "macaroni for dinner four nights a week, with cabbage odors and cracked-plaster walls, in the greatest, cruelest city in the world, Gotham." She stood five feet two inches tall without her shoes in those days and weighed 112 pounds. She had blue eyes and a soft countenance.

Once, when at fifteen, she had tried, and failed, to land a job as a chorus girl in a Broadway kick line, she ran home to Grandma, who listened while Alice poured out her woe, "the tears of her disappointment dropping into the tea."

Salt in her tea, lumps in her throat, mist in her eyes, steel in her will, with "Destiny" stacking the cards in her favor, and her "Guardian Angel" clearing the way, Alice finally got up to "the Big Money."

And now there she was, thirty years later, standing behind the microphone at the party. "I'm thrilled to death," she said softly. "I love you all. Thank you very much."

Lox, Bagels, and Auld Lang Syne

Lox, Bagels, and Auld Lang Syne

There is something strangely affecting about the last hours of long-lived and famous City institutions. Everything goes on almost exactly as it has always gone on right up to the last minute and then suddenly it stops, never to be again. Whatever such places meant in the lives of many people is only a memory from that moment on. Perhaps it is the sheer ordinariness of such an occasion, observed with the knowledge that it is just about over, that gives it that quality. Or perhaps it is the courage of those who, knowing what is about to happen, go about their jobs almost exactly as they have always gone about them, performing their small functions to the end.

I watched this process in two places in the Times Square district, on the last night at Lindy's—September 21, 1969—and the last night at Hector's cafeteria—January 19, 1970.

The Night They Clobbered Lindy's

What kind of a day is today? It's the kind of a day that if you wanted a slice of cheesecake at Lindy's, you couldn't get it.

There hasn't been a day like it since before August 20, 1921, when Leo (Lindy) Lindemann opened the original Lindy's at 1626 Broadway, an all-night deli destined to occupy a special niche in American folklore.

You would have thought it would last forever, but Lindy's is dead. For some people the world changed a little bit at

1:30 A.M. yesterday, when the big neon sign out front on Broadway at Fifty-first Street was turned off and the revolving door was locked.

The last dish could have been, but wasn't, a heaping portion of sentiment laced with treacle. There were some who came in and left unaware that it was not an ordinary day. As far as they knew, there would be other days for fist-sized strawberries smothered in thick, whipped cream.

The final hours were without pretense, without fanfare or formal farewell. No tears were shed, no songs sung, and there was no last-minute seizure of generosity—no last round of drinks or blintzes on the house.

Faithful customers from decades past flocked in. There was a rush in the final hours, and many went away hungry because most of the food ran out.

"They came in here like locusts and cleaned us out of cheesecake and pastry for auld lang syne," said Christopher Rudd, night manager for twenty years. Even the big tins and trays in the desserts display in the window were emptied hours before the end.

A college-aged couple came one-two stepping through the swinging door.

"Got a table?" the fellow asked.

"Table, yes," Mr. Rudd said, "but what do you want to eat?"

"Cake and coffee," the man said.

"No cake," Mr. Rudd said. "Maybe a peanut butter sandwich?"

The couple left.

The waiters went about their business briskly, with their usual blend of insult and geniality. They scribbled their bills and collected their tips and swung out of the kitchen balancing cups of coffee in series up their forearms.

If there was a dominant theme at the end, it was a general agreement, among habitués and employees, that there would not be the likes of Lindy's again. Lindy's has been sold to Longchamps, to be transmuted into a chain steakhouse.

Toots Shor, a legend in the trade himself, was there almost until the closing. On the way out he rasped, with customary directness, "It's a crime to see a place like this being made into a *whatsiz*."

There was only one Lindy's. Its fame ran from Times Square to the Golden Gate and leaped the oceans (there is a Lindy's East in Hong Kong, but it is no direct relation). Lindy's special place in the history of fast-changing Broadway is fixed.

What other restaurant had a customer who ordered cooked spinach with a dollop of ice cream on top, a customer who insisted on eating only female lobsters, a clientele that ran from Bernard Baruch to Ben Blue?

What other place had an owner who used a functioning refrigerator as his only office (he liked the peace and quiet of it, and few salesmen lingered overlong in the chilled chamber) and who spoke of the murals on his walls as the "muriels"?

What other eatery had a biographer like Damon Runyon, whose observations in the place came out, half true, half made up, in tales of the unlikely characters who peopled Mindy's, which everyone knew to be Lindy's in the lightest possible disguise?

The last wedge of cheesecake was served at 12:30 A.M. by a waiter, Irving Weintraub, who had saved it in his locker for himself but served it to a favored patron, Sheldon J. Kravitz, who guessed he had eaten at Lindy's 1,500 times.

"I deserve it, the money I've spent here," Mr. Kravitz said.

A few of the faithful had both lunch and supper in Lindy's the last day, including Peter A. Baldo, a Manhattan clothing manufacturer.

Why had the place gone down? A waiter of long service

was asked, and he replied, "A number of things. A cause leads to an effect, and an effect to a cause, and a cause to an effect, and all of a sudden you're kaput." He jerked a thumb toward Max Stahl, the owner since 1962, who was greeting customers and leading them to seats. "Look at him," the waiter said, "hustling tables. That tells you something."

The locusts stripped the place of menus and ash trays and other mementos. There were conflicting claimants to possession of the last bagel. As a souvenir, a bagel is not much good. It is perishable and it also lacks proof. Anyone can hold up a bagel and say, "This is the last bagel from Lindy's."

Who knows?

The Horn of Plenty Closes

Hector's bustling cafeteria in Times Square, where one helping of strawberry shortcake could make an instant disaster out of a calorie-counter's diet, closed at 12:30 A.M. today.

The cafeteria, in the Claridge Hotel building on Broadway at Forty-fourth Street, is the last surviving Hector's, a New York institution since the early 1930s. Fifteen years ago, there were three Hector's in Times Square—at Forty-second, Forty-third and Forty-fourth Streets—and another just north on Broadway at Fiftieth Street.

The hotel is coming down to clear space for an office structure, the thirty-two-story National General Building. Hector's owners have no plans to open a new place.

Amid the clash of cutlery and the clink of china, Sidney Greenberg, the manager, raised his voice last night and said: "This store here we just hated to give up. We are the last tenants. It's a beautiful store, a terrific store, there's a lot of business. We tripled the size of it fourteen or fifteen years ago.

"People who came into the city from all over, from Pittsburgh and Boston, they used to come in, they loved our cake. They knew we had the best cake on Broadway."

"Good food and plenty of it," said Herman Esslinger, a long-time patron.

"Here you pay something, you get something," another man said, spooning up a valedictory wedge of chocolate cream pie. "Take a piece of cake—let me tell you, I couldn't finish it."

Hector's, no place for a dainty appetite, heaped plates high. For the price of an entree, usually under two dollars, the customer got soup, meat and two vegetables, bread and butter or hot corn bread, cole slaw and seltzer. The dessert counter, twelve feet long and three tiers high, was a gourmand's dream and a diet watcher's nightmare.

Jerry McCarthy, the night manager, rehearsed the construction of Hector's made-on-the-premises shortcake, "Two layers, cream in between, strawberries on top, cream on top of that, and strawberries on top of that." He recalled the night he sold "thirty shortcakes, fifty pieces each," or 1,500 portions.

The cafeteria, often crowded to its 290-seat capacity, was "a very, very quick store," serving 3,500 to 6,200 patrons a day, Mr. McCarthy said. A staff of ninety-eight kept it open from 5:30 A.M. to about 1:30 A.M. daily.

"There's a little woman, lived in a hotel, came here every morning at half past five," said Mr. McCarthy, who worked from 6:00 P.M. to 6:30 A.M. daily. "She liked the seltzer and she liked two spoons of marmalade. So every morning I'd set that out on a table just before she came in.

" 'What am I going to do?' she asked me. 'Well', I says, 'God is very good and He will take care of her,' " the night manager said. A slight brogue told his West Cork boyhood.

The pirogen (egg and flour shell stuffed with potato or kasha), and the cheese blintzes, the strudel and the blueberry cheesecake were sold out before midnight, and, somehow, Mr. McCarthy thought back to the air raid sirens of World War II.

"In two and a half minutes, I'd have all the lights in the house out, and they wouldn't even let me keep the pilot lights in the gas stoves lit," he said.

Mr. McCarthy kept a sharp watch on women with shopping bags. "Everything goes into the shopping bag—salt shaker, sugar pourer, knives, spoons, forks," he said.

There used to be several dozen take-a-ticket cafeterias of the distinctive New York style in the city, with long, heavily stocked food counters running nearly the full length of the premises, starting with a line of twenty-five feet or more of sandwich-making ingredients, then the middle coffee-and-sweets section, the steamtables with their meats and soups and vegetables and hot dairy dishes and great dollops of thick sour cream. Their number has dwindled to a surviving few in recent years, under the pressures created when rising costs cut high volume. One cafeteria went, at last, from ten cents to fifteen cents for coffee, because it cost more than a dime to serve a cup, and lost 300 customers a day immediately. Hector's was among the best of the New York cafeterias, supplying fast service, great variety and hearty portions at moderate prices. Now that the last one has been shut, patrons will no longer wait in that salivary moment of delicious indecision, torn between the peach cake with its thick glazed slices and whipped cream filling, the juicy strudel, the seven-layer chocolate cake or the oversized wedge of blueberry pie.

The Campaign for Jefferson Davis

There is a national election in which scholarship, literary excellence and fidelity to fact count. It is far less noisy than campaigns that fill the City with blatant rhetoric, but it is no less ardent.

Miss Desiree Lucille Franklin was born a long time ago in Augusta, Georgia. She was very old and very frail when I met her, but she was also eloquent and spirited. From an upper Manhattan apartment near the Hudson River she managed a vigorous campaign for the election of Jefferson Davis.

It would be wrong to surmise that Miss Franklin was out of her mind in acting as campaign manager for Davis a century or more after the Civil War. Candidates in this contest are required to have been dead at least twenty-five years.

While Miss Franklin worked to steer Jefferson Davis to victory, an elderly realtor and philanthropist on Fifth Avenue stumped for Lillian Wald. All over the country majors general, some retired, promoted the candidacy of Sylvanus Thayer, regarded as the founder of the Military Academy at West Point.

The election to the Hall of Fame for Great Americans at New York University used to be quinquennial—that is, it occurred every five years, falling as methodically on the decade and half decade as news falls on the hour and the half hour. But now it is triennial, and that is why the election in 1973 came two years earlier than the old schedule called for. Any citizen may propose a name for nomination. The name goes on the preliminary ballot if it is seconded in the senate at New York University. There are always more than 100 electors—138 in 1973—and a nominee must get a simple majority of those voting, close to 70 votes. Since not more than two or three nominees are likely to be elected at any

one time, the various campaign headquarters go into a frenzy of polite electioneering as the deadline for balloting approaches.

Bronze portrait busts of the winners are placed in a long, graceful, open, partly curving colonnade in the Greco-Roman style that crowns a bluff high over the Harlem River on the University Heights campus in the Bronx.

Strolling through the colonnade a visitor sees a precisely ordered series of columns with a sculptured bust on a pedestal beside each column, the graven heads looking inward and set against a backdrop of sky and trees. Under each figure there is an engraved plaque, with a bit about the man or woman written on it. Below the bust of Henry Ward Beecher are the words, "It matters little to me what school of theology rises or falls, so only that Christ may rise in all his Father's glory, full-orbed upon the darkness of this world." There are ninety-four busts in the eloquent display. They include Benjamin Franklin, Eli Whitney, Patrick Henry, Thomas Jefferson, Henry David Thoreau, Thomas Paine, Booker T. Washington, Susan B. Anthony, Ulysses Simpson Grant (he went in as a general, not as President) and Robert E. Lee.

Most of the electors are famous in their own right as university presidents, historians, public officials and "men and women of affairs." Those taking part in the 1973 election included Leonard Bernstein, Walter Lippmann, Margaret Mead, Jonas Salk, Hiram Fong, Grayson Kirk and Leonard Woodcock—an appropriately disparate lot.

One elector, Dr. Robert Gordon Sproul, president emeritus of the University of California was asked if he received a good deal of campaign material. "I certainly do," he said in a booming voice, by telephone. "I have within the last two weeks received about a dozen presentations telling me of persons I should favor and letters telling me something of the background of the men."

In a glass-walled office high in the United Nations Secretariat building, a United Nations official was asked if his role as elector was a busy one. "Oh yes, I'll say," he replied. "Undertaking this service involves a very substantial increase in correspondence."

Miss Franklin's efforts were among the reasons for this. She served as honorary president of the United Daughters of the Confederacy and as chairman of the Jefferson Davis Hall of Fame Committee. In 1960, General Thomas Jonathan (Stonewall) Jackson was elected to the Hall of Fame in a campaign for which Miss Franklin was the cochairman. Davis, whose role as President of the Confederacy eclipsed his earlier achievements, had run badly. He got one vote in 1950 and one in 1955. But with Miss Franklin managing his campaign, he got forty-four votes in 1960 and thirty-eight votes in 1965, far short of election, but quite a respectable groundswell nonetheless.

"My heart is so filled with this," she said in her soft voice at her apartment on West 136th Street. "I have been getting very beautiful letters from great generals, Omar Bradley, General Wedemeyer, Mark Clark and many others." She read off a list of generals and jurists. "You want any more of these?" she asked. "There are three pages of them." Every elector would receive one copy of each of the letters she had obtained endorsing the Davis candidacy.

Miss Franklin sat in her dining room, as fragile in aspect as the many pieces of porcelain and china she had so carefully arranged in the setting. Age had drawn her skin tightly over her strong features making them sharper. She wore a flowered hat, and the distant scent of magnolia seemed to drift into the air with her words.

Few Americans, she said, had served the United States "more selflessly, more dedicatedly, or more gloriously, or enriched it with a greater wealth of achievement" than Davis in his roles as "hero-soldier, architect, engineer, Congressman, Senator and Secretary of War." Whatever he was to anyone else, he was her great American. She set herself to secure his election, but after two stout showings, the Davis vote dwindled to seventeen. Miss Franklin was forced at last to retire from campaigning, and it seemed doubtful that he would make it.

Aaron Rabinowitz, the eighty-seven-year-old philanthropist, acted as the chief tactician in the successful campaign for the election of Lillian Wald. The founder of the Henry Street Settlement entered the Hall when sixty-eight ballots were cast for her in the 1970 election. In his exquisitely furnished office at 551 Fifth Avenue, surrounded by stained-glass casement windows and magnificent portraits, Mr. Rabinowitz recalled an incident before the turn of the century that helped make him a lifelong friend and benefactor of Miss Wald, the originator of the public health nursing profession.

"When I was twelve years old, I had an appointment with Miss Wald," he said. "She was in Rochester and unable to get in touch with me to cancel it, so she came down on the train and met me at the settlement. I was in charge of the refreshments and we discussed the kind of ice cream we were going to have—pink, or white, or green—and then she went right back to Rochester."

Recent campaigns have been conducted on behalf of Ernie Pyle by Senator Birch Bayh; for the bandmaster John Philip Sousa; and for John F. Stevens, esteemed as "the transportation engineer of all time" by men who know about that sort of thing, and put forward by Gregory S. Prince, executive vice president of the Association of American Railroads.

Mrs. Freda Hliddal, curator of the Hall of Fame, occupies offices at One Fifth Avenue and regards it as a high trust. "What people in New York City don't realize is that the Hall of Fame is a very substantial part of society in many parts of the country," she said, explaining why people get stirred up over the election.

"It is the Westminster Abbey of America, although we don't have the bodies—I don't want to be curator of bodies," she said.

Horace Greeley, Paul Revere and John Peter Zenger have failed in recent elections for the Hall, as has P. T. Barnum, but Jane Addams, Oliver Wendell Holmes, Jr., and Sylvanus Thayer have gone in. Fame is not always a foremost characteristic of those added to the Hall of Fame. The busts include those of Asa Gray (botanist), Matthew Fontaine Maury (oceanographer), Alice Freeman Palmer (president of Wellesley College), and Simon Newcomb (astronomer), while persons of far greater public reputation remain outside. The latest bust to be added is that of the physicist Albert A. Michelson, who went in on eighty-two votes, way over the number he needed to be elected.

The World of James Van DerZee

The world of James Van DerZee, which was once as large as all Harlem and as comfortable as the twelve-room brownstone in which he lived on Lenox Avenue, has shrunk to one room.

The photographic record he made of life in Harlem through nearly six decades was cut in half by losses resulting from his eviction from his home and studio on April 7, 1971. At least 40,000 prints and negatives are left, and the Ford Foundation has supplied a grant for the cataloging of this rich residue.

Mr. Van DerZee is the photographer whose work made up the core of the "Harlem on My Mind" exhibit at the Metropolitan Museum of Art in 1969. He is eighty-seven years old now and he lives in a crowded room on West

Ninety-fourth Street, surrounded by cartons of old prints and other memorabilia of his long career.

He had lived and worked in obscurity for decades in Harlem, known only to his clients, until the day in 1967 when a scout for the museum discovered his photographic trove. The exhibition brought his work to a far broader public. Two books of Mr. Van DerZee's photographs have since been published: *Harlem on My Mind* and *The World of James Van DerZee: A Visual Record of Black Americans*.

The irony of his situation is that he has been reduced to welfare assistance just when he has enjoyed a measure of fame as the most prolific chronicler of events both trivial and momentous in Harlem since 1909.

The drawers of the dresser in his room are largely stuffed with cracked old photos. The centerpiece is a table with two big wheels. It is piled high with mementos of his life, including a yellowed birth certificate showing him to have been born to John and Elizabeth Van DerZee at Lenox, Massachusetts, on June 29, 1886.

"My mother and father were maid and butler to General Grant," he said. "I didn't think much of it when I was young. Now there are so many questions I wish I'd asked them about that.

"My first wife thought I was a pretty smart fellow when she married me, but then as she got herself some education, I started getting dumber and dumber to her. Once she said something about my parents, and I told her, 'They didn't pick them out for the general because they were the dumbest Negroes they could find.'

"My mother was a woman of some learning. She knew the evening star and the morning star and she could show you the Big Dipper. She had a big medical book and she was pretty well versed on medicines."

The violin that he played professionally as a young man—with the John Wanamaker Orchestra—sits in a scratched old case in a corner and Mr. Van DerZee still takes it out and runs over the scales on it.

He gave up painting for photography a long time ago.

"I got my first camera when I was twelve years old," he said. "I won it as a premium for selling perfume. I kept running to the express office to see whether the thing was coming in a box or a barrel.

"One day it came. My heart began pumping and beating and my eyes began popping, and I was astonished and amazed when I saw it. The camera was a little thing, about $2\frac{1}{2}$ inches by $2\frac{1}{2}$ by 4 inches.

"Most of my people were painters and sketchers, and I was too, but when I found that with this little box all you had to do was open and shut it, well that saved a whole lot of rubbin' and erasin' and that sort of thing."

He was the only black child among his classmates at Lenox, he recalled, and he became the official class photographer.

Mr. Van DerZee opened his first studio at 109 West 135th Street. He later used locations at 2065 and 2077 Seventh Avenue, and settled for the last twenty-nine years of his professional life in the big house at 272 Lenox Avenue, from which he was abruptly evicted at ten o'clock one night by the city marshall in a mortgage foreclosure.

It was in that G.G.G. Photo Studio that Reginald McGhee, then working with the Metropolitan Museum, discovered the huge treasury of pictures of Harlem.

"When he hit my place, it seemed he hit a gold mine," Mr. Van DerZee said. "The museum spent several weeks picking out negatives, picking out prints. They only scratched the surface."

They found, among thousands of other things, Mr. Van DerZee's trick of superimposing vague images of dead men, their heads floating serenely in the sky, over pictures of their funeral processions, as though his camera had pierced to heaven.

"I made funeral pictures, you wouldn't know they were dead unless you were told," he said.

While the old man spoke his wife, Gaynell, came out of her half of the apartment, where she lives with several unhousebroken cats, and into Mr. Van DerZee's room. She is a rather scrawny woman and she stood behind the interviewer's chair and pointed a bony arm at him and spent the next fifteen minutes accusing him, in a voice choked with hatred, of sundry wrongs. "I had a house, Jim Van DerZee," she said, "and you lost it, Jim Van DerZee, and you don't do a damn thing about," and every time she said his name she pronounced it very carefully and put an extra twist of detestation in it. He sat there, without a flicker of emotion, looking at her with his large, round face and saying very little and finally she subsided, threatening to do him harm. The tempest was over.

Mr. McGhee and other admirers of the man's work have created the James Van DerZee Institute at 103 East 125th Street. The State Council on the Arts has supplied grants for its operation and the Ford Foundation has put up money for the exacting job of cataloging the photos.

Mr. Van DerZee had saved some money, but after the eviction, he and his wife were booked into a Bronx hotel by some well-meaning friends, at $136 a week. Out of it, he learned a hard lesson:

"If you have $1,000 and spend it $100 at a time, it's the same as having $10 and spending it $1 at a time. If I'd got out of that hotel sooner, I'd be better off now. I never thought I'd have to resort to welfare.

"It seems my worst days were my best days and the hardest times are coming when the best days are due," he said with gentle resignation. "If I can make it a few more years then I'll be one hundred, and everything will be easy then."

Wurlitzer Lives!

To stand alone, in dust and silence, in the organ pipe chambers high above the proscenium arch of the Beacon Theater is to hesitate to cough lest the ghosts of the place be awakened. It is an eerie eyrie, not what the mind imagined.

Instead of rank on rank of pipes, as erect and ordered as military cadets, it is a bewildering jungle of 2,500 pipes, some wooden, some metal, some as twisted as coiled serpents. The big pipes are a couple of stories high, the smallest are the size of a cigarette.

Among the pipes is a box containing some steel shot. Far below in the pit the organist touches a key. The box begins to rock, back and forth, back and forth, and the theater is filled with the sound of surf.

Most motion picture theater organs went silent with the advent of the talking pictures, but they are making a comeback now with old films as their foil. It was the prospect of enjoying just such an effect as the sound of surf that drew a large house to the Beacon the other night at premium rates.

By 8:00 P.M., seats in the second balcony of the 2,664-seat theater, on Broadway at Seventy-fourth Street, began to be filled by patrons who had paid three dollars each for admission to a "silent film and organ show." They climbed the stairs because they were expert enough to know that the best seats in the house, for this show, were way up there: The organ pipes play directly out to the upper balcony and the sound is the purest there.

They were, said Claud Beckham, co-producer of the show, "people who are sort of cultish about the theater organ." Scattered among the 1,200 patrons were people indulging a mild nostalgia for the 1920s, when they were young, or looking for an evening of film entertainment that would not jolt their sensibilities.

Jeff Barker was rippling out "Tiptoe Through the Tulips" on a small lobby organ at 8:07 when Buddy Rogers stepped out of the past and into the ornate rotunda of the Beacon. Out front the marquee advertised Mary Pickford and Buddy Rogers in *My Best Girl* with "Lee Erwin at the Organ." It was clear that the evening was going to have a special quality, the quality of innocence.

The Beacon is a huge old cavern—a grind movie house now, but an authentic film palace nonetheless, and one of the few survivors of that endangered species. The great stage is flanked by monumental plaster columns, murals as large as swimming pools, statues of sentries holding javelins, and various ornamental shields, spears, helmets and armored suits.

"It's supposed to be an Arabian shiek's tent or a sultan's tent or something Moorish," Mr. Beckham said. "Roxy built it, 1927 to 1929, as one of his film and stage show houses. It's got a real vintage Wurlitzer organ, and it's back in mint condition."

The organ was sunk twelve feet into the orchestra pit, but soon it came wheezing up by motor to stage level where it stood, painted all ivory with gold leaf edges and curlycues. Bass notes from the pipes were strong enough to send vibrations through the theater's faded red plush seats.

The old Wurlitzers are versatile behemoths. They can imitate an oboe, a flute, or a chamber orchestra.

"This is really quite a good one—a typical Wurlitzer of about twenty ranks," Mr. Erwin said.

The organ was ready for Mr. Erwin because a group of volunteers had worked on it, in a restoration project led by Bon Smith of the Allen Organ Company. "For more than two years we were here, working every single Friday night, from when the show closed until 6:00 A.M.," said James Moe, one of the team.

Joe Vanore poked his head forward from the second row and said, "We did it for the love of an old theater." He estimated that 1,875 man-hours had been put in on the job.

"Re-bulbing the chandelier was also one of our jobs," Mr. Vanore said. "It's twenty feet long, hung on long chains. It has a hand-cranked winch, and we had to crank it down inch by inch. It took us four hours to hand-crank it back up."

Mr. Vanore, a physical education teacher in Fairlawn, New Jersey, explained that to get to the pipes, "You have to walk above the main ceiling on an iron catwalk, then down a thirty-five-foot ladder. We have several people who won't go."

Since beauty of arrangement was no object in theater organ pipes some of the metal pipes are coiled around like a tuba to give them the necessary length for the sounds they must produce.

Mr. Erwin and Mr. Beckham spliced their names into Erbeck Associates and co-sponsored the show with the New York Theater Organ Society, whose idea is to "preserve the theater organ tradition."

"A lot of people associate silent pictures with a tinkly piano, but that's not right," Mr. Beckham said. Mr. Erwin regretted that even so exalted an institution as the Museum of Modern Art had contributed to that myth of overly selective recall.

In the silent film days, "only the smallest houses used pianos," he said. "The largest theaters in the big cities had full orchestras. Every major theater, even in small towns of 8,000 to 10,000 people, had a pipe organ. During the heyday of silent films, the Wurlitzer factory at North Tonawanda, New York, turned out almost one organ a day, pipes and all.

"For almost 1,000 years the pipe organ was a church instrument," the musician said. "With the advent of the motion pictures, the organ began to be something slightly different than it had ever been.

"There's a whole group of percussions in a theater organ—we call them the 'toy box'—that will give you horses hoofs, thunder, sirens, boat whistles, rain—a whole list of claptrap resources," Mr. Beckham said. "It's a sound effects machine as well as a musical instrument." Given the right nudges, the Beacon's instrument will supply castanets, tom toms, a timpani, sleighbells, tambourines, cymbals.

A kinura stop gives a sound "a bit like a bee in a bottle; it's a very snappy little stop," Mr. Erwin said.

Mr. Erwin's training was in classical music at the Cincinnati Conservatory and in Paris, and he played for silent films at houses in Cincinnati and Birmingham, Alabama, before going into radio and later television music. He regrets that "the life span of the theater organ was only about ten years.

"It came in about 1920 and by 1930 it was martyred to the talking pictures," he said. There used to be thousands of good ones in the nation, now there may be a few hundred left.

Mr. Erwin wrote an almost complete new score for *My Best Girl,* with "five songs, five sweet songs," Mr. Beckham said. They included a title song and "Just A Little White House," "When We're Walking" and "I'm In Love With A Girl Named Maggie."

"If you use old tunes to score a movie, the audience laughs in all the wrong places," Mr. Erwin said.

Of the recent release of old silent pictures, Mr. Beckham said, "The silent stars were deathly afraid that all they were going to be used for was poking fun.

"You could take a film like this and make fun of it all the way through, if you wanted to be a musical comedian," the organist said. "The idea is to simply write good music and always underplay it rather than to let it predominate."

My Best Girl is the third silent film that Mr. Erwin has scored. He did *Queen Kelly* and a Valentino film, *The Eagle.*

"I'm taking the Valentino picture on the road next month, going to Atlanta, Birmingham, Knoxville, Rahway,

New Jersey, Detroit, Buffalo, Rochester—there are good organs in all these places," he said.

His score for *My Best Girl* was complete the night before the showing, he said, except for the very end of the film, and he would have to improvise that, using a "reed choir" and various woodwinds.

Erbeck Associates had previously put on a silent film and organ show at the Beacon, featuring *Queen Kelly*, with Gloria Swanson appearing in person. It sold out, and the house was in a near panic when Miss Swanson came on the stage. "Big strong-looking guys in leather jackets would stand up and faint when she came out," Mr. Beckham said.

Buddy Rogers came on stage and said of Miss Pickford, his wife since 1937, "Mary doesn't like to move around much," thereby excusing her absence.

Mr. Rogers had a little patter to justify his appearance on stage so long after his own star had set. It included a tale about "a mean old woman who came over to me and said, 'I don't want to insult you, but I like to sit at home and watch the Late Show and watch your hairline recede.'" Mr. Rogers told the audience he had made two silent pictures before the talkies came in, and they were about to see one of them.

A spotlight blazed down on the organ and Mr. Erwin, a thin, trim man, addressed the four keyboards and began the overture, a medley of five tunes written in the popular-song style of forty years ago—his score for the revival of the ninety-minute romantic comedy. Suddenly it was 1927.

Old movie stars have the means more than most of us of being reminded how they looked and moved and glistened and exuded vitality in their firm-skinned youth, long before their slack-jawed senectitude. There must be something of pride in it and something of pain.

The picture came on—Sam Taylor, director—and left an edge of twenty to twenty-four inches on either side of the wide screen. It was a poor-little-rich girl story of love across the great divide of poverty and plenty, and love, of course, was going to win at last.

"About fifteen per cent of our audience are people who know and love the theater organ, and they bring about ten per cent with them," Mr. Beckham said. "Another twenty-five or thirty per cent are silent film buffs. Most of the rest are looking for solid, old-time entertainment without any need to dodge all the dirty words and find out whether they've got any redeeming social significance."

The audience was predominantly male, with most from thirty-five to sixty years old. Among them were church organists who regard it as a kind of wicked lark to hear the profane Wurlitzer imitate horses' hoofs and other sounds not fit for the pew.

When it was over, and the audience had gone, nine people just sat in silence in the first three rows and gazed at the old organ with a kind of dazzled fondness until the house lights went out.

Jazz City

His Father's Son

His name is Romano Mussolini and he comes, as he says, from "a musical family."

His father, Benito, loved classical music but the son is a jazz pianist, and the posters for his appearance at Town Hall bill him as "Romano Mussolini, a legendary name in Italian jazz."

Mr. Mussolini, who looks quite a lot like his father, has come to New York with his quartet, supported by vocalist Betty Curtis. He will play us some jazz and blues and some folk music and a few of what he calls the "evergreen songs like 'Stardust' and 'Summertime' and 'Over the Rainbow.' "

"The blues is the Via Appia of jazz, the Appian way," he said softly before his first performance in New York. "For me the blues is the base of all jazz and pop music."

The oldies on the program are songs that go back to the distant years when swing ruled the American pop music charts and his father ruled Italy with an iron hand and an upthrust jaw, as Il Duce.

Romano Mussolini is his own man, and he is also, unashamedly, his father's son. He talks about jazz earnestly, as a serious and able jazz musician would, and he talks about his father admiringly and rather fondly, as a son naturally would.

"My father loved classical music, symphonic music, especially Bach, Verdi, Puccini," he said. "He was once a critic of music in Milano. He played the violin, and he was very glad to see that I started to play the piano."

While his father handled momentous affairs of state, Romano fell under the influence, by recordings, of the jazz pianist Jelly Roll Morton.

"When I started to hear music it was in 1932 or '33," he said. "I was five or six years old. I started to play piano by myself, by ear, when I was fourteen years old. When I was young I spent eight, nine, ten hours a day on piano.

"For me the maximum in jazz at that time was Duke Ellington, and for me he is still the number one," Mussolini said.

As for formal education, "I studied at public schools always. We were always with the ordinary people. My family did not want us to be apart, superior." He earned a doctorate in business economics at the University of Naples in 1951 and held, he said, "many jobs in business, in construction." He gave up such work in 1956 to make his avocation, jazz, his trade. He has been a full-time professional ever since.

Of his program, he said, "We make a show. We start with blues and then we make a history of jazz through the years. We do songs of the twenties, complications of blues, songs by Gershwin, Cole Porter. We also have Italian folk music—Roman, Neopolitan and Sicilian songs—adapted in jazz music."

His quartet does "O Sole Mio" in a jazz beat. Mr. Mussolini seemed to be a quiet, relaxed, easy-talking man with a soft manner, both likeable and gentle.

"In Italy my name is well-known," he said modestly. "After the war I wrote songs with different names—Roberto Full, Ricardo Martelli—but since then I have always used my name. In Italy it has helped me."

Joe Valente, who set up the tour of eighteen concerts in twenty days, said, "At the beginning, I thought maybe he'll be difficult to book. But he was very, very easy." After Town Hall, Mussolini goes to Trenton, Boston, Chicago, Hartford and other centers that have significant Italian populations.

In earlier years, he had a passionate nature and when he fell in love with Gioconda Macuso, the daughter of militantly anti-Fascist parents, elders on both sides stood against them. It was Romeo and Juliet updated to 1948. The couple publicly threatened to leap together into the crater of the Elomeo Volcano if they were not allowed to pursue their love.

"When I was young, I like woman. I am Italian, you understand," the pianist said, putting emphasis where none was needed. He has since been married to, and separated from Anna Maria Scicolone, sister of Sophia Loren.

He plays one-night concert stands throughout Italy and takes nightclub dates. "I think only three or four more years in jazz maybe," he said. "I am not tired, but I am not so young." He is forty-five years old.

"I think to write music for the movies. I wrote five or six scores for movies—*Mr. X, Criminal, La Ragazzola.* Now I must write the music for an Italian Western. This is very popular in Italy, spaghetti Western."

Meanwhile, he said, his aim is to "play well, and to enjoy the public and to enjoy myself and to play with good musicians." He introduced his drummer and his bassist.

Because he can get along easily on three or four hours of sleep a night, Mussolini has a habit, of which his fellow players are not fond, of "driving six, seven hours before a concert, then give something to the public, then drive back six, seven hours," all without any rest.

"I die," the bassist said.

"Everybody loves Romano, because he is kind with everybody," the drummer explained. "Many people cry, seeing Romano, because he looks like his father—is the big sob story in Italy. Communists, too, love Romano."

The pianist has a lively interest in public affairs. "I know very well all the Italian politics," he said, "and I like very much to read books of history and politics, but I have never been active in politics. I keep apart because I think it's impossible to be a musician and a politician, and I like very much the music."

"My father was very kind, very gentle with me," he recalled. "Many times I spoke with him—not just personal contact, but political contact, historical contact. My father was one of the biggest journalists, and I asked him many questions.

"If I was good or not good at the school, he would sign what you call the report card. Many times the work was not good—was only five, four—and in Italy ten is the highest. It was terrible for me. My father would say, 'Ah, is not good, you make four, you make five!' "

Four years ago he wrote a book of remembrances called *Apologia of My Father,* as he translated it from Italian, and it had "wonderful pictures of my father, big pictures."

Was there anything his father had instilled in him as a boy that was yet in him? "Yes," he said immediately. "The sense of honesty, and to be good with people."

Dixie-on-Hudson

What is jazz?

"It's like trying to tell somebody what an apple tastes like," the clarinetist said.

Jazz can go from an exaltation of horns down to just the infectious snapping of two fingers by one man in the center of a great stage. It can be a driving, crashing, urgent sound—the cry of brass announcing the apocalypse—or a few light piano notes, dancing on the air like dandelion puffs.

A jazz festival is a multiplicity of musics thrown together in joyous, almost riotous, juxtaposition.

For more than a week, as host to the expatriate spree

called the Newport Jazz Festival, New York City has been the temporary jazz capital of the world, a Dixie-on-Hudson. Thousands of fans have heard jazz indoors, outdoors and on the river. A few held tickets for twenty or more events. They went to jazz sessions in the afternoon, in the early evening, late at night and after midnight. They rushed into restaurants for quick meals in the few free minutes between the "tag" in one hall and the downbeat in the next.

The most ardent partisans heard the sassy, raggedy beat of Dixieland, the more delicate rush of ragtime, the chant-like beat of Africa. They heard jazz variations on waltz music and on swing as well as passages drawn from classical and chamber music.

The purest jazz is an endless exploration of momentary moods. Sometimes a look of sheer happiness comes on other players' faces when a man is hitting a lick the way a lick should be hit.

That does not always happen. Some fans saw Stan Kenton point to a horn player for a solo at one concert, and they saw the player shake his head no. Kenton pointed again, and again the man shook no.

Later, a drummer at the stage door said, "Sometimes I really hit it right on solo, but sometimes I can't get into anything I like. I'll throw an eye at the boss and say, 'Get me out of this. I'm not saying anything.' "

At one concert, the audience let out its breath with pleased excitement when Hoagy Carmichael's "Stardust" was announced. But the first few bars of the melody merely marked the start of a trail for some musical meanderings of uncertain destination. It was its own composition, not Hoagy's, yet it was lovely in its own right.

"When we start, we never know where we're going to go," said Mel Lewis of the Jones-Lewis orchestra. "Where there's a written background, if what we're doing is going well, we'll skip it altogether.

"Generally a man plays as he feels," he said. "You can tell when a guy is happy or when he's depressed; it comes out in his music."

(This report is drawn from extensive hearings of the first two Newport festivals held in New York City.)

*

How big is a jazz festival? With more than 1,000 musicians playing in fifty-six events at thirteen sites for fees close to $500,000, the 1973 festival was the biggest jam session in jazz history, a winging such as the City had never known, upheld by a budget exceeding $1 million.

In seeking to turn the area into a virtual jazzeteria for ten days, George Wein, the founder and promoter, booked his concerts into Carnegie Hall, Philharmonic Hall, Shea Stadium, Radio City Music Hall, Alice Tully Hall, the Singer Bowl, St. Peter's Lutheran Church, a harbor ferry, the Wollman Amphitheater, Roseland Dance City, the Nassau Coliseum, Carnegie Recital Hall and the Apollo Theater. Jazz writers and historians knew of no similar event to match it in scope since jazz was born.

*

A late concert at Carnegie Hall had run loud and long. There was barely time for a bite to eat before dashing downtown to the Radio City Music Hall. It had to be taken in a place with piped-in music the quality of medium-grade broadloom, played by the yard. "Muzak goes to a jazz festival," one fan said sourly, hurrying through his bland snack, apple juice and egg custard, sixty-nine cents.

The midnight jam session at the Music Hall was a smashing sellout. When one ticket-holder got to the Music Hall's wrap-around marquee, he followed a long line stretching toward Fifth Avenue. He traced it all the way to Fifth, then north on Fifth and all the way back on Fifty-first

Street to the northern side of the marquee, a few yards from where he had started.

It was a Pied Piper's line, made up mostly of the young, shuffling three abreast. Ticket-holders were walking from July 3 into July 4 and some remarked on how costly the minutes became after midnight. At six dollars a mezzanine seat, jazz was being lost at a rate of $3\frac{1}{2}$ cents a minute.

*

Bill Chase and the Chase, a group specializing in cry-of-the-banshee-jazz, stood in an electronic forest of eight microphones at Carnegie Hall. Batteries of speakers were trained on the audience and turned up to full cry, and the players let go at full blast, a flat-out attack on the aural cavity at invasion force.

The performance was a kind of nightmare of orange clothes and screaming sounds. One player in this noisome pestilence looked something like a blond werewolf, with a veil of hair growing across his face. Even with both ears fully plugged by thumbs, their shriek came through at excruciating levels.

It was a relief at another session to hear quieter jazz, distinct little ripples and runs of notes, with butterfly endings. A piano, bass and drums skillfully put together a fine mosaic, working with a delicacy that at times suggested lacework.

*

A tidal wave of Dixieland jazz rolled up the Hudson River and nearly 6,000 jazz lovers were swept along with it. It carried most of them exactly where they wanted to go—to shores of ecstasy or isles of euphoria. The jazz of an earlier era came pulsing and throbbing from bands that have mastered the form—two from New Orleans and one from Copenhagen—in three consecutive cruises.

Close to 2,000 people boarded a truant vessel of the Staten

Island Ferry line for each unaccustomed run, from the Battery to Dixie, by way of the George Washington Bridge.

That impossible dream of the movie musicals, where everybody suddenly breaks out singing and dancing, came as close to happening in real life as it's ever likely to on the ride. The music spread a kind of rhythmic contagion among the passengers. At times they were singing, clapping, stomping, dancing, swaying or simply bobbing up and down.

A ship's officer, a policeman, a beer hawker and scores of passengers danced—or at least jiggled—in the aisles, on the stairways and on top of the seats.

On its first run, the 285-foot *John F. Kennedy,* newest boat of the line, tooted one toot out of its berth and then tootled up the river, churning up a syncopated wake. Cruise admission was five dollars a person.

"From five cents to five dollars in one day, with no squawks," said Jim Snyder, a deckhand, in a reference to the ferry's regular five cent fare. "Next time the city contemplates raising the fare, I suggest they give 'em Dixieland music with it."

Kid Thomas, the seventy-six-year-old trumpeter, led his Preservation Hall Band of New Orleans in jazz that went from sweet to sizzling. His men rotated with the Papa French Original Tuxedo Band, also of New Orleans, and Papa Bue's Viking Jazz Band of Copenhagen.

The members of the boisterous six-piece Danish combo proved to be fully as faithful custodians of the cadences and moods of the black jazz of the Old South as the men from Way Down Yonder. They had picked it up, they said, from American records.

The Vikings were a bearded, husky and barrel-chested lot to a man, but the trumpeter, Keith Smith, is British. He sang out, "Swing yo' baby to and fro/ Don't you ever let 'er go/ Ohhhhhh!" in a syrup-thick, deep-throated borrowed Bayou accent.

The styles of the three groups were broadly similar. They pumped out earthy jazz with more than a hint of wheeze in it and plenty of underlying razzamatazz. One man blew his horn into a brass derby. The players made the cruise a trip back almost to the origins of jazz, as they beat out some of the classics of the genre, songs like "Won't You Come Home, Bill Bailey," "Ol' Man Mose," "Basin Street Blues" and, inevitably and triumphantly, "When the Saints Go Marching In."

On the second run, an officer in white hat came down the steps from the bridge deck, bouncing at the knees at every beat. He held both hands upraised and was jiggling them in V-signs, and when he stepped off the bottom step he hooked an arm and swung around twice with a girl who was dancing there and walked off.

Three policemen stood near an exit. Two were erect and sober-faced, but one had succumbed. He was slapping his hands together and grinning in pure delight.

The beer counterman's uniform seemed just right for a Fourth of July—red and white striped shirt and a blue-banded straw boater. The music got to him, too, and he did a kind of dip-step in his narrow alley.

The metal ceiling made the second deck a brilliant acoustic chamber. But a Staten Island ferry is essentially a seagoing street car, filled with subway-like narrow benches, and the staid commuter vessel was not built to be a floating jazz hall.

The musicians sat in a straight line on a bench in a rather small seating area, in which at most eighty people could sit and about 250 more could stand tightly jammed together. The effect of the musicians on the passengers was essentially that of a magnet on steel filings. As many people as could crowded in close to the bandsmen. A few others caught fragmented glimpses through narrow openings; one slot gave a good view of the back of the piano player's head and the top of the bass.

Big amplifiers had been placed at points throughout the two upper decks. A few freeloaders held tape recorders near the speakers and reeled in a big catch of Louisiana jazz.

Anyone who had standing-space big enough for his footprints had room to stomp in. There were a few cleared spaces of two square feet where people could dance, mostly just shoulder and elbow action. "When I was in college and went to a dance, you had to know how to dance," a passenger said. "You had to know what the fox trot was. Now you just stand there and have the fidgets."

A fat woman with a Shirley McDimple hair-do, all curls and blonde, turned her saucer eyes toward heaven on the wah-wah-wah sounds and made her frame shake like a tub of yogurt. Some loud and beery fellows of advanced middle age were more interested in the sounds of their own voices than in the sounds of New Orleans.

The Louisianans, all elderly blacks, sat in their straw hats, eating ham and cheese sandwiches and sipping beer, while the Copenhagers played. One of them, Albert Burbank, said he had been playing for fifty-three years. He let loose on his b-flat clarinet at the Paddock Lounge on Bourbon Street for twelve years, working six nights a week for six hours and on Saturday for seven hours. "I was born in New Orleans—never did move out of the seventh ward either," he said.

Mr. Burbank came of musical age during World War I. "I used to whistle so good. I could whistle anything," he remembered. "I always did love the clarinet, but the good men were all too busy to teach me, so I took some lessons with Big Eye Louis. Sometimes it got so there wouldn't be a job in a month." He has been working at Preservation Hall the last four years, a steady job that pays a steady wage.

"Saints!" "Saints!" the crowd cried near the end, and "Saints" it was! The musicians got out of their seats and led an uproarious march through the aisles. Passengers fell in after them. Almost all were singing or clapping, swaying and marching, and some were whistling, behind the band. It was a show-stopping apogee, as the players knew it would be.

Some passengers were so absorbed in the jazz that they had only the vaguest idea of where they had been. "I wasn't even aware of moving," a woman said. "I was just watching the show all the time."

"Let's go again," a young woman said to her escort at the end of the second cruise. "Don't you think twice is enough?" he asked.

*

Charles Kivvi Helleman, "The Count Basie of Basel"—a title quite gratuitously conferred on him by other jazz fans in spite of the fact that he can't play a note—had come from Switzerland to attend the festival. His interest in jazz was awakened as a teen-ager and he owns about 500 jazz records. He modestly explained that his fluency in English had come from his vocation as a motion-picture projectionist, "because we play the original sound track with American B-pictures with subtitles."

He had learned English by watching "Dracula, Frankenstein and Gene Autry," he said, naming them in descending order of menace.

*

The Alvin Jones Quartet was on stage, and Alvin Jones went from long calms to short storms on the drums, as the tempests seized him. The globe-shaped Wein, no foot tapper, was standing in the wings watching with stony mien. He is egg bald on top. He listens to jazz standing stock still, very impassively. But a long drum solo by Jones finally cheered him up.

A singer undertook to present "The Legacy of Bessie Smith," one of the most famous of the jazz and blues singers. She did not lack the equipment for it. The least that could be said was that she did it from an amplitude of voice and a plenitude of bosom.

*

"It's a change for us to be able to play for more than thirty seconds at a time," said Bobby Rosengarden. His television studio band shared the platform at one concert with another television band and the Jones-Lewis Orchestra of Manhattan. "There are so few bands left in the world, they went around and got television bands," Mr. Rosengarden said.

"These guys are the unsung heroes of jazz," he said of the players. During the performance, particular attention was drawn to Al Klink, a saxophonist, long a brilliant but sidetracked jazz player. Klink, with a sharply cut beard and rimless glasses, looked like Freud. He was sitting in.

"Al's a marvelous musician," Mr. Rosengarden said. "He was in the original Glenn Miller band. He was my idol, and here he is playing for me." In his regular job, with the Tonight Show orchestra, Mr. Klink is a builder of musical bridges, running from quips to commercials, and of musical tunnels that go under a station break and come back up on the other side.

"All men are not created equal musically," Mr Rosengarden remarked after the show. He was asked why his extremely polished music was played less stridently than that of most big bands. "Anybody can play loud," he said, "the hard thing is to play soft."

He was followed by another television band, with Billy Taylor at the piano, who introduced "I Wish I Knew How It Feels to Be Free," a clear note of Old South Gospel twisted with jazz. The speed of jazz pulled hard against the slowness of yearning, putting a fine tension in the music. The applause had a liquid quality—it flowed easily and often at the session.

Before it is over a jazz session discloses everything, hides nothing, holds nothing back, tells all, or very nearly all.

*

The Jones-Lewis band, indigenous to Manhattan, had made a triumphant swing through Russia. Three young men with Afro bush cuts were sitting near an old man with fleece white hair—Grandfather Jazz. The band is made up of eight blacks and nine whites; the only discrimination is that of the sound a man makes. They played in an intimate classical style, then switched to a big band focus, Chicago style. They split the air with "Don't Get Sassy."

Just to see Roland Hanna at the piano was worth the price of a seat. How Hanna coaxed humor out of the keyboard, one listener did not know, but he had and the audience laughed in delight at what were, after all, extremely subtle musical suggestions. On solo, he did interpolations, changes of pace, variations on form and explored one-finger melodies.

All of his humor flowed through his fingers. "He plays with much humor, yet he is one of the most serious piano players I know," Mr. Lewis said. "He'll go into a very heavy creative thing, then all of a sudden out of the blue he'll drop into a pixieish way of playing. It's not an act at all."

Each band that came on seemed to be a little better than the last, and the first had been superb. When it was all over, all three bands had rearranged the air, but none had rearranged it as riotously as Jones and Lewis. The first two bands had got away, almost by surprise, but when Jones-Lewis finished, the audience came to its feet and hollered for more.

"It's all emotions," Mr. Lewis said afterward. "It's music and emotions. It's at-the-time. All the elements have to be in place—the audience, the hall, the acoustics, the players. We had a small but very emotionally strong audience. We reach them and they reach us, so anything can happen. It can go exactly the other way."

The Jones-Lewis band is a brilliant aggregation with a strong reputation in the trade. "Economically, it's been a losing proposition," Lewis said. We've had to take money out of pocket to keep together. We all do some studio work and small group work, to keep us going. Jazz is the only art form America has given to the world, yet it's treated second-class here. But in Europe it is given great respect."

*

After the concert, Harold Mayburn, a free-lancer, was standing with nine other players out by the mailboxes at Broadway and Sixty-fifth Street, "unlatching," as one of them put it.

"We got men among jazz musicians who could set down and write a symphony and then play it," he told a stranger. "Composing—that's what playing a solo is—spontaneous composing." He said that medicine, law and music were similar in that they could more or less engage a man's thought all the waking hours in a day.

What is jazz?

"It's like trying to tell somebody what an apple tastes like," a clarinetist said, explaining why he could not readily define jazz.

"Playing jazz is like learning how to speak a language really," another man said. "Once you know how, you can speak it."

"If you like it, that's what counts," still another said.

Listening to jazz is its own best explanation. Jazz men sometimes have a language of their own, like the scat singer who came out and let go with, "Bob-a-deeba-aba-loob, oh, man! A-doobee-doobee-doobee-doobee-do!"

In jazz everything depends upon what the player is doing at the moment. The best of it is like a gorgeous sunset or a particularly lovely cloud formation; it is there for the moment and then it is gone. At other times there will be other cloudscapes, and yet it is never likely to be quite the same again.

*

The dean of jazz men in Australia, Don Burrows, left the stage of Carnegie Hall to long applause. He is a wiry man with the deeply bronzed face of a cowboy and, while he was packing his instruments backstage, he talked through tears.

"If I never play another note again . . ." he said, choking off.

"It might seem a long way to come to play for forty minutes," he remarked, "but that's not the point. You might go to an Olympics game and make only a couple of jumps. It's the kind of a jump you make that does it."

His jazz style was highly original, not imitative of the American sounds. A priest described it as "some Australian snake-charming jazz"—a different idiom, cool and slightly dissonant and highly-pitched, with an Eastern hint in it. It was, at the same time, distinctly more melodic than most atonal jazz.

"The last thing I wanted to do was go out there and sound like another American group. So what?" Mr. Burrows said. He could recall the time when "the standard by which my performance was gauged was not how much I sounded like Don Burrows, but how much I sounded like Benny Goodman."

"It's only latterly that we've been able to throw off that shackle," he said.

Mr. Burrows was recently made an M.B.E. in the Most Excellent Order of the British Empire, an honor that rewarded his years of fidelity to the cause of jazz in Australia far more than money ever had.

It has been a thin life, with long stretches of no work, and years of playing in a dark subterranean hole, the El Roco coffee lounge in Sydney for eight dollars a night, until it was turned into "a pizza joint" without live jazz. "We've stuck together for thirteen years," he said of his quartet, "and we've made no money at it." His men have picked up some cash doing "studio gigs" and "playing chase music for juggling acts" on television shows.

"See this little b-flat school flute?" Mr. Burrows said, before packing it away. "I got it for $1.85 when I was a kid. I was determined to stand here today and play that little flute in Carnegie Hall. Without that, I might have been a soda jerk."

The jazz situation in Australia is "terribly fragmented," he said. "You'll have a man in Sydney who's great on tenor saxophone, and maybe there's a great drummer in Adelaide, and a great piano player in Perth, which is 2,000 miles away." It's hard to get them all together.

"We're all self-taught and we play strictly by ear," he said. The Sydney Conservatory of Music, "the seat of classical music in Sydney—it's like your Juilliard," invited him to come in and set up a jazz faculty. "Not that I by any means think that you can teach anybody jazz," he said. "You've got to have it first."

There is a reason why jazz has lacked the more formal recognition and institutional status that has come to opera, symphony and chamber music, Mr. Burrows thought.

"Jazz is not a What, it's a How," he said. "If it was a What, you could teach 'em a What, but you can't teach 'em a How."

That, he guesses, is why jazz is far more easily caught than taught.

*

When the last sweet notes of his first refugee Newport Jazz Festival in New York floated into the air, George Wein knew that he would never return to the uncertainties and tumult of its place of origin at Newport, Rhode Island.

Wein, whose life as a jazz festival promoter was full of

hazards in New England, fled the disruptions of Rhode Island for the safety and serenity of the City. He did so after hordes of young people had swept down from their perches on a hill overlooking—and overhearing—the festival to rip down yards and yards of chain-link fence; 15,000 of them swarmed onto the field, cutting the series off two days early and, indeed, ending its eighteen-year stand in the resort city.

In New York City, police protection for the festival proved to be about as necessary as sheet music at a jam session. At Lincoln Center, a quartet and a trio of policemen stood—the quartet near the fountain, the trio close to Philharmonic Hall—with nothing to do but stand and chat.

Eddie Condon, an old warrior of jazz who came out of retirement, played in the first midnight jam session in New York. "It looks like he guessed right," he said of Wein's City schedule.

Festival attendance surged from 70,000 in the later years at Newport to 102,000 and 133,000 in its first two years in the City. "This town has been so wonderful to me," Mr. Wein said, "that they'd have to run me out of here on a rail before I'd leave."

*

Jazz men, accustomed to adversity, blew lilting choruses of joyous affirmation across the face of a sodden afternoon in Central Park. Cool zephyrs of jazz with occasional gusts of up to about eighty-five miles an hour, came with heavy bursts of rain on a small audience in the Wollman Amphitheater in the southeast corner of the park.

Gerry Mulligan, standing in front of a seventeen-piece band, sent the first enunciations of brass into the air a little before noon in a diverse and crowd-pleasing program that brought the drenched audience to its feet at the end whistling and cheering.

It was with a hope of recapturing the approximate ambience of the outdoor concerts at Newport, short of the riots, that Mr. Wein had booked the festival into the Wollman arena for seven generous noontime sessions, each of nearly four hours duration.

But it rained on and off, brief deluges descending with tropical suddenness, throughout the concert. The fans raised and lowered their umbrellas in appropriate accompaniment, and one put a bright streak into the afternoon, spinning a six-color model into a painter's-palette-blurrrrr.

Skyscrapers looming above the tree-rimmed amphitheater were wrapped in silken mists. Fans coming in had to wade through ankle-deep puddles or step up and walk on bleacher slats. Thunder answered the attestations of the players several times. As if to mock the occasion, the sun broke through a few minutes after the concert was over.

Several select committees of the great congress on jazz conducted hearings through the dreary afternoon.

"The medium is the message," Mr. Mulligan told the crowd after leading off the program. He got deep inside one listener by delivering a slow and sinous, and profoundly nostalgic version of "Waltzing Matilda" in solo. If the message was not misread, its mysterious expressiveness—every long-held note imparted a sense of poignant loveliness—came from a longing for something that was missing. It was almost as if, after the funeral was over and the others had left, a lover had gone back alone to a fresh-made grave to play one plaintive and wailingly tender song.

When Mr. Mulligan left the stage, he was followed by Margie Joseph, a lithe and winsome young singer from New Orleans. She was followed by the festival's founder, George Wein and his own Newport Ensemble—Mr. Wein belonging to the very select company of impresarios who can artfully do the very thing they so skillfully promote. The producer's rotund form hunched over the keyboard and his fingers danced, and James Spaulding came forward and made his flute sound like an inspired tropical bird. The Charles Lloyd Quartet and the Gato Barbieri group took off from recognizable idioms and explored some unfamiliar, beguiling zones of jazz.

The variety of the program, with its Latin, soul, rock, modern and Eastern themes, was an index to the disparate tonalities of the whole festival. The roster for the 1973 festival sounded like a hall of fame of jazz, including Cozy Cole, Eddie "Lockjaw" Davis, Gene Krupa, Illinois Jacquet, Roberta Flack, Dizzy Gillespie, Kid Shiek Colar, Eubie Blake and Wild Bill Davison.

In a lineup running alphabetically from Abdullah and the Aboriginal Music Society to Reggie Workman and Josef Zawmul, names such as Big Joe Turner, Doc Cheatam, the Brotherhood of Sound, Sun Ra, JuJu, Max Kaminsky, and Natural Essence helped at least to indicate how spaced-out the offerings were on the musical spectrum.

As a man who has managed to put jazz into the fanciest concert halls, Mr. Wein shares a memory with many of the older players of days when jazz was too often confined to low dives and saloons. As he would tell one audience in Philharmonic Hall:

"When I was fifteen years old, I used to play in joints, and I mean joints—places like the Blue Moon Cafe in Lynn, Massachusetts, and Jack's Cafe in City Square in Charleston. You had to know songs, and that was it. If you didn't know songs, you were nowhere in those joints."

The joints have become a lot sweller since George Wein began booking jazz into houses that match his estimation of its stature as an art.

*

It was the night of the "Thirties Ball." Members of the generations born in the first half of the twentieth century—some in their vibrant twenties, others in their heel-kicking seventies—flocked to the Roseland Ballroom, where three big bands with plenty of brass set them spinning until they became a nearly homogenous whorl.

Half an hour before the shindig was to begin at 9:00 in the huge dance palace on West Fifty-second Street, a long line reached almost to Eighth Avenue. The flashing neon of the marquee tinged faces and dyed clothing as the generations shuffled off Fifty-second Street and into the 1920s, past a ticket taker who evoked the era by saying, "Hold your stubs, please—there'll be a door prize."

On the way in, they passed the Wall of Fame, made up entirely of old shoes—the actual dancing shoes of people like Mae Murray and Tony DeMarco and Adele Astaire.

As a time machine set for the 1930s, Roseland is practically perfect. It is a kind of living museum of the big band pop culture that flourished then. It has succeeded in defying the changes that have blighted that culture and in keeping the tradition alive.

Among the crowd there were some gorgeous old dolls who had made castles of their hair, standing very straight and obviously belonging to the age and to the place. Decades were hidden under their layers of pancake makeup. There were also much younger dancing doll types, all dimples and fresh frozen smiles.

They had come—some to dance, some just to listen—to hear the big, bold, brassy sounds of Woody Herman and his "Thundering Herd," of Duke Ellington and Count Basie at nine dollars a person. Though their ethnic and age variety was great, they were predominantly a nice crowd from the working middle class, people who believe in bowling alleys, beer, baseball and ballrooms.

Roseland is structurally as square as a freight depot, but long strips of plastic curving down from a central point in the ceiling give it a tent-like appearance, and the whole place is suffused in a low reddish glow. The centerpiece of the ballroom's decor is an electrified red, white and blue picture of Old Glory that hangs over the band stage, full of flashing stars that blink on-off-on-off, until the house goes dark.

The ballroom seemed to be crowded at least to its 3,450 capacity by the time a young man in a white linen suit came in, escorting a girl in a tight gown of flaming tropical orange. At times even a dance floor said to measure 10,000 square feet was crowded to the density of an IRT subway platform at the rush hour.

Even at that, Woody Herman had the place jumping by 10:00 P.M. The jammed floor was full of shoulder and high-knee action, head-under-arm turns, arms'-length spinaways and spinbacks—to use strictly nonterpsichorean terms. Later, when some couples drifted out and space loosened up some, a few dancers really let go with loose-jointed, swivel-hipped, limp-wristed, free-form flying.

A man of advanced age with a gray and graven face had danced for a while with a woman of his own age, half-stepping in an area about four feet square, until she retired. A few dances later he was out there fast-stepping with a slender chick forty years his junior, but evidently more his speed. She was dressed in a half-blouse and a mini-skirt.

"How do you like it?" an old buck with silver hair was asked.

"Heck, I expected to come in here and see Ruth Etting sitting up on the piano," he said.

An eye-catching young couple in their early twenties headed for the door. He was short and sharp-bearded, compactly handsome, and she looked as fresh as a meadow at daybreak. Why had they come to a Thirties Ball?

"Change of pace mostly," said John Gross, a college senior.

"My mother wore this dress in the 1930s," Lynn Urstadt said, before flowing out in her silver lame gown.

One couple came dancing off the floor and went dancing right out the door.

The Roseland tradition is a venerable one. The ballroom is a place where sweet sixteeners from the 1920s can renew the illusion of their youth. A telephone call to Ade Kahn before the ball turned up some vital facts and some pretty unvital ones, too.

"This would never have happened if there hadn't been a college coed named Dorothy Faggen, who loved to go dancing in 1916 in Philadelphia," he said, still struck with the continuing wonder of it all, "because her now husband, then boyfriend, Lou Brecker, opened the first Roseland for her sake. In those days, college kids who wanted to go dancing had to go to some dismal holes, places with benches around the walls and a bulb hanging from the ceiling. He figured if somebody put a little decor into a place—decor and soft lights and sweet music—it would be a success. That's what made him a millionaire."

The original Roseland opened in Philadelphia. "He got the name because a fellow who lived in his sweetheart's apartment building told him, 'If you have a name from nature, you'll have a theme to decorate with.' It's lucky he didn't call it chrysanthemumland, because the decorations on the neon lights would cost us a fortune."

Roseland opened in 1919 at Fifty-first Street and Broadway, surrounded by brownstone houses. The place ran continuously until 1956, when the owner moved a block north and took over the Gay Blades skating rink at the present site.

Roseland is particularly proud of its agency as a social catalyst. "From 1919 on it's become a dynasty of romance," Mr. Kahn said. "You'll notice when you go in the door, there's a roster of over 500 married couples who met at Roseland. We have sworn affidavits from all of them. Not only that, one couple met here and got married, and their daughter met *her* husband here, too. Those couples would never have met if this hadn't been here. You can figure that.

"You don't have to listen to all this," Mr. Kahn said, "but if you hang up, I'll keep talking."

He explained that the owner named the place Roseland Dance City "because he hates the name 'dance hall'. It's a ballroom. He figured if he named it that, people wouldn't call it Roseland Dance City dance hall—it's too much." Roseland is open every night except Monday, usually from 7:00 to a little after midnight, with mid-afternoon openings on Thursdays, Saturdays and Sundays. The restaurant at the west end of the dance floor seats 600 people. On Sundays families come in the afternoon, stay for dinner, and dance again after dinner.

"On the coldest winter night, when you've got a blizzard and you figure people would be crazy to leave their homes, you get 200 or 300 in here," Mr. Kahn said. "Some people are religious about dancing. Somebody pointed a woman out to me and said she's your champion customer, because she's here every night. So I went over and said, " 'Are you the champion customer?'

" 'What makes you ask that?' she asked.

" 'They say you're here every night of the week.'

" 'I'm not here on Sunday,' she said.

" 'Why not?' I asked her.

" 'I figure I should spend one night at home with my husband,' she said, 'and he doesn't like to dance.' "

A little after midnight, George Wein called the house to order and drew a stub out for the door prizes, $200 record sets.

"It's a Ticketron stub—7-0-2," he said carefully. "Does anyone have that ticket?"

"Yeah," a young man with curly blond hair called out.

"Oh, wait a minute—it's a wrong number," Mr. Wein said, but the young man cried, "Wait!" and rushed up front. He came back a little later, prizeless.

"A lot of other people had it, too," he said of the number. "It was the date."

The suave, handsome, empty faces of professional dance teachers came out in a fashion show of dancing models. The men seemed too perfectly good looking, the women too statuesquely beautiful to be warm-blooded creatures. They looked like Lord & Taylor window mannequins briefly touched with life.

The music went on—"Basin Street Blues," "Hello, Dolly," "April in Paris." A woman about thirty gave a stranger a good crack on the elbow and said, " 'Scuse me—do you know which band is playing?" through her gum.

"This has got to be one of the funkiest places I've ever seen," Debbie Pearl told her escort, Henner Wachs. Miss Pearl, a 1972 graduate of Barnard College, paused to explain what magic the occasion held for her. "I had a sense of feeling just like my mother tonight," she said. "I just kind of flipped back and felt this is the way it must have been.

"It was fun just to sit there and watch them bouncing. It's wonderful that they can come back here and bounce, when you think of all that's gone on. I was bouncing the whole night, really grooving."

Del Markoff of Westport, Connecticut, came strictly for the music, and the evening took him back to the night of the Harvard-Dartmouth-game ball in the Somerset Hotel in Boston in 1938, when he was a student at the Harvard Graduate School of Business Administration.

"The Duke was there that night," he said, "and the place was filled with kids and they were just listening to him mostly and they wouldn't let him go. They were really responding, and the Duke stayed there and played all night. He would do that for his own people, but he wouldn't do that for a white college crowd, but that night he did."

At least 500 people crowded close to the Roseland stage and watched the musicians play. Sonny Payne, the drummer, did his juggling act, throwing his sticks in the air, doing a spin-and-catch behind his back, and never missing a beat. "You see that?" Mr. Markoff said. "They're not dancing. They're just standing there mesmerized. They're all mesmerized."

At 1:30 A.M. it was over and the people went out, hundreds more among the 56 million admissions that have been counted since 1919. Having discovered that there "is a pot of gold at the end of the mambo," Mr. Brecker, the founder, owner and impresario, barred the twist and the frug from his premises as anti-romantic.

"When you dance miles apart, you're not even spending the evening together," he explained. "You have to send smoke signals up when you want to say I love you."

*

The Newport festival hit on a hugely successful formula in "A Jazz Salute to the American Song." The concert filled Philharmonic Hall, and if credit is given where it is due the editors of the Oxford University Press would have to take a bow. They published the book on which the concert was based.

Jazz campaigners of the first rank—Dave Brubeck, Mabel Mercer, Earl Hines and Jimmy McPartland among them—found their stomping ground in the rich fields of American popular music from the first five decades of the century. The idea was taken directly, if rather loosely, from the 536-page book, *American Popular Song: The Great Innovators 1900–1950,* by the composer Alec Wilder. The concert was a happy union of all-star jazz players and the works of such composers as George Gershwin, Cole Porter and Irving Berlin.

It was a departure in form for the festival's producers. Mr. Wilder, who sat anonymously in the audience, said afterward, "This is the first time any jazz festival has ever considered song that I know of." Several of his songs were played by Gerry Mulligan and Marian McPartland as the concert finale, and Mr. Wilder was grateful that his melodies were not improvised out of existence. The composer is at home in the classical as well as the popular idiom—he put both in partnership in his octets—and his "It's So Peaceful in the Country" is an enduring jazz standard.

"I was very impressed by Mr. Mulligan playing my tunes exactly as they were written before he improvised. Then he worked his way back through a brilliant improvisation to the original tune again," he said. "He was the only one who did that tonight."

That is the sort of thing that sets such jazz players as Mulligan and Joe Wilder and Stan Getz and Zoot Sims apart for a composer like Mr. Wilder. He knows by experience that to trust jazz music to most classical players is disastrous, while to trust written music to many jazz players is rather like handing a ballet choreography to a basketball player and expecting him to go by it.

"When you write legitimate music for jazz men, they're interested," the composer said. "But only a few carry it through with the control and responsibility of concert musicians.

"Many of them are marvelous improvisatory jazz players, but they get terrorized when they are up against a concert situation in which they can't fall back on improvisation to cover their nervousness when they're faced with nothing but written notes. They don't know how to shift gear. It's not that they're not able; it's purely a psychic problem.

"In some jazz, you write a few notes, and just leave a lot of open spaces, and in those open spaces they have their own security."

It also works in reverse. If jazz music is given to a concert player "it will sound so square unless he happens to love jazz," he said. "You cannot write a jazz phrase down on paper. It's absolutely impossible. It's an impulse, it's a way of phrasing, it's a way of attacking a note, a way of releasing a note, letting it go."

All a composer like Mr. Wilder can do is put the music down and mark it, right at the top, "jazz style." Then he hopes the playing of it will not be "a disaster."

The question, of course, is who you give it to—jazz or concert players. "Some of the jazz men, if you write an absolutely legitimate movement, make it come off as a kind of funky, raunchy misplaying" that is an acute embarrassment. "It's rare when you get the combination in one man," he said.

"The ideas in jazz are so loving and so tender and so witty that I tried to employ thematic material taken from the jazz area and put it in my music," he said. "I don't claim it's jazz—it certainly isn't, because once you make it formal, it ceases to be jazz."

Once he had an unusual opportunity to demonstrate the just affinity between jazz and classical music. He wrote a jazz quintet and a woodwind quintet "for a jazz group and a legitimate group" to play on a television program. They occupied two platforms in the studio. At first the camera cut from the concert group to the jazz combo and back. "Then they interlocked, these two. They kept moving closer and closer together until the camera locked them into one picture." As the jazz group infiltrated the concert group "they became absolutely one piece," he said.

"I love jazz players because they play with more passion and vulnerability," the composer went on. "They have a kind of emotionalism that, except in the case of the great concert instrumentalists, I seldom hear.

"In the ballad playing of a great jazz man, there is something that happens with no other kind of musician. The jazz player reveals more of himself and therefore more about life than any legitimate soloists, except the greatest of them.

"Improvisation is a miracle to me, but it's second nature to jazz men. They can slip into it without any effort at all.

"With Mulligan, I turned over one entire movement in a piece, except four measures which I wanted played exactly, and I left it absolutely wide open for him. It was totally legitimate music, and I wanted him to make a jazz commentary on that, and I knew his musical sensibilities were so acute that he wouldn't sound like a patch on a pair of pants.

"The first rehearsal of his improvisation was so good that I said, if this piece is ever published, that movement will say baritone part by Gerry Mulligan. I told Gerry, and he said, 'Oh, I was just fooling around.' "

"It's instantaneous, and they never do as well on a record date. Some of the most miraculous moments of jazz have gone right up the flue, because no one got them down on tape.

"Let's go back to Bach, who used to improvise six-part fugues at Sunday church. I mean—how?

"Jazz players create instantaneously highly imaginative music without any time to think about it. You never know what's going to happen; they themselves don't know. Of course, they can suddenly go dry. There are times in the middle of a piece when a player is forced to use a cliché, a conventional phrase, but other times some incredible intuitive process is at work. When I listen to these people, I am in literal awe of them.

"I have heard Charley Parker create very rapid passages that were fantastically considered and responsible melodic lines, harmonically perfect—and doing it at the speed of light. You'd think he was just showing off a lot of digital dexterity, but it was not just a series of chromatic runs and pyrotechnics. Behind it all, the notes made sense. If you slowed them down, they all made sense.

"I once said to Marian McPartland, 'What on earth did you do in the middle of that piece where the harmony became so enormously complex and the rhythms became so complex,' and she just looked at me and said, 'I don't know what you're talking about.' "

*

Earl Hines came on stage to play in a "Tribute to Fats Waller."

"My heavens, he must be one hundred years old; he looks

about twenty," a middle-aged party said. "I used to see him for thirty-five cents at the Paramount." Hines, born not long after the turn of the century, had been a star with Louis Armstrong in Chicago in the 1920s. He seemed a brilliant figure on the stage nearly fifty years later, trim and raven-haired and firm-fleshed, looking like a major league pitcher—which is exactly what he is, brother; it's what he is. The old man was full of kinetic energy and athleticism and dramatic force. His twenty or thirty fingers went skittering over the keys in a jazz-quick version of "Two Sleepy People." A bit later he moved into a racing, lilting, lively "Honeysuckle Rose."

The festival presented some very serious preservers and recreators of styles, none more impressive than Bob Greene whose approximation of the delightful, tinkly sounds of Jelly Roll Morton verges on perfection. Greene, the only gifted narrator of a jazz program in the festival, began by reminding the audience that "Jelly" was thirty-two years dead and that, for all his reputation, he had gone out of the world "alone, broke, forgotten." He then set himself to writing a sort of musical biography of the jazz pianist on the keyboard, interspersing the selections with brief, affecting words that were placed with an artist's spare, sure sense of the appropriate.

There is a difference between a man whose imitation is designed to show how well he can do the thing, and a man whose imitation is honestly framed to show how well the other man did it, and it was not until sometime after the concert that Greene's own gifts were realized, so successfully had he drawn all the attention to his beloved "Jelly."

*

A jazz concert is most satisfying when it moves an audience out of its ordinary reserve, beyond a normally enthusiastic response, to a kind of mild hysteria. There is a point at which people are so roused by the music that they are up on their feet, clapping, whistling, shouting, grinning like Irish sweepstakes winners. It is very hard to predict when a response like this will come, or just what will set it off, though certain five-alarm renditions in the Dixieland style are more reliable in this regard than almost anything else.

A response of this kind is most likely to come at the end of a performance, but sometimes it occurs repeatedly, so that three or four numbers are played to an audience that has become fully primed for uproarious acclamation. The phenomenon was seen in a blues concert, in a Dixieland-ragtime-stride session, at a Sarah Vaughan concert, and elsewhere, including a Benny Goodman concert whose prelude supplied a nearly perfect demonstration of differences in the quality of response.

The capacity audience for the B.G. reunion in Carnegie Hall was by all odds the one least likely to blow its cool. It was markedly older, more affluent and more sophisticated than other audiences, and it was more fashionably dressed.

The first half of the concert—the introductory public performance of the extremely well-matched Ruby Braff-George Barnes quartet—was a conspicuous triumph that attracted a singular amount of critical attention in reviews that were expected to attend to Mr. Goodman and his illustrious cohorts. Indeed, in some cases, the new quartet ran away with the bulk of the notices—a remarkable fact. Yet it never came even close to stirring its admiring audience to anything like pandemonium, while the augmented Goodman quartet—five strong men and true—roused them mightily. It was not done on the strength of recollection, either.

The audience sat there in white linen jackets, rose-flowered dresses, trim beards, silk shirts, pearl necklaces, sash gowns and sheath dresses when the Braff-Barnes group walked out in black tie attire, with black velvet lapels and shoes polished to a mirror gloss. They rolled easily into their low key, highly rhythmic music—salon jazz, not saloon jazz, all smoothed out with no hint of a washboard effect in it, sedate supper club jazz of an entirely practiced and brilliant kind. At times the players went skimming low over green meadows and glassy ponds, or gliding over citrus groves or looping out over coral reefs. The lead player had a slightly elegant, French dinner table way of touching his pocket handkerchief to his lower lip to free it of moisture. The performance was admirable, flawless, enormously competent and emotionally unexciting.

There was more magic in the first three bars of Benny Goodman and the first two jazz-drum flourishes of Gene Krupa than there had been in all that went before.

Goodman came on looking like a retired banker—the chairman of the board and chief operating officer of the National Jazz Fiduciary Trust. Smiling with a vast benignity and playing his revelatory clarinet, the old master bent way, way back on his stool and blew some very fancy lines and phrases into the hall. He gave every impression of working by pure instinct and feeling, now and then putting his clarinet to his lips for just the briefest interpolations, at other times sailing freely into long and rippling refrains. Several times he got into intimate dialogue with Lionel Hampton on the vibes and the other players, recognizing that, receded until the clarinet and the vibes had said all that they wanted to say to each other. The basic quartet—Hampton, Goodman, Krupa and Teddy Wilson at the piano—had not played together in the hall since 1938. And while it was perfectly true that they were now playing solid old standards—pieces they may have played hundreds of times—it was equally true that they were not playing them as set pieces, but were doing a lot of ad libbing. That is what gave their performance its wonderful sense of loose-jointedness and unpredictability.

The fifth player with Goodman was Slam Stewart on bass, who was brought in, Mr. Goodman told the audience, as "a designated hitter." He has an act all his own on solo, in which he makes his voice as one with his bass and manages to sound like an instrumental duet.

A fire engine went by outside; its siren pierced the hall and there was Mr. Goodman cupping his hand at his ear and smiling quizzically, as if to ask who was horning in on his quintet. And there was Mr. Goodman twirling his clarinet like a baton. They could do nothing wrong, of course, but aside from doing everything right, they exceeded all the norms of their accomplished rhythms and moved into areas of pure genius. Mr. Goodman's entire mastery of the clarinet enabled him to do things with ease that very good players would be unable, or unwise, even to attempt. Before it was over the audience was on its feet, filling the hall with a din that ran for minutes.

A far younger audience made up chiefly of members of the jeans-and-sandals set was highly spontaneous in its reactions at the B. B. King rhythm and blues concert, now chattering, now whistling or giving out high-pitched "whooos!" Sometimes the whole house stood through numbers while many people danced in place or beat their palms rhythmically or stamped to the beat. Muddy Waters sang. So did Eddie "Cleanhead" Vinson," Big Mama Thornton, and Clarence "Gatemouth" Brown. One girl got clap-happy and attacked the back of the seat in front of her as if it were a set of drums, grinning, slapping, hacking, snapping her head from side to side. Near the end, without any effort at all, the musicians and singers had the audience reacting the way a football crowd would at a game-saving eighty-yard touchdown-run seconds before the clock ran out.

Afterward, in the colonnade outside Philharmonic Hall, a young man had after-effects similar to those experienced by Charlie Chaplin's factory hand in *Modern Times,* who could not stop tightening the bolts with a wrench-jerking motion even after he had come off the assembly line. The young man was a rhythm-freak and he was still beating his palms and goose-thrusting his neck in and out of his collar fifteen minutes after the concert had ended.

*

Some 800 fans filed into Philharmonic Hall for a dinner-hour concert, and the free-form fall of gold splinters high in the glass walled entrance seemed like a kind of static jazz in sculpture. The concert, titled "Stan & Woody," brought together two of the old masters of big-band jazz who had survived, by sheer stubbornness and guts, the shoals of public indifference that had sunk other bands long ago.

The Woody Herman band came on first, with its leader, a showman to the hilt, looking bouncy and vibrant and trim-waisted in a white jacket and black slacks. His men wrote some reminiscences on the air in brass, things they had done, he said, "Oh, a little while ago."

He introduced a new member of his "herd." "His name is Gregory Herbert and he plays the tenor saxophone *thusly*," Herman said.

He called a New Zealander forward from the bandstand, then told the audience he would give them "an example of his penmanship." The leader showed a nice economy in the use of gestures, too. He produced great stabs of music of almost symphonic grandeur at times. In one passage, thirteen horns seemed to be pointed straight at a fan in the audience, like thirteen trains with headlights coming on.

The pointed white shoe of an old party—a woman in her late sixties with blue-white hair—switched back and forth, left-right, right-left, to the pulsing tempo of the music.

A small woman of some age, who had been a star with bands in the 1930s, came out to take the microphone, and she soon showed that she had lost none of her savvy. She was a genuine show-biz doll, a silvery blonde in a pink blouse over a shiny rust long-skirt. She had a big, slightly husky, sure voice, strong gestures, a big smile and hard eyes.

The silhouette of her head was thrown perfectly onto the face of a bass drum by the spotlight. While she sang, her head and one hand were etched in sharp shadows on it.

Stan Kenton came on next in a screech of trumpets. He soon had his horns flying in V formation. He is tall and loose-limbed and when he turns around suddenly from leading the band, he is grinning with delight at the sound he is producing.

A round butterball of a player hit the rim of a tambourine with his chubby hand just every now and then— exactly when he felt it was right, not on any regular beat, usually giving it two short slaps at a time, sometimes one. The player was coiled in tension between the hits and somehow it was always exactly right. When he held off and when he hit it—it was right.

During the concert, a "conversation of horns" was presented, made up of declarations, protestations, expressions of surprise and reproach. "I like you," one horn distinctly said. "Is that so?" the other replied.

One of the unexpected pleasures of the concert was the gleam and glint of shattered light that streaked one wall in the hall—a reflected spotlight beam. It bounced off a cymbal and did a wild dance at times.

When it was over, the members of the Kenton band made their way through back areas of the house and out the rear exit on West Sixty-fifth Street, into the inevitable bus that waited for them, its door open at the end of a canopy that runs from exit to curb. Jazz is still in the bus age.

The band had come down from Poughkeepsie and would go on to the Monticello Raceway and then to Brielle, New Jersey, before making two stops in Connecticut and swinging around to head for Ohio and then to roll all the way west to California.

If it is going to make such important occasions as a concert in Philharmonic Hall, a band has to survive. In offhand remarks between numbers Woody Herman had given a glimpse of the kind of life a jazz man has to live when he said, "We did all those gigs together, you know the one-night stands, to kind of string things together."

"We go fifty-one weeks a year, seven days a week," said nineteen-year-old Phil Herring, who plays the bass trombone and tuba in the Kenton band. "We get off a week at Christmas.

"If I stayed in the City, I'd be playing dinner music. Most jobs in town are a drag. There's a few cats in town who have good jobs, but they're people like Stan Getz and those cats.

"You take the Jones-Lewis band—that's a great band to be with in New York, but they don't make much money. All those cats do studio gigs, Dial Soap commercials. I'm playing music that I want to play."

A knockabout life of bus runs from date to date is the price he pays for playing the music he believes in.

Jazz has no great hall or home of its own, no continuing place. It is always passing through.

Yet jazz belongs anywhere: in a wharf's end bar, in a hotel supper club, in a band shell, on a riverboat, in Philharmonic Hall.

In the jazz business, survival is the greatest triumph. Jazz may or may not be a living. To the men most dedicated to it, it is a calling.

Bright Lights

Open Call

There are few institutions as cruelly democratic as an open call for tryouts in a Broadway show. Anybody can come and everybody who shows up has an almost perfectly equal chance to be rejected. The casualty rate at an open audition is slightly higher than that of the Flood.

If that were all, it would be dull and futile. What makes it as taut and exciting as drama is that everybody who steps onto the stage has at least one fleeting chance to break through.

An open audition is a time of hopes raised high and quickly dashed, of short, snap judgments, of discovery and of sudden, unexplained rejection.

Sometimes the candidates are jostled together, the rankest amateurs, fresh out of their high school musicals, lining up with anxious semipros and working pros, quite against union rules.

More than 200 young men in their teens and twenties showed up at the stage door of the Majestic Theater on West Forty-fourth Street for a stab at the lead role in the musical *Pippin*.

It was a big chance with a promise of hundreds of dollars a week, a name posted in lights on Broadway, a position at stage center for most of two acts. In it, a young man could step from anonymity to stardom in a night.

Over 200 professionals had been auditioned and no one had seemed to fit the part, so the word went out and the door was thrown open and the candidates trooped in by the score, stardust in their eyes.

A boy with a bushel of hair sang his suspenders right off

his shoulders. A pale boy almost as thin as plywood, who looked as though he could hardly peep, came on and belted out a song with terrific authority in a kind of rooty-tooty Al Jolson style.

A strapping, handsome young man with a strong profile came out in a faded rose sweat shirt, flashing a smile that lit up the house. There seemed to be a star quality there. He subverted his chances almost instantly when he started to sing because he had effeminate gestures.

"Thank you very much," came the prompt, terminal compliment. The piano died in mid-phrase and the young man walked off to join the losers.

But all this was later in the day, after the first eliminations. The process began a little after 11:00 A.M. when thirteen candidates marched out of the wings and stood in a long line, facing an almost empty house of red velvet seats. Three bare electric bulbs, two of them roughly the size of cantaloupes, shone down on the stage.

There, in the first couple of rows of the orchestra, stood the brain trust of the show—Stuart Ostrow, the producer; Bob Fosse, the director; Michael Shurtleff, the casting director; Stephen Schwartz, who did the music and lyrics; and Roger O. Hirson, who wrote the book.

There was very little ceremony. "We know exactly what we want, so we're going to type you out first, save you a lot of time," a voice came up at the stage from somewhere in the dark house beyond the orchestra pit. "Find the light—it's always good at an audition to stand in the light."

"Number 9, will you step forward please," another voice called. "Number 3, step forward."

In a scant two minutes, five of the thirteen had been asked to step forward and eight others were told to go home, with hardly a word said by any of them.

As soon as the one line had walked off, the next came out. "We're going to type some of you out," the voice said, and then a moment later it was saying, "Okay, that's it, thanks for coming. Thanks a lot for coming."

This time, seven survived and six went out. It was all so fast and nobody was told on what basis he had been selected or rejected.

There were twelve in the next line. "Who's really a terrific singer?" Mr. Fosse asked, and eleven hands shot up. Modesty is not the foremost virtue of show business, and in novices at an audition reticence is unseemly.

The candidates came from many places, from Washington, D.C., from Chicago, from Philadelphia, from Queens and Harlem. They were wedged together in narrow spaces backstage, among the ropes on pulleys, in every state of dress—tee shirts, military jackets, corduroy jackets, levis, turtlenecks, red suspenders, floral shirts, suits. Most were from eighteen to twenty-three, with some a few years older or younger.

"How old are you?" a voice asked from the dark.

"Fourteen and a half," said a boy still in the blessed season when age is boasted of almost to the latest minute.

"What have you done?" the voice wanted to know.

"I've been in numerous plays," the boy said, causing a burst of laughter on stage. He paused to let it die. "Good plays, by Strindberg and Shakespeare," he went on.

Every individual in the lineups got a good, hard, assessing look of perhaps four seconds duration.

"Looks like a lineup—a police lineup—but there's no other way of doing it," Mr. Ostrow called out amiably. Some of the candidates were given the chance to make a short pitch—two or three sentences about what they'd done.

The eleventh lineup came out on stage and already more than half had been dismissed without having the vaguest idea of what the criterion was by which they were judged—some chimerical essence, dimples maybe.

The lead part in the show is the eldest son of King

Charlemagne, about A.D. 793, which is reaching centuries further back into history than Mr. Ostrow did for his hit musical, *1776*. This time, he said, considerably more liberties are to be taken with the facts for the sake of musical comedy fun.

The part is about equivalent in its size and demands to the role of Fanny in *Funny Girl*, according to Mr. Schwartz, who wrote the music and lyrics for *Godspell* and collaborated with Leonard Bernstein on *Mass*.

"The boy has to look aristocratic," Mr. Ostrow said in a spare moment.

"You get to know every motion, every sinew of the part in your mind and you form a perfect picture of what you want the boy to be."

"We're just looking for a boy who's young and fresh and charming and has a sense of humor and a voice to fit the songs," Mr. Schwartz said. "That sounds awfully easy, doesn't it? It's impossible.

"We've seen hundreds of boys. Actors all think we're their enemies, but it isn't so. We're just as desperate as they are."

Mr. Schwartz said getting cut from the lineups was mostly a matter of "just luck."

"If there's any fire in them, they're going to get it across to you" during the lineup Mr. Ostrow said. He spoke of subtle qualities of "endearment" and "innocence," for which he was looking, as well as talent.

Robie Sacco, eighteen, had come up from the Allentown, Pennsylvania area where he is a student at Kutztown State College. He guessed there would be about $800 a week in the part. "But I'll settle for a dollar and a quarter an hour," he said.

There were fifteen lineups in all, with twelve to fourteen in each, and seventy-five out of the 201 candidates were called back. In the afternoon they came on stage one by one to sing, with help from a pianist in the pit.

A good looking young man with a big smile and a strong, sure voice seemed to have it all—stage presence, voice power, personality. Unfortunately he had too much. "Too slick," one of the brain trust whispered in the dark.

Most of them had three minutes to win—or lose. Only about a dozen were cut off before finishing their songs.

Number seventy-two, Jonathan, a curly-haired chap with a lot of charm and a pleasing voice, cut himself off after forty seconds.

"Is that all?" Mr. Fosse called. "So short?"

The boy had almost bluffed himself out, but they asked him to sing again and he was one of only three who were handed the script and told to come back in twenty minutes to do a reading. Jonathan did, and he read it superbly.

On and on it went through the long afternoon.

"Nobody yet. Nobody yet," Mr. Ostrow said, shaking his head when it was over. "There's a romance going on, but we haven't fallen in love yet."

"What about these fellows you called back to read the script?" he was asked.

"Well, we need an understudy," the producer said.

Barbara Loden—Up from Daisy Mae

One of the high rewards of reporting is the opportunity to spend private hours with uncommonly interesting people, and by it to have brief privileged access to their minds and lives and spheres. It fell my sudden lot one afternoon—in newspaper work almost everything is sudden, if not by necessity then by *habit* —to interview a woman who is in her appearance virtually the sum total of any man's dream of loveliness. Such a circumstance obtrudes upon the interview a factor that might, if it were not checked, hinder it from reaching the best levels of ideation possible.

Barbara Loden is a classic American beauty, not austere in the Greek vision, but pliant and as soft and warm in exterior as fleece. It would be impossible for any man, unless he had been hewn from marble, not to be aware of that fact. The actress had quite a lot on her mind, most of it wholly surprising to me. Behind her softly radiant exterior there were perceptions and resolves of a serious, even steely, character.

The occasion of the interview was the opening in New York of the film *Wanda*, which came in under banners of international critical praise. Miss Loden wrote it, directed it and played its central role. As the story said:

"More than merely a film she has made, Wanda is the woman Miss Loden might have become, before she discovered who she was."

Her film was made in express rejection of Hollywood techniques. It was also made in express rejection of national values as Miss Loden sees them.

In its blighted atmosphere, *Wanda* discloses the poverty and ignorance of Appalachia. It tells of a passive, slatternly young woman who abandons her family and drifts, like a piece of wood caught on a slow tide, through a series of dreary events in motels and bars.

"She's trapped and she will never, ever get out of it and there are millions like her," Miss Loden said.

At first her declaration that the film is in some respects autobiographical seems unlikely, but the improbability dissolves as she talks. Much of her mature life has been, perhaps only half-consciously, a flight from categorization.

"I really hate slick pictures," she said, coiled in a green chair in the sitting room in which she presides as Mrs. Elia Kazan, wife of the stage and film director. The film was edited in a back room of their spacious townhouse near Central Park West.

"They're so slick they're unbelievable. I don't just mean in the look. I mean in the rhythm, in the cutting—everything. The slicker the technique is, the slicker the content becomes, until everything turns into Formica, including the people. Everything is calculated to manipulate the audience. I think people subtly resent this. But I don't subtly resent it—I really hate it."

Miss Loden is made up of no parts Formica. Her countenance glows without a trace of cosmetics. She has wide, innocent eyes, strong cheekbones and a turned-up nose. She wore brown corduroy slacks.

"I tried not to explain things too much in the film, not to be too explicit, not be be too verbal, especially because of my subject matter, which is of people who are not too verbal and not aware of their condition," she said.

"I've been like that myself. I came from a rural region, where people have a hard time. They don't have time for wittily observing the things around them. They're not concerned about anything more than existing from day to day.

"They're not stupid. They're ignorant, but they're ignorant from not being educated, and I don't mean in a formal sense. Everything is ugly around them—the architecture, the town, the clothing they wear. The food they eat is unnourishing.

"What example they set for their children is on a very low level of awareness, of what people are and what life can be."

"It's not a matter of money," Miss Loden explained, describing what she regards as the produce-and-consume-and-produce treadmill. "It's the same in Detroit. They work in the factories to make all those ugly cars that don't last so they can get paid to buy a few of those ugly cars and to buy the things that others are making in other factories. It's a whole aspect of America."

"Do you have any answer.?"

"No," Miss Loden said quietly. "Just to change the whole society." The revolutionary currents that are running are evidence of a terminal distaste for the entire setup, she believes.

"People are always saying, 'Why don't they work within the system?' They don't because the system doesn't work, you see," Miss Loden said.

"This country is so rich, so wealthy, and everything is wasted. The richest country in the world. It's shameful we have all the poverty we have. We have no in-between. Everybody has to be fantastic, or you're nothing.

"I sort of made my way up, but I know if I had stayed where I came from, I would just be a wasted person. I came up here to get away from down there." Miss Loden remembered that she began her public career by having electricity shot through her in Brown's Science Circus at two dollars a jolt.

By leaving her rural setting near Asheville, North Carolina and coming to New York, she escaped the life of ignorance and drudgery into which she is certain the cycles of life would have trapped her. But she was immediately caught up in another banal categorization.

Since she had "a figure approaching perfection" as one reviewer put it, and a face that undeniably suggested both the beauty of Bergman and the sensuous glamour of Monroe (whose image she reflected in *After the Fall*), Miss Loden was credited with exterior assets only.

She danced at the Copacabana. She had spots on television with Jackie Gleason, Martha Raye, Martin and Lewis. Ernie Kovacs, who knew a good thing when he saw one, dressed her in very scanty tights and had her romp through television slapstick parts, in which she was subjected to various indignities, such as appearing to have her head sawed off, or seeming to have water spouting out of her eyes, or smoking a cigar, or being hit in the face with pies. While that was going on, she was studying acting in the Actors Workshop.

She sees both of these circumstances—the drab and hollow life at home, and the glittering and hollow life here—as having a single root in a misorganized society.

"I got into the whole thing of being a dumb blonde—sort of an object, as they say. I didn't think anything of myself, so I succumbed to the whole role. I never knew who I was, or what I was supposed to do."

"Do you know now?"

"Yes."

After years of doing Daisy Mae turns, Miss Loden at last got larger opportunities. "Barbara Loden's performance is all fireworks and whirling razor blades," the *Times* critic wrote of her work in *Splendor in the Grass* by Inge. And in his review of *The Glass Menagerie*, Jack Gould said: Barbara Loden played the shy and limping Laura. The vision of her glowing face after her lips had been touched by the caller will stand as a closeup of almost unbearable loveliness. In Miss Loden's touching tenderness of expression there was embodied all the agony of one human yearning for another and all the ecstasy of being wanted."

"Everybody was so surprised that I could do a dramatic part because all I'd ever done was get hit in the face with a pie," the actress said.

"I really feel very strongly about this girl Wanda. I wanted just to sort of make people aware of the existence of this girl, just to see her everyday life. The people who have control of the film business, they don't want to see her in the cinema, or if they do, they want her spiced up with some sex, or they want her made interesting with some redeeming qualities, but I wanted just to show her as she is."

Since her film has a documentary quality and is implicitly

accusatory, Miss Loden was asked—who is guilty?

"All you can say is society. It's the mythical 'they,' " she said.

"We're all brainwashed. From the time you're little, you get brainwashed. What you have to do is to continually, intentionally re-educate yourself and what you're doing, and it isn't easy."

Miss Loden wrote *Wanda* nine years ago. "It was a story I had in mind for a long time," she said. "I was pregnant, and not doing anything, and I decided to write it in screenplay form. It wasn't my main interest at the time. It was just a little side thing. I never had any ambition to make a film or direct one.

"In those days everything was Hollywood and big productions and large crews." The actress saw no way to film the story until she became aware of the underground filmmakers and their far simpler techniques.

"Wanda" was shot in 16 mm and printed in 35 mm. "The camera is so much lighter. You have mobility," she said. "With 35 mm you have to have a lot of people, you have to carry around a lot of equipment and accessories."

The casting process was catch-as-catch-can. "Sometimes I would see people on the street. I would go up to them and ask them if they'd like to be in a movie. Either they said okay right away, or they'd say no right away. You'd run into people who thought it was sinful to be in a movie."

Miss Loden picked up props and costumes in thrift shops. "My costumes were from Woolworth's and the Salvation Army store," she said. "The film was done in very simple ways."

The picture was shot in Carbondale and at Scranton, Pennsylvania. "Everything in the picture was a real place." Miss Loden said. "Most of the people I used were not actors, so they couldn't read lines. You can't rehearse them. The more you rehearse them, the worse they get."

In the lower hallway, near the film-editing room, there

was evidence of the work that had gone into the making of the picture. There were 212 film cans piled in seven stacks that fitted into the curve of the stairs, like so many silver dollars on Paul Bunyan's poker table. Of the 212 cans of film shot, only five were used, Miss Loden said.

The Chaplinesque series of credits that bears her name fails to encompass all her work.

"Writer, director, player—I don't divide the job that much. I just say I made a film. I want to continue to make these little movies, to make them for myself and not to make them to please other people's tastes."

"I was also cleaner-upper on location," she said. "I did the casting, and since I had no scouts, I went out and found the locations.

The obligatory question was, "Did Mr. Kazan help you in this picture?"

"He helps me every way he can," she said. "It's good to have an expert around. What he tried to do was to get me to do what I wanted to do, and that's not the way he would have done it. Anybody who sees the picture knows it's so much me.

"I wanted to make an anti-movie," Miss Loden said. Her picture won an International Critics Prize at the Venice Film Festival as the best foreign film.

Miss Loden talked on about the simple way of making films. "It's not a new wave," she said. "It's the old wave. That's what they used to do. They took a camera and they went out and shot. Around that this whole fantastic apparatus grew up—the Hollywood albatross. They made a ship out of lead. It won't float anymore."

The Monks and the Bells

It is 5:00 A.M. in a monastery in Burgundy. To the east, the pageant of the morning bursts. An impartial sun pours its bounty on fools as well as kings.

Slowly, phantom shapes emerge out of the diminishing blackness of the belfry; four long ropes hang in motionless suspension from the tower overhead. There are lumps on the floor; but they stir, betraying life. They unfold, revealing monks.

In a moment, they will herald the day, and waken their brethren with "Frères Jacques." But first comes a season of yawning and stretching and of shaking the sleep from the limbs.

In this delicious interlude, one of the monks hears music. Not the honest cadences of "Frères Jacques" but a subtle, beguiling corruption. It has the style of New Orleans, among cities, and of Thelonious only, among Monks.

He succumbs to sly temptation. He switches a foot from side to side. He snaps his fingers. Intimations of jazz subvert the cloister.

The time has come to ring the bells. And, O, how those bells are pealed that morning!

Around and around the monks go in widening circles, running, skipping, leaping, twining their ropes together! Into the air they go, denying their last inhibition, greeting the new, the hilarious morning!

It is this scene—sometimes called "The Monks," sometimes "The Bellringers," sometimes just "The Bells"—that conquers the audience in the French revue *La Plume De Ma Tante*, as it has done before in Paris and London and as it did for the 600th time in New York last night.

The skit was born in pious circumstances at the village church at Héry in Burgundy. Robert Dhery—writer, director, player—and his wife, Colette, were chatting with the pastor after mass. It was a small church and the pastor had to ring his own bell for the succeeding service.

Abbe Mast was an old man, not very heavy, and following each long pull on the rope he was carried a foot off the floor.

"That's a good gag you have," Robert said.

"It would make a wonderful sketch, a ballet," Colette said later.

"We can't put priests on stage," Robert objected.

"Ah, no, but monks!" she said.

Monks it was. Robert decided that there should be four, "with a big, fat monk" to play the role of the disapproving abbot. They nursed the notion for several years.

The act was worked out one night from sketches by Mr. Dhery. "We started at nine and by three in the morning it was finished," he said, groping for cheese popcorn in a dim hotel bar.

"The best things come like that, from A to Z immediately. We didn't touch it. It's wonderful when it happens like that," he said. The scene, billed in the program as "Frères Jacques," has been in previous revues by the author and was carried into *La Plume* by acclaim.

One of the actors, Jacques Legras, has played it 2,300 times. Like the others, he finds it keeps him fit. Despite a look of easy spontaneity and abandon, it is a rugged chore that puts muscle where fat was. Except on Ross Parker, who plays the ponderous abbot.

Mr. Parker, who hasn't lost a pound, comes abruptly upon the monks' mad festivity and freezes it, practically in mid-air. He reproves them with a scowl, but he leaves a moment later, an unconfessed convert, syncopating secretly.

Songbird of the Automat

There is something new in Times Square—a floor show at the Automat. Edna Thayer, a sometime vaudevillian and movie bit player, has won her first big part on Broadway, topping a bill that also includes seeded rolls, coffee, lemon meringue pie and lukewarm chicken à la king.

The old trooper is now starring as the golden-haired songbird of the Automat, the Jenny Lind of the steamtables, belting out songs three nights a week in the Horn and Hardart cafeteria on Broadway near West Forty-sixth Street.

Her presence in the first floor show in the sixty-year history of the fast food chain signifies the start of a major departure in its operations. The move is toward adding fun to the food. Last year, just on food alone, the chain lost $10.3 million.

Miss Thayer, a character who deserves to have been invented by Damon Runyon, is four feet eleven inches tall and about half as wide. She has the face of a kewpie doll, with big blue eyes under yellow curls that cover her forehead, and she looks like an ice cream parlor Sophie Tucker. Her act is free.

"No cover, no minimum, no talent," one customer grumbled, with perhaps typical New York ingratitude for largesse. He did not know that Miss Thayer is a comedienne who has held back most of the surefire elements in her novelty act to do the one thing she was hired to do—sing.

Her voice has a four-note range—some say three—and sounds like a piece of sandpaper being rubbed across the top of a xylophone. She easily makes up in verve what she lacks in musicality.

"I do twenty to twenty-five songs a night, and I get a ten-minute break," she said. "I get my meals free. I stipulated that. All actors and actresses like to eat, and I'm allergic to starvation.

"I'm an old trooper, I'm sixty-five-years-old and I'm fat," she said in her accustomed flat-out manner. "I dance when I sing. I'm a hoofer, too."

An Automat habitué off and on for forty years, she was just another face in the cafeteria crowd, as expert as anybody at stretching two cups of coffee and a sticky roll into a convivial afternoon of spirited repartee. Then she met Fred Guterman, the new president of the company, and the rest is Cinderella in a size $4\frac{1}{2}$ C. Miss Thayer has already signed to record a couple of her songs.

Her booking in the Automat is especially sweet to Miss Thayer because she had not always felt welcome in the place. "I used to eat here a lot," she said, "until they got the bouncer. He bounced all my friends out. He was like a gorilla."

"Now the waitresses are jealous of me," she said. As she spoke, an Oriental-looking man at the next table opened a case and began playing a guitar, Hawaiian style. "Everybody wants to get into my act," Miss Thayer remarked.

"One time I went to an agent and he said, 'Can you yodel?' and I said, 'Sure,' and he put me in a club and I yodelled and I got paid for it.

"Sammy," she said, turning to the man next to her, "if I told you how I learned to yodel, you'd die laughing, but I won't.

"I do dialects," Miss Thayer said. "Jewish, Irish, Scottish, Bronx. I do sound effects and jungle noises—aaaawk, aaaawk—and barnyard sounds. I can do roosters, chickens, ducks, dogs, cats, parrots. I do instruments—trumpets—raaaah raaaah raaraaraanee—violin, guitar and saw, musical saw.

"I do Popeye," she said, lowering her voice to a bass rasp. She got some of her savvy working in "The Kookie Follies," an imitation of "a small-time vaudeville act" on television.

"I came from a theatrical family. I was born in Worcester, Massachusetts," she said. "Jack Harney—he's the golden-voiced tenor of New England—is a cousin. I was a big hit in stock in New Orleans in 1927. I did a newsboy number that tore the house down. Afterward I went into comedy. I did a flash act on the R.K.O. circuit for nine months, with eight people in it, like little miniature musical comedies. I was the old landlady. I always got the obnoxious parts. I once played an old-bag woman, no makeup on, with Red Buttons. That was in movies. I was in *Girl Fever* in 1960. I was in *French Connection* but you can't find me. I was just an extra in that."

Miss Thayer's stage is a space near the entrance of the glass-fronted establishment from which a couple of tables are pushed aside. Al Grenier, her accompanist, sits at an old upright piano, marked in gold letters "Horn and Hardart Memorial Post #1192," and plays a ricky-ticky style to go with Miss Thayer's songs.

Bouncing her bulk to the beat and occasionally doing the shuffle, Miss Thayer sings out loud and clear, mixing a little patter with the tunes. She strolls between the tables, bestowing her attentions on customers. "I'm a big fat mama, I'm big and fat. I got that way from eating at the Aut-o-mat!" she sings, autobiographically.

She fingered one man's crewcut hair and sang one of her accusatory blues numbers: "I get a hamburger, baby, when I'm out with you/I get a hamburger, baby, you know it's true/You know I like steaks and chops/But with you, baby, a hamburger's tops."

Miss Thayer—"I'm Miss, I missed," she said jovially—has a whole kaboodle of original songs inspired by forty years of eating self-service food—"The Doughnut Song," "The Coffee Song," "The Bean Song,"—ten others.

Her lyrics have a sort of Mother Goose quality, which makes them catchy and about as easy to remember as they are to forget: "Oh my gosh, I like squash/Yes, indeed, I do/Oh my gosh, I like squash/And you will like it, too."

"What else are you going to rhyme squash with?" she wanted to know. The customers sometimes sing along. Her appearance draws a crowd out on the street, onlookers curious about the phenomenon inside. "I've got them dancing in the streets," Miss Thayer bubbled. Actually, most of the gazers were standing stock still, peering in through the glass, their faces screwed up in puzzlement.

"I guess you'd call her a combination singer and entertainer," said Gus Hardart, a grandson of one of the founders, groping for definition. "She makes people happy, and that's what counts. It makes our customers laugh, and it makes our help laugh."

"Beans, beans, golden brown," Miss Thayer sang. "Got the best baked beans in town/Where do you get them *at?*/No place else but the Auto-*mat!*" Sammy had just signed a contract with Miss Thayer for the publication of twelve of her songs. In numbers like "Ipsy-Pipsy Papsie-Wapsie Boopsie-Boopsie Boo" and "Wah Wah Da Dee Dah Boo Boo" he thought he spied the makings of a possible novelty hit—a latter-day "Hut Sut Ralson" perhaps.

"I can't read a note of music," Miss Thayer said.

"She'll sing 'em for me and I'll write 'em down," Sammy said.

"Next we'll do 'Jazz at the Automat,'" Mr. Guterman said. "Get a nice young crowd in here." He talked of similar plans for other spots in the twenty-two-store chain, designed to make the Automat "a fun place." Miss Thayer sings on Thursday, Friday and Saturday nights in the original Automat and she may be booked for other dates on the budding Horn and Hardart circuit.

Vaudeville Days

Vaudeville is dead, long dead, but a few vaudevillians live on. Some still stay in the nearly anonymous hotels off Times Square—a stroll from the lights of Broadway yet decades removed from the days when the brassy pit bands piped them on.

One woman, a singer, came back to the square after nearly half a century because, even in old age, there was still the mysterious pull of the theater that she had felt so keenly as a girl. She is there by choice. Others are there because they have no choices anymore.

Most live on welfare, just above the poverty line.

In the more spacious years, before television, before radio, they had moved across the largest music hall stages—sometimes dancing, or juggling, or flipping cartwheels or just strutting with a cocked hat and a cane. Now many are squeezed down to a few crowded square feet. The days, the years, the times have passed them by.

For the most part, each one lives alone in a box of walls called a room.

The old variety players starred briefly again at Lincoln Center, in a show of documentary photographs called "The Vaudevillians of Times Square," in the Amsterdam Gallery of the Museum of the Performing Arts, where they could be heard as well as seen.

The thirty-eight photographs of mostly mural size by Marcia Keegan tell a story of their own, and the visual display is amplified by three hours of tape-recorded reminiscences, including bits of singing and comedy. Miss Keegan asked the men and women to tell about themselves, and what they say shows that a few of them are living in the present, while most are living in the distant, irreclaimable past.

Some old players keep the photographs or the showbills of their days behind the footlights on walls or dresser tops, things that seem to say, once I was wanted, once I worked, once—a long time ago—I heard laughter and applause.

An observant stroller in the cross streets off Times Square finds many old hotels, usually five to fifteen stories high, with names such as Somerset, Crown, Normandie, Remington, St. Francis. A faded blue sign, reading "Rooms from $3.50," is high on the exterior of the Knickerbocker on West Forty-fifth Street.

Places such as these, and rooms in tenement flats west of Eighth Avenue, shelter what Miss Keegan calls "a loosely-knit and diminishing colony of vaudevillians." She made this discovery in the winter of 1969 and spent part time in the following three years finding her subjects. The result, in pictures and text, will be published in a book called *We Can Still Hear Them Clapping*.(Avon).

The photographs are eloquent, in a cinema-verité style, and they often show the tokens of a former gaiety or glamour set in a present bleakness. "I think that when you're older you really show what you've done with your life," Miss Keegan said. "I think the karma really shows."

There is an old woman with bony hands and a face full of lines in a room just big enough for a bed and a chair and a small table, with a hot plate on its upper shelf, and six beer cans, a jar of peanut butter and a roll of tissue on its lower shelf. She has a large portrait of John F. Kennedy and she wears her room key on an elastic around her small-boned wrist.

Another elderly woman had set up a sort of altar on her dresser, very neatly arranging a photograph, a crucifix and other objects, including an old mayonnaise jar as a vase for flowers.

A few have made brave if pitiful attempts to add a touch of elegance to their ill-painted rooms. There is a woman with an exquisite white candlewick bedspread so carefully smoothed over her bed, in a room whose bare walls are streaked and cracked.

"Worked thirty-five years I did," said Emma Hyman, who remembered a big success she had had in 1915. "I worked with my husband, man and wife. He used to balance me on the bridge of his nose on a chair, like I'm sitting on now, with the back across his nose and me sitting there. I can't think back all those years.

"I had the command performance to show before the Queen of England. When he went to balance me on his nose, the Queen came up and said, 'What is he going to do with her now?' He didn't take a bit of notice of her—he went right on balancing me. I was there on his nose. I sat on four legs on a chair and tilted back across his nose. That was show business. I don't remember anymore.

"This was a clever man, he had a mark on the bridge of his nose. We had a beautiful act. He had a mark on his nose like a corn from the weight."

In one photograph, Miss Keegan shows an old woman in bed as seen through the mirror on her dresser. A crack in the wall runs behind the mirror and comes out the other side. "Like anything that hasn't existed for a great many years, it's really forgotten," she said of vaudeville, "and so are the people."

"My name is Philip M. Foote," a voice from the amplifier says. "At the present time, I'm going on seventy-four years and I've been in the business for sixty-nine years. I was born in Kewanee, Illinois, which is 165 miles southwest of Chicago. Now I actually played with the original production of *Sweethearts*, written by Victor Herbert. Well, anyway my job was simply to chase ducks onto the stage and across and then off again. I got seventy-five cents an afternoon.

"I started in vaudeville in the lower part of Columbus, Ohio, and I got my piano training with some of the New

Orleans greats up there. We'd go down and ride the scene bridge and we'd pack trunks, things like that, just so I was around show business.

"I sang 'Moonlight Bay' the first year it was out, which was 1909."

The trouper remembered working as an extra with the Hartman and Shubert chains, "and I tell you something funny about the Shubert chain, they had so much trouble with the ballet boys that they put pansies in all the way through it. Shubert never had anybody but pansy boys in that whole thing. Well naturally, I mean, when a girl would jump at you, you were bound to excite each other. That's true. And Shubert never had anybody else except that."

Mr. Foote played the Keith Orpheum circuit and, west of the Mississippi, the Pantages circuit. "The owner was a Greek and he had one pet expression that I loved. He said, 'When a dog growls throw that dog a bone, and if he growls again, put a little meat on it, my boy, put a little meat on it,' and that was his success. He had over fifty theaters."

The entertainer went out to India with an oil company for fifteen years, organized a symphony orchestra of about fifty players there and "wrote gobs of stuff," which led up to the fact that he "had a hit in 1924, a thing called *Get On Your Dancing Shoes.*

"I had my own yacht then and I don't know what else. I had a wonderful time out there," he said.

Cleo Lewis lives in an apartment just off the Square, where she has been for forty years. "I was an old show woman years ago," she said. "Singing, dancing, acting and contortionist." She began in show business at eight years old and she recalls the era of ten shows a day in the nickelodeons. "You could see four big acts and a big moving picture for a nickel. That's why they called it a nickelodeon—five cents," she said.

"I quit show business in 1966 and took a cashier's job at the Penny Arcade and I was in the booth in Forty-second

Street, Times Square. A friend came up and said, 'Gee, Cleo, you look tall.' I said, 'You would too if you were standing up.'

"He said, 'Get a chair for this woman.'

"I was seven years in that booth, and got my Christmas and vacation. So they switched me to Fifty-second Street and they didn't give it anymore. I worked all night long 'til 5:00 in the morning, no extra money, no nothing.

"I traveled all over the country in vaudeville, cabaret. I was five years understudying Mary Pickford. She got the big money and I done the hard work—the rough horseback riding, swimming, acrobatics—she didn't do that.

"I wouldn't go back in show business for anybody. Today show business is crummy, it is vulgar.

"I outlived all my husbands. This one here was killed in Chicago, and the first husband was killed in Chicago by gangsters. I could write a book if I could write.

"I met my first husband, the Irishman, when I was working in a cabaret in Chicago. He was a waiter and he was hanging around me and hanging around me. He didn't ask me, he just took me down and we got married, that's all. He didn't say a word. . . . Then he turned out to be a bum and I had to leave him.

"Mr. Lewis was in show business. He had a band and I used to sing in front of the band. Then he died and I was alone again. Then I had the policeman. He died in '47. So if you kill three of them you don't take the fourth one do you? No, I had my share, I guess—gray old world.

"I used to have a lot of fight, but I don't anymore. I shot my second husband twice. He was working up on the campus. He was running around with this woman, and I told him when I married him, 'If you want someone, leave me, go with her. Don't fool around while you're with me.' So anyhow, he goes with this woman and he was up at the campus. I walked in and I had a .38 gun. When I went to go to the bathroom, he tripped me. I said, 'You're not going to get away with that Mr. Lewis.' He said, 'No, I don't think I am.'

"So I went to the bathroom and when I came back he was in the bar downstairs and he's talking to the bartender. He looked at me and I said, 'You ————,' and I shot him half an inch from the heart and they took it out of the shoulder blade. Masonically speaking—do you know what the Masons are? Well, that's how I got out. They stick together. See the people of the campus were all Masons. My second husband was a Mason. We were living on Forty-third Street and still he wanted to come back, the bum.

"I didn't like show business. I was in it to make a living, but I never liked it. It's all right for giddy people that flies here and there."

A woman who wished to remain anonymous remembered coming to Times Square as a girl of fifteen, in the days when there was no pay for stage rehearsals. "Times Square looked so good to me," she said. "I loved it—I still love it. It's very exciting, even though its passé, almost passé, with all those big buildings and office after office after office. In those days when I was a young girl—why, oh, those bright lights, those theaters, one after another. The dressed up ladies and men—oh, there was such gaiety. Seems to me, you know, we always like to think that the past was always the best, but there was such a gaiety that's stayed with me all these years. I loved every moment of it. I did 'Old Heidelberg' and 'Student Prince,' and then I worked in a night club. That was 1921—way back when.

"At the time I didn't have an agent and I had no one to—to discover me, let's say, although the producer of my first show told the crew and cast that I looked like a million dollars out front and that someone should get interested in me and, you know, launch me. Well, nobody launched me.

"I had to find some way to make a living and pay my room rent and get something to eat. So I went to what they used to call a Dime-a-Dance hall.

"Well, it was ten cents a dance and we got four cents out of the deal and management got six cents. We danced—oh, to midnight and for each dance we got a ticket. 'Course, when I first worked at this place, it wasn't filled with hoodlums and cutthroats, you know, holdup men and mafias and what have you. It was just a nice clean place. As a matter of fact, when I applied for the job, Mr. Wilson looked at me and says to his partner, 'Take over.' His partner's name was Prince, and he said, 'Take over. I'm going to take this little beauty out for a ride in a hansom cab and show her off all over Broadway. And we rode—oh, I had a big picture hat and my hair was all in curls and I had golden hair at the time. And I must have been pretty—they all said so. They all said so.

"Well, this one evening half a dozen sailors marched in and they bought tickets and this man, he looked—oh, well, he must have been imbibing a bit and he leaned up against the wall there and he looked.

"I said, 'Do you want to dance or don't you?' Well, he said, 'I don't know how.' I said, 'All right, I'll show you.' Well, we danced and he said he was going to one of the islands and how would I like to get a bird of paradise, and I said, 'Oh, all you boys are the same. You promise girls the moon and you just don't give it to them.'

"To me he was just one more man who gave me a ticket for a dime. Oh, I wasn't aware of it, of course, but this friend of his said that when he first saw me, he turned to his friend and said, 'You see that little girl there with the blonde curls and the big feet—I'm going to marry her.' And we did, ten months later.

"Actually, I didn't have big feet, but my feet used to be sore from dancing with so many of the boys. I had to get large shoes naturally, about two or three sizes larger than my feet. And to him I had big feet.

"For the next forty-five years I did nothing. I stayed home, of course, and my audience was my husband and all the applause I got was from him for whatever I did. He was a sailor when I met him, but after we got married, we went to Chicago and he learned a trade and became a projectionist, a motion picture operator, so he was more or less in the industry—show business.

"Then suddenly my beloved, he just passed away, and I found myself completely lost. We were married for forty-five years, till he passed away—the tragedy of my life. To me he was just the stars and the moon and the sky, because I was so very young when he married me. He was such a gentle soul, just a wonderful, wonderful darling."

After his death, she said, "I was like a homing pigeon. I came right back to the place I love so well. . . . And once in a while I break down, and I try—I try not to think of the end of the road."

Clown

Otto

Is it possible, in the excesses of the American three-ring circus, for a single performer to steal the show? I know that it is because one man did it under the tent in an empty lot in Baltimore in 1952 for me. He did not steal a part of it, an act or a segment, but he ran away with the whole show for me that night. What is more surprising is that, in the midst of all that noise and commotion and athleticism and daredeviltry and grace, those scores of performers, he stole my attention chiefly by doing a few small and seemingly ordinary things.

I don't know what others were watching that night, I suppose they followed the spotlight, but my eye followed the clown Otto Griebling as far as it could, as often as it could, and I let most of the rest of the show dissolve into the middle-distance as a backdrop.

Clowns, with their obvious and well-practiced and exaggerated routines, probably deserve about what they get in a circus—a glance or perhaps twenty or thirty seconds of undivided attention. As soon as a clown has yanked the baby out of the baby carriage and snapped it between his legs like a football quarterback, or has had his pants ripped off by snagging them on another clown's umbrella, he has shown me all he has to do and has spent my patience with the gag. It is a good thing that he is off to the other side of the arena to repeat it there. But Otto Griebling held my attention all that night.

The more I watched the simple things he did the more completely I enjoyed them. An artist was at work in that

arena, daring to do things no other circus performer would regard as having even the smallest possibility of comic effect.

Griebling could do the broader things better than most, but he did not rely on them. Instead, he spent his time in the arena limning a character—a totally worried man in the grip of very small affairs. He could invest in the act of sewing a button on a coat all of the intensity and concentration and apparent peril of a physician engaged in open-heart surgery.

Griebling's clown was harassed and futile, truly pathetic, yet he was also limitlessly patient and persistent and devoted. The things that menaced him were entirely unseen; they were private torments locked within some chamber of his consciousness and showing only on his face.

For a circus clown to seek his effects in *implied psychology* rather than in plain and overt acts; for him to rely on a *suggestion* of an inward state rather than an outward showing of things, is virtually a defiance of the form. While other clowns ran away from men waving huge clubs, Griebling's clown walked under the unseen shadows of unspoken woes. His round-shouldered form was just a little weary, a little slumped under the weight of them all.

It should be remembered that not even actors in that most intimate theater of them all, the television screen, attempt such delicacy, and here was Griebling doing it in all the frantic hurly-burly of the circus!

The act was not straight comedy, nor was it pathos, because it avoided the excesses of both. It was a very close blending of the two so that the line between them could not be discerned, or probably even suspected, by the spectators.

I never went to the circus again without giving my primary attention to Otto Griebling. With the wave of a hand, in effect, Griebling was able to steal my attention from lions, from trapeze artists, from high-wire walkers, from elephants on their hind legs, from slapstick artists, from chorines twisting on ropes in their aerial ballet routines.

Yet no one but circus people and circus buffs ever talked about Griebling or even knew his name. He got almost no public attention, while performers of an entirely different order were made famous. When the circus came to town, I would write a memo to the editors and suggest a feature on Otto Griebling, the clown, but they never responded to the idea.

One year I was able to write two paragraphs about him that got into the paper, and I was glad for that. On a slow day in 1961 the circus advance man walked into the office in an adjectival frenzy. As a result, I was asked to do a short piece on the circus, and I wrote that it was about to open "in a glorious burst of oompah, hyperbole and precision timing." The story said:

"The ninety-first edition will be, by self-estimate, 'extravagant, spectacular, exquisite, elephantine, gaily caparisoned, near-fatal, death-defying, unbelievable, delightful, hilarious, awesome, peerless, resounding, scintillating and a choreographic tour de force.' "

Midway in a piece only nine paragraphs long, these short lines appeared:

"Otto Griebling, a dour clown who wears the perpetually worried expression of a self-defeated man in a world too busy to care, will again find himself abashed and perplexed at every turn.

"Mr. Griebling, who has circus admirers who do little else but watch him thread his ineffectual way through a performance, is an unusually subtle actor who achieves his effects not by pantomimic overstatement but by a precise and satiric mimicry. He reaches the top of his form when he undertakes to assist, or interfere with, every unit of a long procession circling the arena."

That was the sum of my writing about Otto Griebling, a man whose bewildered face and distraught manner added a new dimension to comedic portrayal in the circus. I learned that there were others who had felt the same way. The spotlight would sometimes hit a streak of fire in a diamond ring on Griebling's right hand. A business man the clown had never met died in Denver, Colorado, in the early 1940s and the final sentence of his will read: "A little tramp clown named Otto Griebling made me laugh. I bequeath him my diamond ring, valued at $500."

Griebling never confined his work to the short bursts of erratic nonsense known as the clown walks, though he had every right to do so. He made himself a part, often a deliberately secondary part, of almost the whole performance, sometimes half-hidden in the shadows beyond the spotlight, doing something that most people probably never even saw.

Subtlety in a clown is an extremely precarious bent, particularly in a setting where nearly everything is done at cannon-burst power, but Griebling practiced it constantly, never stooping to conquer and probably thereby eluding the attention he might have won more cheaply.

He was, in fact, a magnificent slapstick performer, better than most of those who made it their specialty, and two or three times in a performance he would do something in that bigger-than-life vein, but then he would go right back to doing what no one else would do. That was essentially to portray a single, oddly believable character on a level almost of inference.

With Griebling, it was not what he did that counted—what he did had virtually nothing to it; his outward actions were as ordinary as buying a pack of gum at a newsstand—it was the way he did it. He somehow invested each simple action with a whole sense of character.

An early Griebling device, which he did not use in his later years, was the performance-long running gag. If it was funny, it was not funny by what he did at any given point but by the cumulative suggestion of frustration and futility and absurdity that it conveyed.

Griebling would walk into the seating areas dressed as a youthful Western Union messenger, full of bounce, crying up and down the aisles for "Mrs. Jones!" That was all. Later, he would come back, perceptibly older, still calling for "Mrs. Jones!" With each succeeding appearance his uniforms grew more worn, his face more aged, his desperation more profound. Finally, he would come on as a bent old man, thwarted, but still crying for "Mrs. Jones!"

In one of those exercises of corporate humorlessness that make the world a little grayer place to live in, the telegraph company warned him that if he persisted in this portrayal, he would be sued. Griebling came up with a new invention. He came into the audience carrying a big block of ice on his shoulder, searching for his customer. Each time he came back, the block of ice had melted down considerably. At the end, he held an ice cube, and he still hadn't found his customer.

Think about it for a moment and you will realize that, in this way, Griebling worked out something that no other circus performer had ever attempted. The circus is supremely episodic, a long succession of quite unrelated things hurled at the audience in rapid sequence. Griebling violated that basic form by stitching the strand of a single and developing idea through an entire performance. He built a comic situation by successive stages and, ultimately, suggested something about the busyness and wastedness of some men's lives. In later years he lost his voice box in an operation and did not have the power of speech. Irvin Feld, the producer of the circus, in what I can only believe was a genuine tribute, called him "one of the funniest and most touching clowns of all time."

The biographical facts of his life are simple: Born in Coblenz, Germany, brought to America in 1910 at fourteen-years-old. Otto soon thereafter saw an ad in a German language newspaper for an apprentice bareback rider with the circus, which he answered. He started training, but was not very good at it and broke some bones. It was a legend in the trade that he had once had his own long-running gag with the circus.

One evening in Madison, Wisconsin, the trainer gave him a five dollar bill and told him to go to a nearby store and get two loaves of bread and two bottles of milk. But Otto, who by now feared his humiliations and injuries in the circus, walked off, hopped a freight train and rode out into the dairy country. He worked for a farmer for two years, until he saw that the circus was in Madison again. He rode the train back into town, went to the store, bought two loaves of bread and two bottles of milk and hurried to the circus lot. He delivered the milk and the bread to the trainer, with no explanation. The package was received wordlessly, and he never defected from circus life again. For a while he worked with the M. L. Clark show, a mule-drawn wagon circus.

By 1952, when I first saw him, he had been a clown for thirty-seven years, which is a very long time, if you think of it. I can only suppose that, since he always did much more than was expected of him, he had used every performance through those years for the most exacting expression of his art. What is the impulse—if it is not simply integrity or love—that can keep a man working that hard that long in what was, for Griebling, a nearly anonymous occupation?

"His art," one man said, "was essentially that of the tragic actor." Yes, and it was practiced within the perimeters of a circus where everything went against that and where it was essential to be funny. It is that, I think—his absolute joining of opposite forms in an entirely original portrayal—that must have won me so completely that night in the tent in Baltimore.

Have you been to the circus once or twice, or maybe six or ten or a dozen times, in the last quarter century? Did you ever notice him? Were you aware of who Otto Griebling was or what he did?

He would walk slowly through the aisles among the

spectators, scanning the rows for an attractive woman. When he found her, he would go to her seat, close his eyes in blissful expectation, pucker his lips, and lean forward for the kiss, which never came. He would open his eyes and cast a look of mournful reproach at the woman and walk away. Later he would come back to the same section, now clutching some scraps of paper. Again he would stare at his failed lover. But this time he would take a stubby pencil and, with one fast motion, strike her name from his list. (Usually he would touch the pencil to his lip for just a second before the decisive act, and in that gesture there would be a hint of hesitancy and regret.)

In the spring of 1972 when the circus came to New York, I wrote to the editors again and suggested a story about Griebling, hoping that they would say yes, that many would read it and make it a point to watch his performance and perhaps to find him, as I surely did, a man of nearly Chaplinesque portraiture. The memorandum said:

April 13, 1972

Mr. Kramer,

During a parenthesis in life when I wore a khaki tuxedo in Baltimore, I saw the circus under a tent on a lot on the edge of the city and made a discovery—a clown named Otto Griebling whose artistry is quite unlike that of his peers, though I think he has none. I was so caught by the subtleties that ran all through his performance that I later bought a ticket solely to watch him work.

Griebling does what other clowns do—he juggles, takes terrible blows and spills—but he does things that no other clown would think to do. Small things. He takes a bit of chalk and a tape measure and walks around the rim that divides audience from arena, marking off two and a half foot lengths. There is nothing to it, but Griebling invests it with comic effect and something more. With slight gestures he portrays any little man who bears more of the burdens of the world than he can quite endure and who is absorbed to the exclusion of everything else in some immediate, unimportant task.

Griebling combined such a look of entire worry about what he was doing with such concentration on it as to leave me as limp with admiration as with laughter.

He is the butcher whose wife is a shrew slicing off the bacon, he is the cop who is about to be caught for bigamy directing a line of left-turning traffic, he is the barber who cannot meet his debts trimming hair out of the nose—a man whose troubles are almost cosmically overwhelming concentrating with picayune precision on the small task at hand and suggesting by it a contradictory state of abstraction and absorption.

To do that, it seems to me, requires a high degree of artistic surety, because there is nothing inherently funny at all about marking off two-foot lengths with chalk.

While clowns of massively less creativity have been made relatively famous, Griebling has never got any public attention. Emmet Kelly's cartoon hobo with his half-dozen surefire turns and Felix Adler with his classic face and unmemorable performance are in that class.

Griebling dresses as a tramp, just faintly overdrawn (for a tramp). He spends more time in the arena than the rest because he does not work only during the clown walks. When an aerialist is working high overhead, sometimes Griebling is walking below, holding his battered old fedora directly under the wire walker, ready to catch him when he falls. He does this with total worry and total diligence.

During the spectacle parades, Griebling takes a stand somewhere on the line of march and does a bit of business as each element of the parade passes by. He tries to help in some wonderfully futile, overconscientious way. He takes umbrage. He mocks certain elements in mime. In each case there is a lovely appropriateness to the thing he does.

Griebling is an old man now but he goes on. There is, to me, a quiet and touching heroism about an artist who practices his craft with entire consecration, and goes on doing it for decades, with very little care to whether anyone particularly notices or not. Should we not do a story on him?

Within half an hour, the answer came. "This sounds fascinating," the editor said. "By all means do it."

I was immediately on the telephone to the circus. They were delighted, but I would have to wait a few days. Otto Griebling was sick and he would be out a little while. As soon as he was ready to go back, they would let me know.

Otto Griebling died on April 19, 1972, in St. Clare's Hospital, New York, at seventy-five-years-old, having been a circus clown for fifty-seven years and having been, I am persuaded, an actor so far ahead of his medium as to be essentially lost in it.

I doubt that any visual record of his work exists. It survives only in the memories of those who discovered it there among all the glitter and the noise and high excitement of the arena; but I shall never cease to wonder at it, and, if I ever go to the circus again, I suppose it will seem a pretty empty place.

Epilogue:
Beyond City Limits

A Winter Walk Along the Shore

A city dweller fleeing the pervasive afflictions of his setting begins to think that he may have driven far enough when he reaches a point named, not inappropriately, Promised Land, Long Island.

To the south, facing the sea, a man can have a five-mile long ribbon of sand to himself on a wintry day. He can enjoy ocean therapy—a long, meditative walk along the shore, the salt mist stinging his face at every step.

A single bird wheeling overhead is an event in this setting, to be celebrated by at least a lingering look. The only really obtrusive events are the breakers, which curl to shore in a series reaching back to a very distant age. The sky is infinite and the sea is eternal, or if it is not, it is enough beyond the measure of man to seem so.

Up beyond the sand, long stretches of eastern Long Island seem lifeless now, a sere and silent wilderness, awaiting spring. Blind houses dot the bleak landscape. They are shuttered and empty, as are most marinas, bathing houses, seafood restaurants and inns.

"At this time of year, people come out here not to be annoyed," a resident said. "We're over one hundred miles out to sea—the next stop is London."

Dusk on the beach in mid-February is an intoxicating hour. Everything has the gloss of pewter, the sky, the sea. The "walking dunes" troop above the tide line, shapes of sand governed by the winds. They have the name because their bulk sometimes shifts overnight. The early morning stroller finds them heaped in shapes unlike those he had seen in early evening.

The city dweller is tempted almost to tears—or to wild, mocking laughter—when a resident falls to talking about local conditions and utters the lamentive phrase "our clam problems."

No joke is intended. The man's face is etched with lines of sober concern. He really does have "clam problems."

He does not emphasize the words, they just tumble out in the long flow of his conversation but they seem to emphasize themselves—as if a man with two compound fractures and a concussion were listening to a man describing the discomforts of a touch of indigestion.

Others told of rabbit problems, deer problems, raccoon problems. They were encountered in two days of poking around in the thirty-five-mile beachfront stretching from Southampton Beach at Shinnecock Bay out to the famous old lighthouse that has beamed at Montauk Point since 1796. The visitor learned why shrubs have to be trussed up in burlap and wire, why people put screens over the tops of their chimneys, why tulips cannot survive here.

There were two half-decent half-days in the two-day span; the rest was fog, hail, wind, snow and rain. In the worst of it residents were seen in homes, restaurants and stores.

The simplicity of life as it is sometimes lived out this way is hinted at in a red-lettered sign in the window of a bakery in Montauk: "No Bare Feet" it warns customers.

One resident told of the pleasures of hawk-watching through his picture window. "I'm up in the morning for coffee and, at 7:30, that hawk is here, working the field outside my dining room window," he said. "He covers the field methodically. He goes up and turns, and comes back and turns, and goes back up and, all of a sudden, he just drops—I can't see what he gets."

Some morning that punctual hawk will come as usual and find, not a wild field, but a building plot. His astonished eye will see earth-gouging machinery and the first chews of excavation.

Epilogue: Beyond City Limits

There is perhaps a prophecy, written in wood and mortar, of things to come, in the sight of six motels in a row, with no spaces between them, lining one side of the Old Montauk Highway—the Umbrella Inn, Kris Ann Cabins, The Beach Plum, The Breakers, Twin Pond, The Beachcomber. Here and there in the scrubby terrain garden-style apartments, the first hint of the Queens look, are sprouting.

Yet these are isolated incidents on the landscape amid vast tracts that remain hospitable to wildlife, including pheasant flocks.

"We have pheasants galore," a resident said. "They're so tame your damn cat can go get one. Our three cats have got ten bells between them"—a sort of Pheasant Early Warning System.

Odd reminders of urban reality occur here and there. Rolling along a winter-deserted beach road, passing no other vehicle for miles, a driver comes upon a large "No Parking—Tow Away Zone" sign, a token of municipal zeal far exceeding present necessity.

The promise of sheer solitude was shattered by a major coincidence on the first evening out. Some 220 automobiles were parked where 100 would have been a quorum, on the grounds of Gurney's Inn, a resort whose buildings cling to a terraced hillside that slants down to the oceanfront.

Inside there was a crowded, noisy, smoke-choked scene—a little bit of midtown Manhattan exported almost to the tip of the island.

The annual charitable bash of the Lions Club was going on in a spacious enclosed deck called the Admirality Room, whose eighty-foot wall of windows looks down on the surf. Some 500 people had come for cocktails, dancing, canapes and raffle prizes.

"A bottle of champagne, a turkey and twenty pounds of potatoes—all for a dollar," was the repeated prize offer, a special that seemed to cater as much to elegance as to plain necessity.

A portly man in a crew cut named William De Pouli, a local lumber man, was handling the cash and he turned out to be president or chairman of practically everything.

"Bill's treasurer of the Lions, he's president of the Montauk Chamber of Commerce, director of the Montauk Youth Club, chairman of the Boy Scout dance," a retired businessman confided. "He's a sweet guy, but very shy."

"We have this every year," Mr. De Pouli said. "We help the blind, and we've got a project going on in Guatemala where we're bringing water into a village. They can't tell a Lion from a leopard there, but they need the water. This is the biggest party we've had."

Loud laughter and dance music made the shouted raffle calls hard to hear, and one had to step carefully to avoid the plastic cocktail glasses that rolled empty on the floor. Retreating to the restaurant two visitors escaped the din on the dunes, one of them complaining of a headache.

"You Jewish?" another diner asked the man with the headache. "We've got a lot of Jews out here—five to be exact. I'm one of them. In a population of about 2,000.

"Come out and join us. Life is something here. One day the dogs chased a deer into the water. It was up off the Sound, and we got involved in corraling a deer in the Sound. First time I've ever done that. We spent an hour and a half in a boat driving that deer back to the shore."

That act was carried out in spite of a much-discussed superfluity of deer, and it illustrates the peculiar love-hate relationship of the people to the herd here. The deer are deplored in the aggregate yet catered to as individuals.

"We're overrun with deer," a man said. "They come into your yard, they chew up all your foliage." That is why prudent gardeners sheath their best growths in burlap and wire. Homeowners put screens over their chimneys to keep the raccoons out. "They'll come down your chimney when you're away and wreck your place, rip the stuffing right out of your chairs and sofa," he said.

The deer remained a rumor, often spoken of, never seen. "When you least expect to see them, they're suddenly there. When you go out and want to see them, you never see them. You can search for hours," explained a resident wise to the elusive ways of deer.

Throughout a sullen afternoon, the ocean was the color of lead under a sky that could not resolve its own conflict between gray and cobalt. The moonless night offered an eerily lovely spectacle. The beachfront was a sleeve of black velvet and nothing could be seen, neither sand nor water. Yet on that dark void, long lines of white were continually written. The foam of the breakers looked like liquid lace.

Early the next day sky and sea were dissolved in a mist of their own making, a mist that laid a wet slick over everything—leaves, roadways, tree limbs, rocks.

At Montauk Point, the throaty blast of a fog horn sounded at ten-second intervals. It was necessary to walk within a few yards of the mouth of the on-shore horn to gain access to the beach, and passersby could feel each blast reverberate in all their bones.

A narrow, twisting sand path through thickets of low bushes led to a steep and rocky descent which, when negotiated, permitted exploration of an inhospitable beach. Cautious feet had to find a way over boulders and great jagged rocks, some partly in the brine.

Love yearns to express itself in heroic ways and others had climbed over this moonscape to paint their troth in bold strokes on the rocks.

"BOB LOVES CAROL" one rock asserted, while another bore this unsigned piece: "Each Day As the Sun Rises Above the Sea, May Our Love Grow Stronger and Deeper."

West of the boulders, on a serpentine strand of waterfront, smaller rocks lie in a peculiarly orderly pattern. The waves sort the rocks. A bed of pebbles about twenty feet wide near the waterline gives way to a four-foot-wide swath of thumb-sized stones succeeded by about five feet of fist-sized rocks and, beyond these, a more mixed batch twenty-five feet wide, in which rocks the size of grapefruit predominate.

Walking across this millenial rubble, the visitor enjoys the thought that he has just been made a geological multimillionaire. Dull red stones lie scattered among others of gray, speckled, pink, brown, pale blue.

Rocks are individuals. That one there—long, slim, milky white, almost translucent—is a lovely maiden. There are contradictory rocks, including one with a gray top and an orange bottom. Beyond the stones, there is sand.

Two men stepping on the sand leave oddly different tracks, side by side. One is five feet eight and weighs 170 pounds. He leaves an impression $1\frac{1}{2}$ inches deep with every tread of his size $8\frac{1}{2}$ shoes. The other is six feet five and 195 pounds and he makes a barely perceptible dent with his size thirteen boots and feels, for a moment, lithe and graceful beyond probability.

The gulls, swirling in the wind, are nature's masters of aerodynamics. They sweep low and belly across the ruffled surface of the water, instantly adjusting their flight to every minor variation in the waves.

A man in a loud orange rain suit comes along the beach—a pillar of fire on the tan sand. A mile or so downshore, a man and a dog appear. "I walk my dog every day and I look at twenty-five houses, just walk by and check for fire or evidence of thievery—if there's snow you get tracks and if there's no snow you get mud tracks," said Rollei Waterman. "There's not a lot of thievery, but it's coming out. I check doors.

"The summer residents are becoming spring and fall residents, and some of them are turning into winter residents. Out here they can uncork. They like to dress casually and live casually, go for walks on the beach, kick some pebbles around."

The land is yielding to the wind and the sea up near the

point, and one of the heroes of the battle to save it is a sixty-year-old woman, a summer resident, who devotes something close to full time to the problem.

"She read that somewhere in China they use levees of reeds, and she spends a terrific amount of time collecting certain reeds and making these levees to save the shore," said Harvey Edelstein, manager of White's Drug and Department Store.

"We're on the route of most birds," he said, "and we have cardinals—beautiful, beautiful birds. And swans. You see three or four of them and the sound of their wings is really something to hear. We even have parrots, green parrots, don't ask me how.

"March 15 is the day the osprey come to Montauk, right on the day. If you don't know what day it is, you can tell by that. I was raised in Brooklyn and I moved to Stony Brook and then here.

"When we lived in Stony Brook, we'd drive out here and say, 'How can people live like this—nobody around you?' Now when we drive back, we say, 'How can they live like this—everybody on top of each other?' My kids have a little skating pond of their own in the woods."

"I'll tell you this, when I came out here I was an atheist," another resident said. "But I have seen a lot of things out here that make me think different."

In a winding cove in the Hamptons a flotilla of seven ducks of the purest white was seen. They were perfectly tame, very curious and exceedingly gabby, and they came right up out of the water to greet a pair of strangers. On a vast, flat farm a few miles west, about 350 pheasants in a field took off virtually as one and made a wheel in the sky.

There is a point lookout near Shinnecock where drivers stop to gaze at the lonely shoreline. Suddenly up from the sloping beach came three radiant girls, about seventeen or eighteen, laughing and chattering, their long hair trailing in the wind. The rewards of nature at a moment like that can seem very rich. The girls scrambled into their beetle and drove off. Two city dwellers watched them for a while, then headed back toward the urban haze, passing a place called The Quiet Clam on their retreat.

About the Author

McCandlish Phillips, a member of the staff of *The New York Times* for twenty-one years, was born in Mount Vernon, New York, and he was reared, quite literally, practically everywhere. His earliest academic distinction was chiefly nomadic—attendance at thirteen grammar schools in seven years, a process by which he acquired an extremely infirm grasp of the multiplication table, among other things, and obtained "the peculiar notion that the Civil War had somehow preceded the War of 1812, it having occurred in that order in my training." The baffled stripling took refuge in words, and he has never abandoned them, a fact for which a good many readers of his work are grateful.

Mr. Phillips is six feet five inches tall (a fellow reporter once described him, not altogether accurately, as "he of the graceful phrase and the awkward gait"). He worked for *The Boston Sport-Light, The Brookline Citizen,* and, under patriotic constraints, for the U.S. Army. He has lived in and written about New York City since 1953. At *The Times* he won recognition as the best newspaper stylist writing about the city since the late Meyer Berger.